INTRODUCTION

If a person wishes to participate in the sport of diving he normally goes about it in one of two ways. He is either 'shown' by a friend, which usually means he is taught very little of the theoretical aspects of the sport, or he undertakes a course of instruction through a school, club or shop. The second method results in a safer and more educated diver and one better equipped to cope in an unfamiliar environment.

Regardless of the method of instruction, the level of scuba theory taught throughout the world varies considerably. There are many excellent books on diving covering most aspects of theory at this level. However, none of these books is a standard for they do not outline what is essential knowledge and what is not.

This book is the first serious attempt to standardise theory at a particular level — i.e. the World Underwater Federation (C.M.A.S.) — Two Star Diver Award. We do not intend to cover the practical aspects of a scuba course for two reasons. The first major reason is that no matter how detailed the text on a practical subject is, a competent and qualified instructor is required to ensure that the learning process is safe and efficient.

Secondly, we believe that a practical course outline is too dependent on the facilities available, staff, equipment, and the personal approach of each instructor.

What we have included is that which we consider is the minimum knowledge required of a scuba diver.

ACKNOWLEDGEMENTS

To the many people who have helped us in the preparation of *International Scuba Diver,* we thank you very much.

Special thanks must go to: John Butler, Simon Jones, Jane Langdon, Jenny Mosse, Peter Mosse, David Parsons, Clark Smock, Dr. Peter Sullivan, Dr. Warrick White and Dr. John Knight.

Cover photograph by Peter Barker

"Brine Snorkel" cartoons by John Butler

Illustrations by Sandy Parker

FOREWORD

SCUBA diving is a potentially risky sport. To understand the many dangers of diving, and why they occur is a major step towards being able to avoid them, and to enjoy SCUBA diving in safety.

The novice diver will find in *International Scuba Diver* all that he needs to know of the theoretical aspects of SCUBA diving. In fact, it would be an excellent supplement to his instructor's lectures during training.

It will be equally valuable to the experienced diver whose theory knowledge is no longer what it should be!

The authors, Hugh Morrison and Steve Sinclair have excellent credentials for authorship of a diving text book. They are both instructors with the Federation of Australian Underwater Instructors, who in their many years of diver instruction, have made significant contribution to the sport of diving both instructional and sporting level.

Each has held office at both state and national levels with FAUI. Their personal diving skill and knowledge is unquestioned, as Hugh was Australian SCUBA champion in 1977 while Steve won the title in 1981.

As dive shop and dive school proprietors, Hugh in Perth and Steve in Melbourne, they are well versed in the current needs of the diver, and the theory requirements of the student.

International Scuba Diver reflects that knowledge and experience. I commend this book to all divers.

Stan Bugg

STAN BUGG
NATIONAL EXAMINER,
FEDERATION OF AUSTRALIAN
UNDERWATER INSTRUCTORS

CONTENTS

		Page
	INTRODUCTION	iii
	ACKNOWLEDGEMENTS	iii
	FOREWORD	iv
SECTION 1:	**PHYSICS OF DIVING**	1
	A. The Physical Environment	3
	B. Gas Laws	16
SECTION 2:	**EQUIPMENT**	30
	A. Skindiving Equipment	32
	B. Buoyancy Compensators	41
	C. The S.C.U.B.A. Unit	47
	D. Tools and Accessories	61
	E. Care and Maintenance	68
SECTION 3:	**MEDICAL CONSIDERATIONS**	71
	A. Respiration and Circulation	74
	B. Barotrauma	79
	C. Gas Poisoning	94
	D. Decompression Sickness	101
	E. Hypothermia	113
	F. Miscellaneous Complaints	116
	G. First Aid	120
	H. Resuscitation	125

Page

SECTION 4: DIVE PLANNING 128
A. Dangerous Marine Animals 129
B. Understanding Water Movement 140
C. The Dive 147
D. Specialist Diving 156

APPENDIX
A. Useful Addresses 162
B. Diving Metrics 163
C. Hand Signals 165
D. List of Recompression Facilities 166
E. Bibliography 167
F. Decompression Tables 168
i. Royal Navy Tables 168
ii. U.S. Navy Tables 176
G. Procedures for Administration of Pure Oxygen in an Emergency 182
i. Administration of Oxygen Using Standard Equipment 182
ii. Administration of Oxygen Using Non-Standard Equipment 185

Index 191

Section 1: PHYSICS OF DIVING

1A: The Physical Environment

1. Pressure
2. Buoyancy
3. Temperature
4. Light
5. Sound

1B: Gas Laws

1. Gases
2. Boyle's Law
3. Charles' Law
4. Dalton's Law
5. Diffusion
6. Henry's Law

Section 1: PHYSICS OF DIVING

1A: The Physical Environment

1. Pressure
2. Buoyancy
3. Temperature
4. Light
5. Sound

Section 1 PHYSICS OF DIVING

1A The Physical Environment

A sound understanding of basic physical properties is essential for safe diving. Inherent properties of water, the diver's environment, will result in physiological changes during a dive. The importance of such properties as pressure, buoyancy, temperature, light, sound, and density will become evident during that dive.

For instance, with or without scuba a duck dive in water to a depth of two metres will cause discomfort in the ears. This is a direct result of changing pressure.

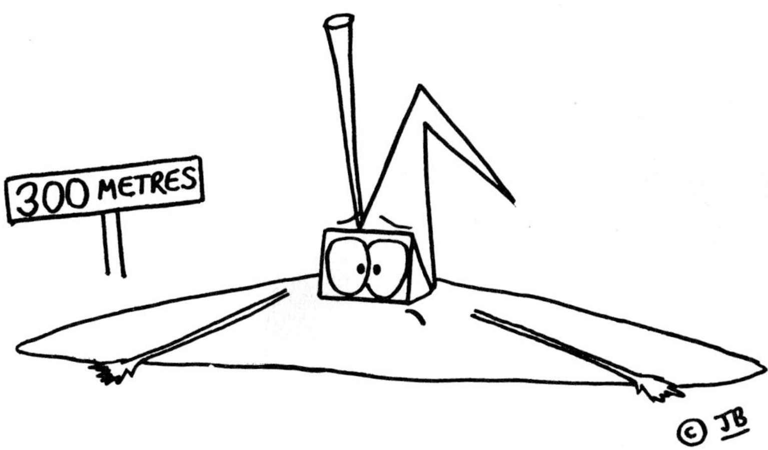

1A: 1 Pressure

When diving, the depth travelled through the water is relatively unimportant when compared with the pressure changes which occur as a result of such movements.

As a land animal we have evolved in an environment which is relatively stable when considering pressure changes. Our atmosphere, 320 kilometres high, only produces a total pressure of one atmosphere or approximately 100 kilopascals. One needs to travel 6,000 metres upwards to halve this pressure.

Water, being more dense than air, creates a hyperbaric (high pressure) environment. As a consequence, the increased pressures encountered in the underwater environment are readily noticeable. A depth of only ten metres is required to produce another atmosphere of pressure. At ten metres the "total" or "absolute pressure" is two atmospheres (200 kilopascals) i.e. one atmosphere of air plus one atmosphere of water.

To calculate the total or absolute pressure at any depth, the depth in metres is divided by 10 and one atmosphere of air is added to it.

Pressure can therefore be equated with depth as a depth-pressure relationship.

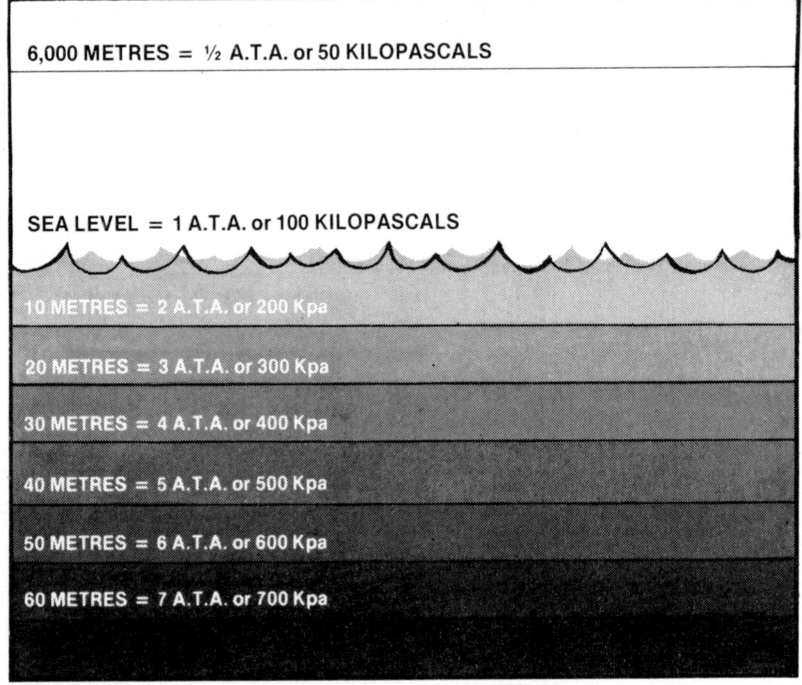

The Depth-Pressure Relationship

"For every 10 metres of water an extra one atmosphere (100 kilopascals) is added to the total pressure."

i.e. Absolute Pressure (ATA) $= \frac{\text{Depth(m)}}{10} + 1$ atm

To convert atmospheres to kilopascals multiply by 100

Problem: What is the absolute pressure at 37 meters?

Solution: Absolute Pressure $= \frac{\text{Depth(m)}}{10} + 1$ atm

Therefore Absolute Pressure at 37 metres $= \frac{37}{10} + 1 = 4.7$ ATA

Another term which can be used for absolute pressure is "ambient pressure" — that is the total pressure surrounding the diver at any one time.

If depth gauges, contents gauges, and other pieces of equipment for measuring depth are to be used, they need to be calibrated to read zero at the surface, ten metres at ten metres and so on. That is, these instruments are calibrated to ignore the one atmosphere of air.

Depth-pressure readings which ignore the one atmosphere of air are known as "gauge pressures" and are only used with measuring instruments.

All of the work with pressure and its effects on the body will have to take into account air pressure, so all future reference to pressure will be in *absolute units* unless otherwise stated.

Instruments which are used to indicate depth or pressure usually ignore the atmosphere of air pressure. They read in gauge units.

1A: 2 Buoyancy

When objects are placed in a liquid they will either float, sink or occasionally appear to be neutral — that is, they will neither float nor sink.

The two factors which decide if an object sinks or floats are its mass (weight) and its volume. These two factors give us an indication of the object's density. It is the object's density when compared to the liquid in which it is placed that will decide if it is positively (floats), negatively (sinks), or neutrally buoyant.

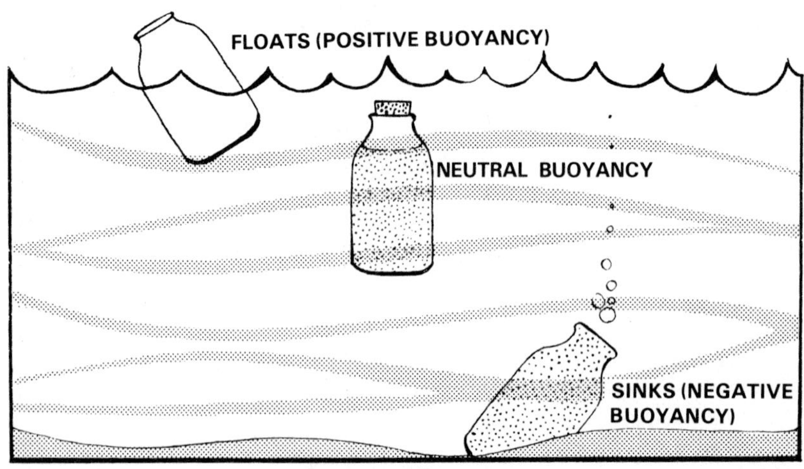

Degrees of Buoyancy

As the object is placed in the liquid its volume will cause an equal volume of the liquid to be displaced or pushed aside. The weight of the liquid which has been displaced will equal the upward lift or buoyant force given to the object. The more liquid displaced or the greater the density of the liquid displaced, the greater the uplift given to the object.

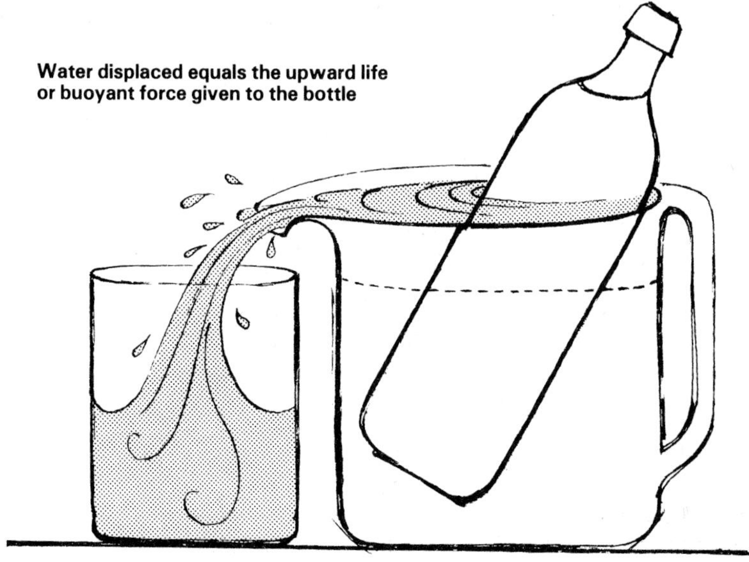

Water displaced equals the upward life
or buoyant force given to the bottle

Because salt water is more dense than fresh water, an object placed in salt water will have a greater buoyancy than when placed in fresh water. It will have less tendency to sink in salt water than in fresh water.

The human body has a density very close to that of salt water. This means when

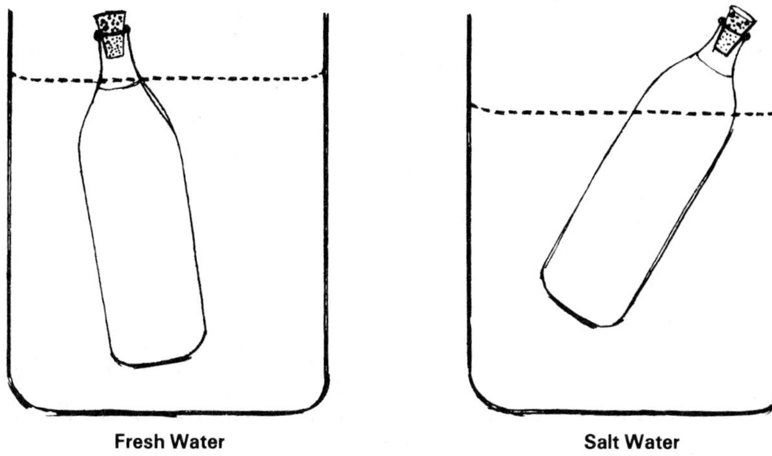

a diver is immersed in salt water he usually just floats with the top part of his head out of water. If he exhales then there is a slight decrease in chest volume and he will tend to sink because he displaces less water.

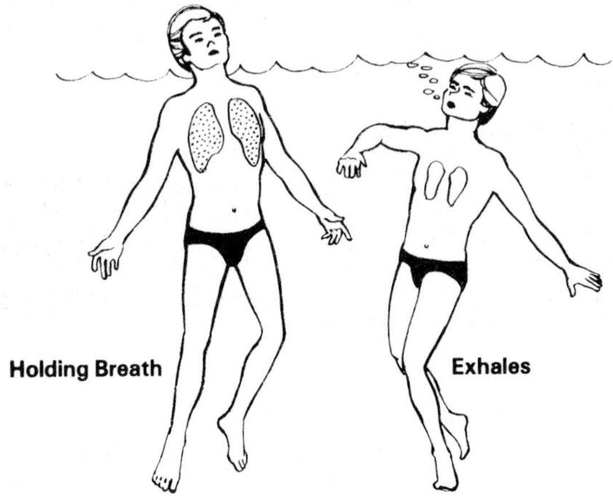

If we now place the diver in a wet suit which has considerable volume of gas filled rubber neoprene but little weight, then his overall volume has increased markedly while his weight has not. He will float much higher out of the water. To compensate for this problem, a belt with lead weights is worn. The lead has very little volume but considerable weight. The diver will now return to neutral buoyancy provided the correct amount of weight is worn. If the amount of weight is correct, then when the diver breathes out while wearing his wet suit and weight belt, he should be able to sink.

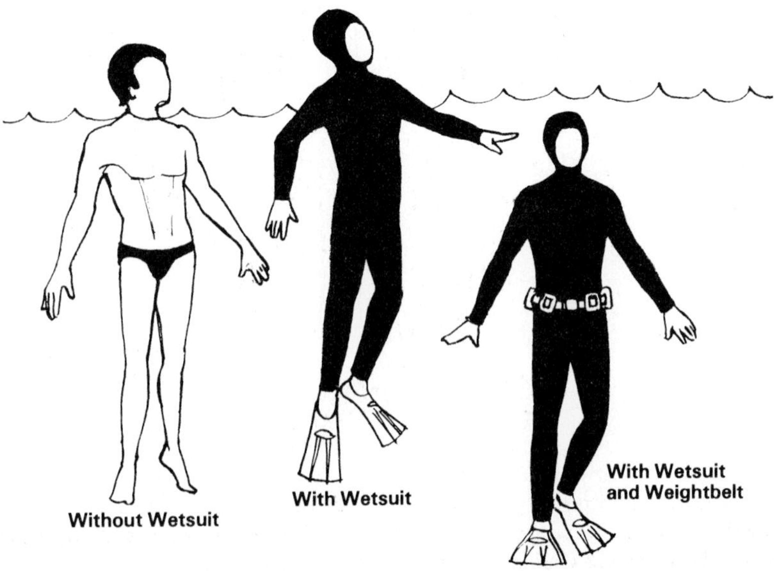

There are other factors which will affect a diver's buoyancy during a dive. As he collects objects during the dive his weight will increase without a significant increase in volume. Therefore, he will tend to sink. If he descends the gas bubbles in his wet suit will be squashed by the increased water pressure and so compress the suit. He will now have lost some volume without losing weight. Therefore he will tend to sink.

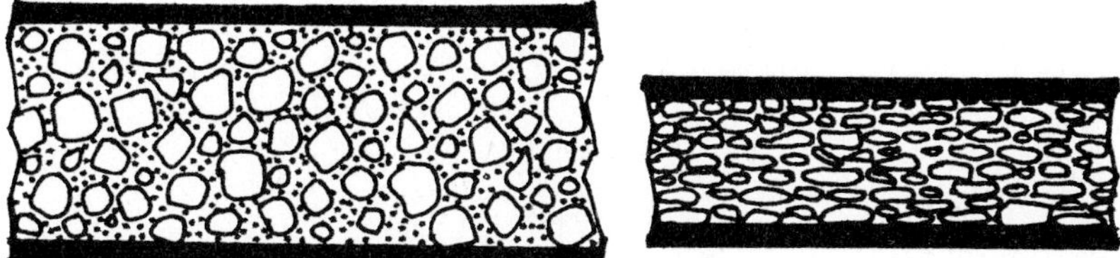

Wetsuit compression at depth

Inflatable vests or buoyancy compensators (see equipment — section 2B) can be used to increase buoyancy by adding volume but not weight. Other factors such as empty scuba cylinders or breathing more deeply will automatically increase buoyancy. In the case of the empty cylinder it is loss of weight not increased volume which causes the buoyant effect. This loss of weight can be from 1.5 kilograms to 5 kilograms depending on type and capacity of the cylinder.

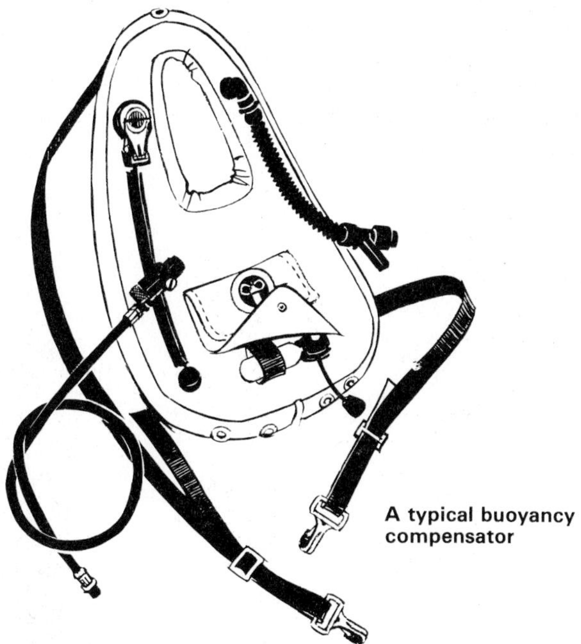

A typical buoyancy compensator

A well trained diver should be able to adjust the equipment being used to obtain neutral buoyancy. From then on minor changes can be made by either altering depth of breathing or using a buoyancy compensator.

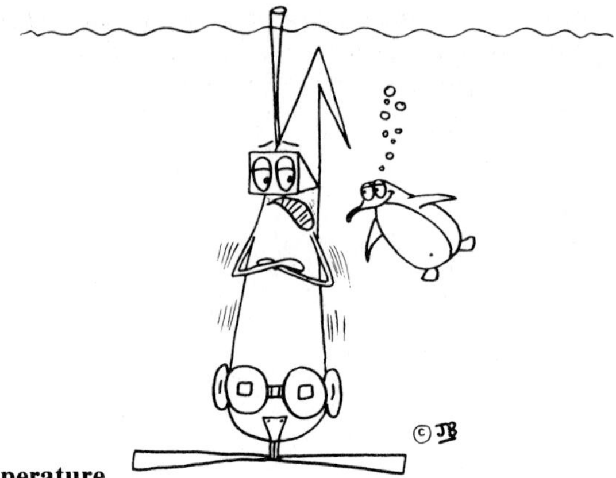

1A: 3 Temperature

The body's internal (or core) temperature is approximately 37° Celsius but skin temperature can be much lower. In air a person can tolerate temperatures as low as 15° to 18° Celsius without great discomfort because air is a better thermal insulator than water. Providing strong winds are not blowing the warmed air immediately surrounding the body away, heat loss to air is not great.

Water on the other hand has 25 times more thermal conductivity (i.e. temperature carrying ability) than air, and tends to carry the body heat away from the diver at a very rapid rate. A diver can become dangerously cold in a surprisingly short period of time if the conditions required are present.

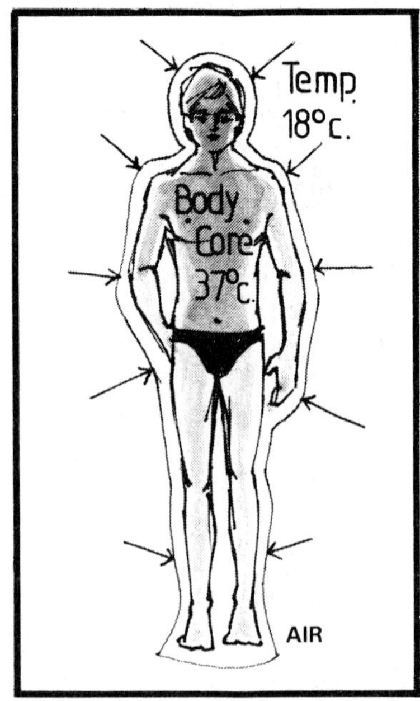

Still air tends to insulate the body

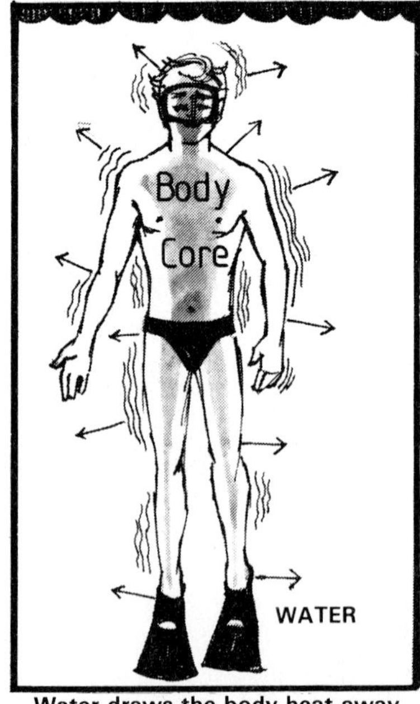

Water draws the body heat away

Water can drag heat away from body 25 times faster than air does

Some form of thermal insulation such as wet suit is usually required in most waters if prolonged periods of immersion are anticipated.

The dangers of cold water exhaustion and lowering of body core temperature (hypothermia) will be discussed in section 3E.

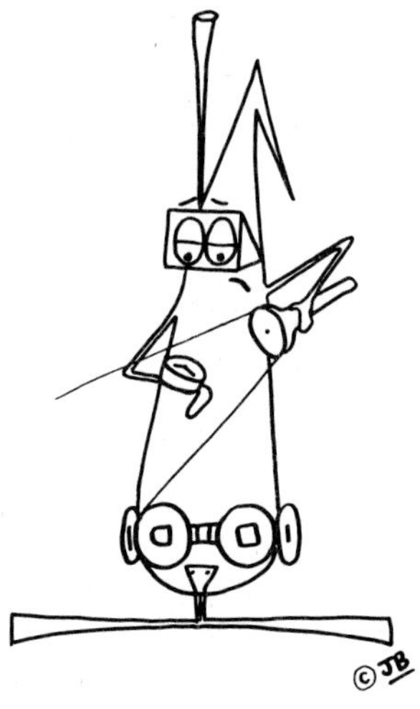

1A: 4 Light

As light enters the marine environment it is distorted due to reflection, refraction and absorption to such an extent that the diver's ability to see is partially impaired.

a. Reflection

The majority of the light striking the surface is reflected back while only a very small proportion will penetrate to any significant depth.

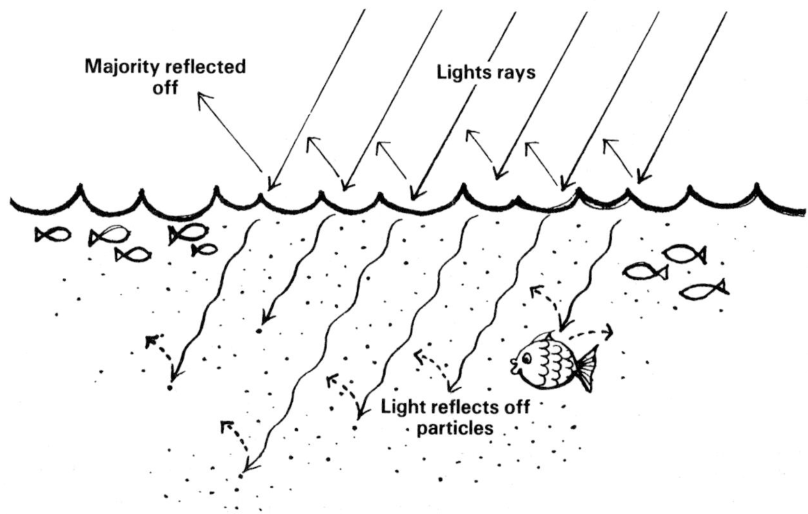

The first effect noticed by the diver is the reduced light level giving a gloomy, almost twilight effect to the underwater scene. Once light has penetrated the water it will be reflected or bounced from the floating particles in the water therefore reducing visibility even further. Generally, suspended material will ensure that light is reflected into caves and ledges reducing to some extent the shadows and darkness that would otherwise be expected. However, because the total level of light intensity is so low, the penetration into caves and ledges is very poor resulting in the need for artificial light if these areas are to be viewed.

Lack of penetration of light under ledges

b. Refraction

As light travels through media of different density it is bent or refracted. When light enters our eyes the rays are refracted or bent so they will focus at the back of the eye.

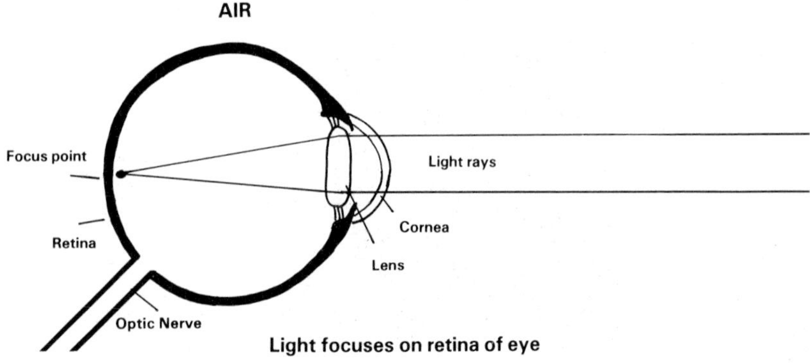

Light focuses on retina of eye

The eye has a similar density to water, so when underwater without a mask the rays are not bent and the viewed object will therefore appear blurred.

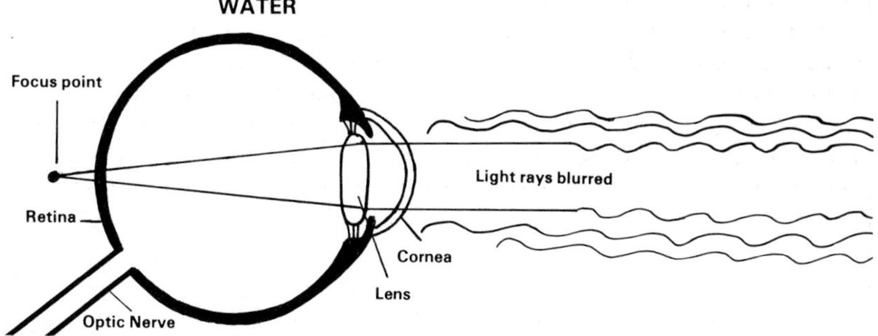

Water has same density as eye.
Light does not focus on retina of eye — vision blurred.

In order to be able to see clearly underwater a mask must be worn to introduce an air space in front of the eyes. By wearing a mask, three points of refraction are now introduced; the water-glass interface, the glass-air interface, and the air-eye interface.

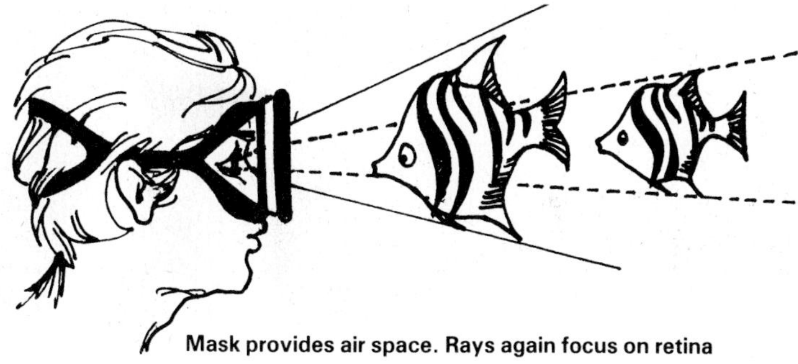

Mask provides air space. Rays again focus on retina

The eye is unable to adjust the refraction due to the glass and so the object appears larger and closer. As the angle of the light hitting the mask causes differing amounts of refraction the distortion of an object will be greater towards the outer edges of our field of view. This is known as the 'pin cushion' effect.

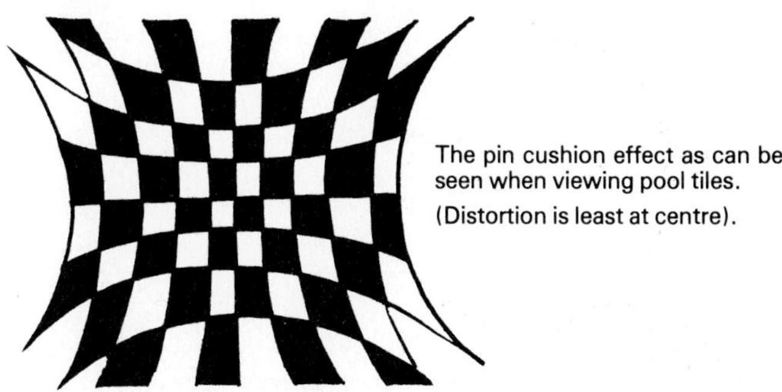

The pin cushion effect as can be seen when viewing pool tiles. (Distortion is least at centre).

c. Absorption

As well as being refracted, light is absorbed when it enters a media of greater density. The degree of absorption will depend to some extent on the colour of the light. White light, in fact, consists of a series of colours — the spectrum. The colours are red, orange, yellow, green, blue, indigo and violet. Red light has the lowest energy level and violet has the highest. Water acts as a blue filter so white light will be seen as varying hues of blue until eventually even this colour is absorbed. As a result an object which appears red or orange at the surface, very quickly loses its colour as it is taken deeper until it eventually is perceived as black.

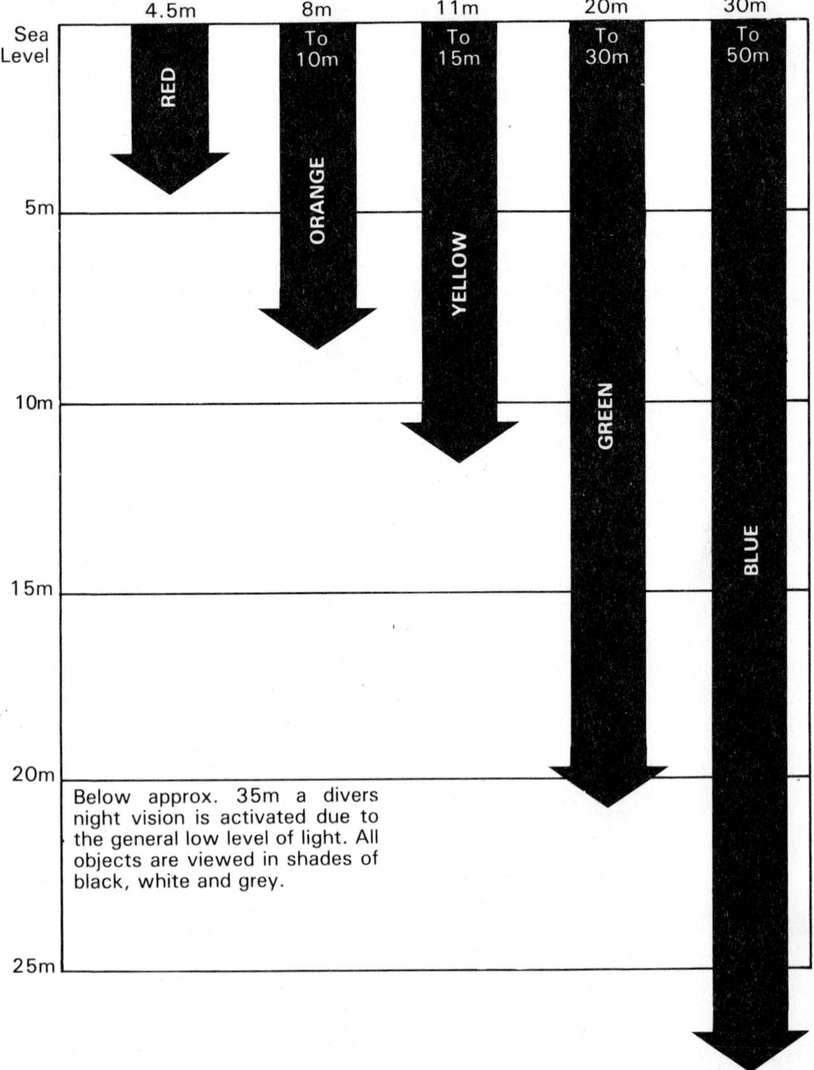

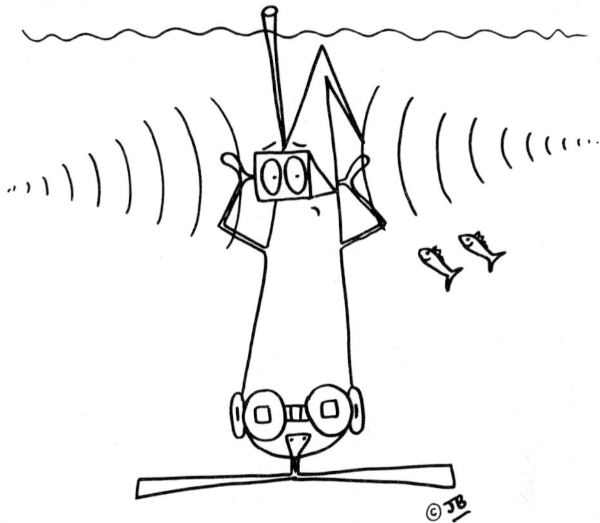

1A: 5 Sound

The transmission and perception of sound through water is a problem for the sport diver. If sound is produced in air, very little will penetrate the water and that which does is distorted due to the increased speed of sound in water. Sound travels at 1550 metres per second in sea water, four times faster than in air.

The source of sound produced underwater, such as the noise from an outboard motor is difficult to locate as the ears are adapted to locate direction of sound in air. The increased speed of sound underwater and the fact that the bones of the skull act as a conductor make sound location marginally accurate only after considerable practice. Wearing hoods and the natural reduction of sound intensity underwater will further reduce the efficiency of the diver's hearing mechanism.

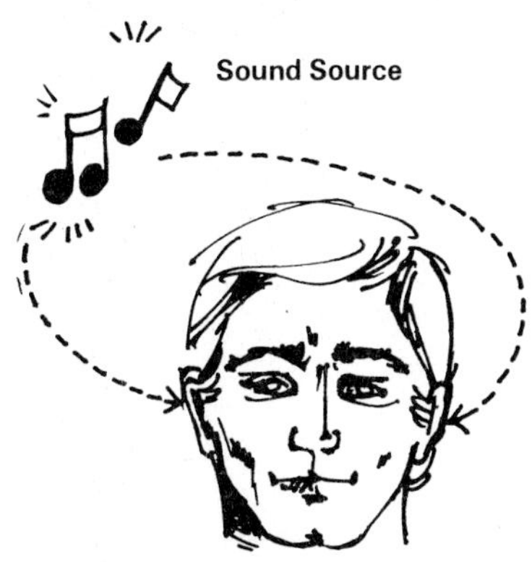

AIR

The ear can detect the difference therefore we can locate the source of the sound.

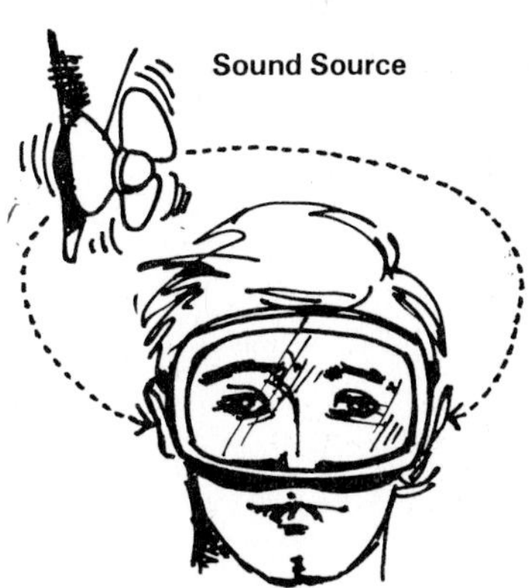

WATER

Sound travels 4 times faster. The time difference cannot be detected therefore we have difficulty locating source of sound.

Section 1: PHYSICS OF DIVING

1B. Gas Laws

1. Gases
2. Boyle's Law
3. Charles' Law
4. Dalton's Law
5. Diffusion
6. Henry's Law

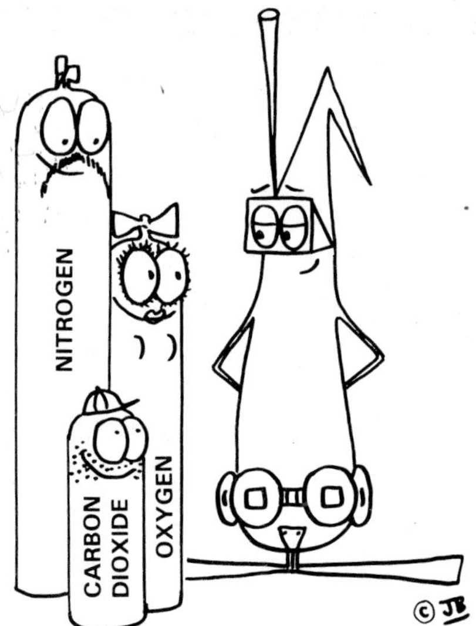

1B: 1 Gases

All matter is composed of atoms and molecules and can exist in three states: solids, liquids and gases.

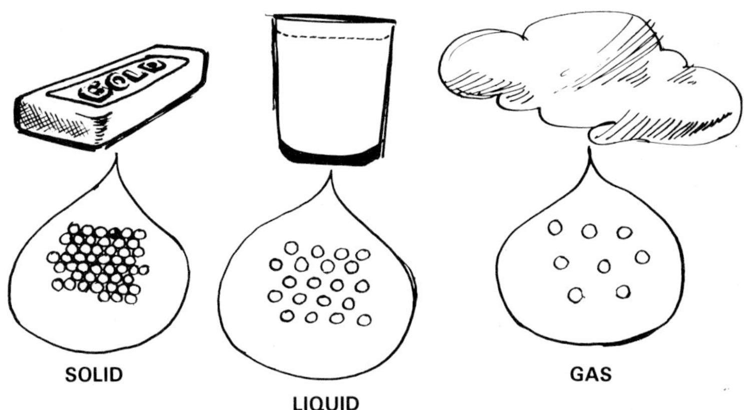

In solids and liquids the molecules or atoms are very close together relative to their size and hence are incompressible and have distinct volume. As a result of this incompressibility, they do not change volume when pressure is increased, and the pressure will be transmitted evenly through the substance (Pascal's Principle). The diver's body which is 79% fluid or solid will therefore assume the same pressure as the surrounding environment.

Gases, however, are greatly affected by pressure because the distance between the molecules is great in relation to their size. Hence they can be compressed. Also, due to this great distance, molecules do not assume any definite shape or volume and must be stored in a container. As a result of these properties of gas the human body's air spaces such as lungs, ears, and sinuses require considerable

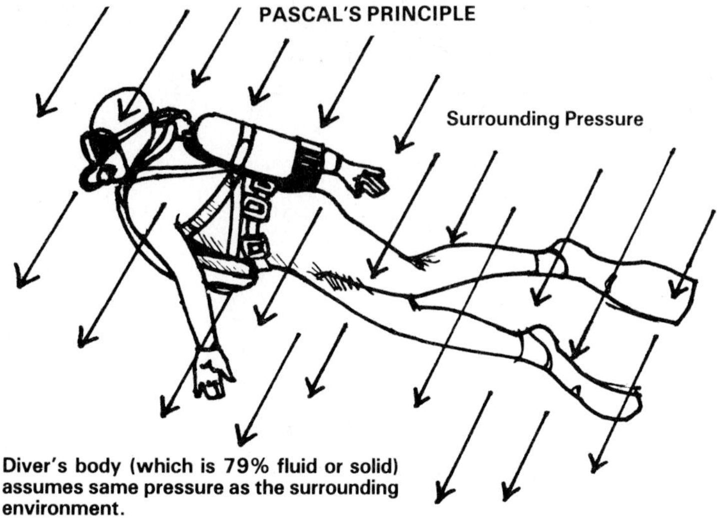

attention when diving so as to avoid adverse physiological changes during the dive.

When discussing the properties of a gas it is assumed that the gas molecules are in constant motion and when they strike the surface of the container an instantaneous pressure results. Of course when the millions of molecules present in even a small volume of gas strike a surface a constant pressure is produced.

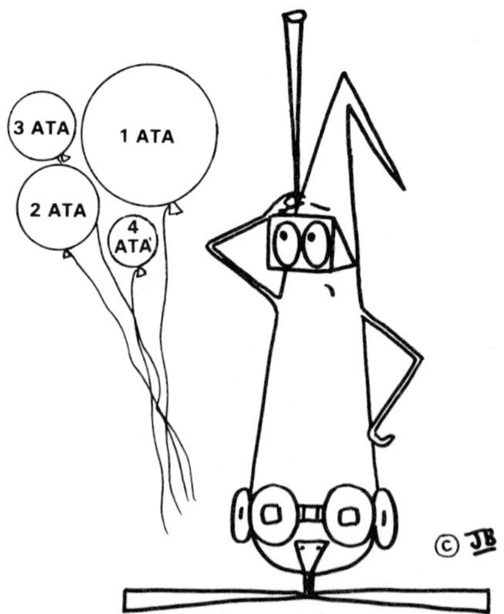

1B: 2 Boyle's Law (Pressure - Volume Relationship)

If ten molecules were placed in a rigid container they would move around randomly striking the walls thereby generating a pressure.

Let us define this pressure as one unit of pressure.

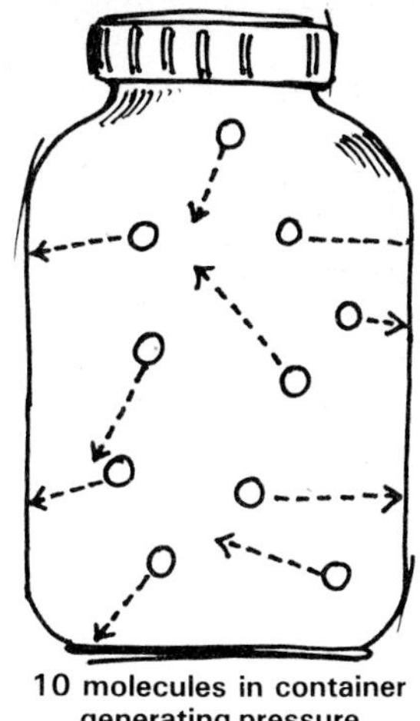

10 molecules in container generating pressure.

Now, if the volume of the container were reduced to half then the ten molecules, still travelling at the same speed, would only have half the volume in which to move. Therefore the molecules would strike the walls of the container more often, in fact, twice as often. Therefore, the pressure would double.

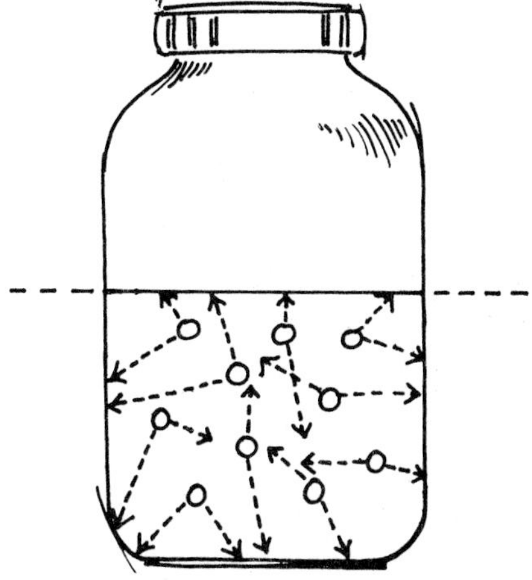

Volume halved, pressure doubled.

In other words, if the volume is halved, the pressure will double. If the volume were doubled then the molecules would have twice as much room in which to move. Therefore, the molecules would strike the walls less often. Hence only half the pressure will be exerted on the container walls. In other words, if the volume is doubled, pressure is halved.

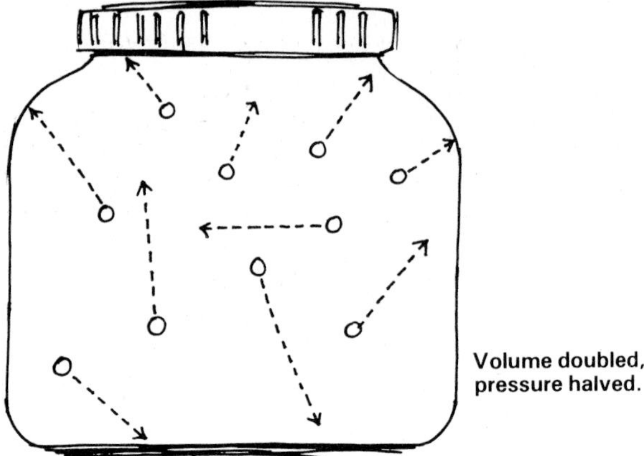

Generally, if the volume a gas occupies is increased the pressure will decrease. This is known as Boyle's Law.

If we now consider a flexible container such as the lungs the implication of Boyle's Law can readily be seen. When a diver holds his breath his lungs contain a volume of air (approximately 6 litres) which will be reduced as he descends because of the increasing water pressure surrounding him.

Thus at ten metres (2 atmospheres absolute) the pressure has doubled and so the volume of the lungs will be halved. As the diver ascends the pressure will fall and the volume of the lungs will increase again.

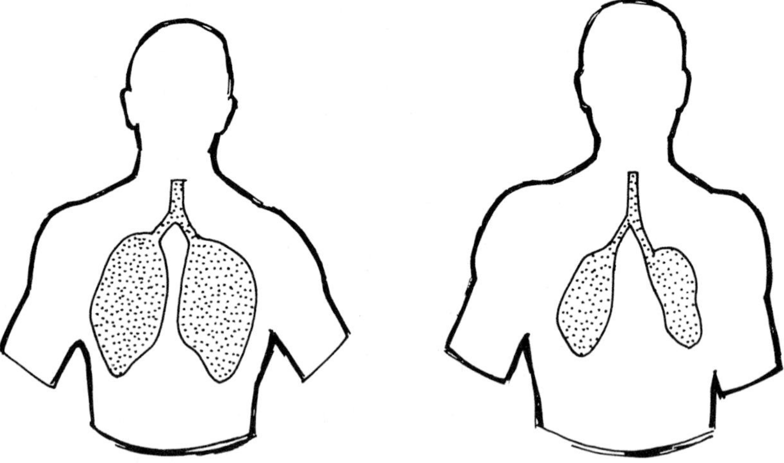

Lungs at surface (1 A.T.A.). Lungs at 10 metres (2 A.T.A.).

All other gas spaces within the body can be expected to do the same as the lungs. However, in the case of the middle ear, volume expansion or reduction cannot be tolerated and so ambient pressure air from the lungs and nasal passages needs to be introduced into the middle ear via the Eustachian tube to avoid damage to the middle ear (see Section 3).

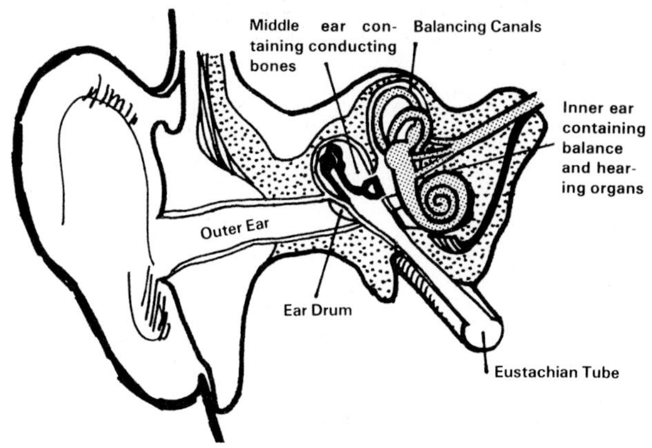

As the rate of volume change is dependant upon pressure changes, it can be seen that the major area for concern is in the top ten metres of the water column. From ten metres to the surface there is a fifty per cent pressure reduction thus producing a fifty per cent increase in volume. Compare this reduction to that experienced when travelling from the surface to 10 metres with that experienced from 30 metres to 40 metres where the volume change is only twenty per cent.

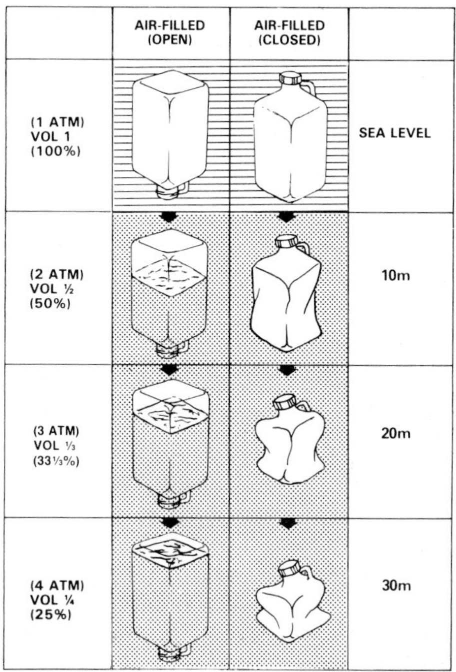

The effect of Boyle's Law on sealed and unsealed volumes of air.

It is therefore likely that most cases of pressure related injury (barotrauma) would occur within the top ten metres of water, and this is found to be the case.

1B: 3 Charles' Law (Pressure - Temperature Relationship)

If the same rigid container used in the previous discussion is now considered in relation to temperature we will find that as the temperature rises the ten molecules begin to move faster. As they move faster they will strike the wall more often and so exert a greater pressure.

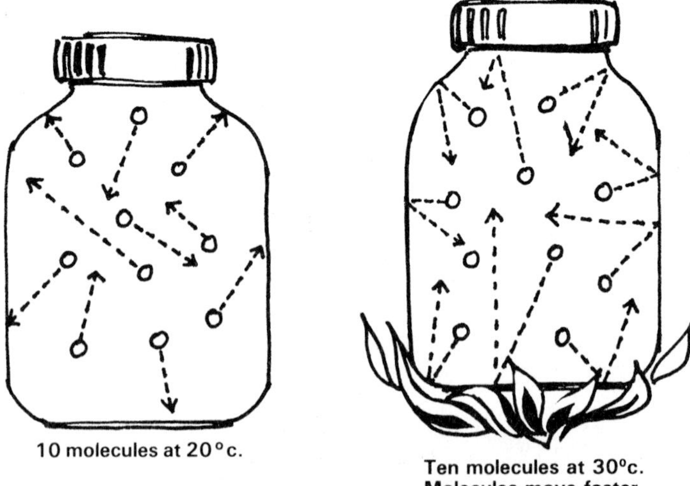

10 molecules at 20°c.

Ten molecules at 30°c.
Molecules move faster.

Hence as temperature increases the pressure of a gas within a rigid container will increase, conversely as the temperature falls so will the pressure. This is known as Charles' Law.

Flyspray tin in fire exploding.

If the container is flexible the increased pressure within the container will cause the gas volume to expand and so the container will increase in size.

This law becomes of major concern to divers when one considers the properties of scuba cylinders (rigid metal cylinders containing high pressure air). These cylinders contain air at a pressure of up to 250 atmospheres (25 Megapascals). If left in the sun for long periods of time the already high pressure becomes excessive because the cylinders are not flexible and the volume is forced to remain constant. If in a weakened condition the cylinder may explode.

Another consequence of Charles' Law can be seen during the filling of scuba cylinders. The process of gas compression produces heat and therefore the cylinder will heat up while being filled. However, after filling the cylinder will cool and hence gauge pressure will drop. To determine the true contents of a scuba cylinder always gauge it when cool.

1B: 4 Dalton's Law (Partial Pressures)

Air is a mixture of gases with the two main constituents being oxygen, O_2, approximately 20% or $^1/_5$, and nitrogen, N_2, approximately 80% or $^4/_5$.

If the container previously under discussion still at a pressure of one unit now contains these two gases in the above proportions, then of the ten molecules present, two are oxygen and eight are nitrogen.

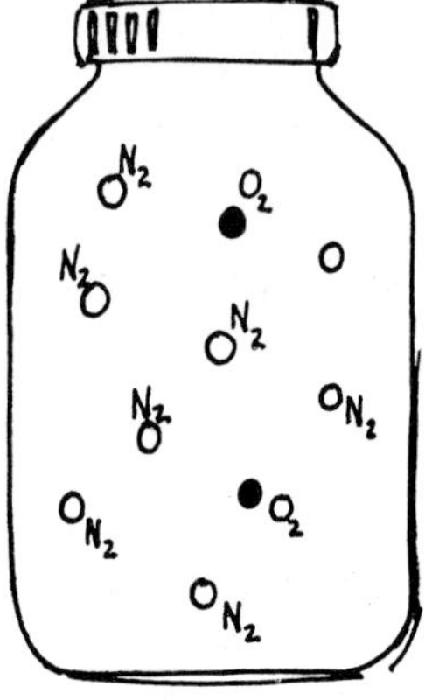

If the 8 nitrogen molecules are removed then the pressure due to oxygen would only result from the 2 molecules left. They still have the same volume but only 20% (1/5) of the original ten molecules will strike the walls. Therefore, the pressure due to oxygen alone is 20% (1/5) of the original total pressure. If the 8 nitrogen molecules are replaced and the oxygen molecules removed the pressure due to nitrogen will be 80% (4/5) of the total pressure as there are now 8 out of 10 molecules striking the walls of the container.

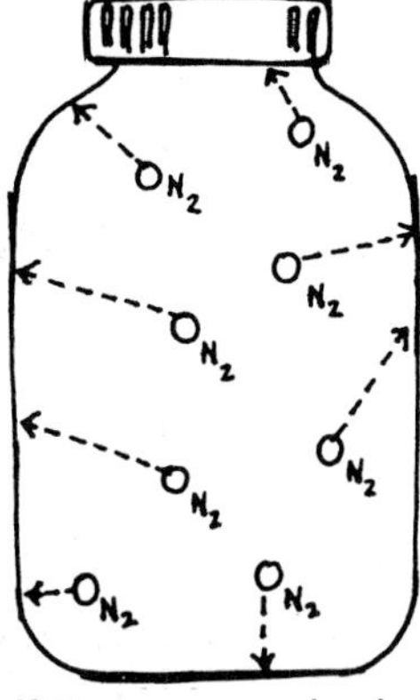

If the oxygen molecules are removed the pressure will be 80%.

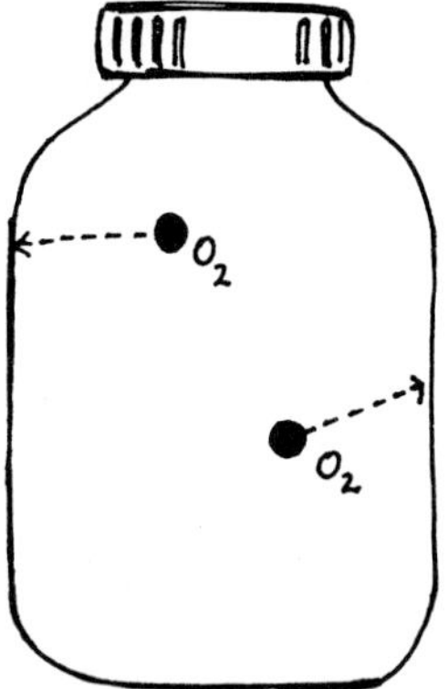

If the nitrogen molecules are removed the pressure would only be 20%.

If the total pressure is one unit, the pressure due to oxygen will be 20% or 1/5 of the one unit, i.e. 0·2 units and the pressure due to nitrogen will be 80% or 4/5 of one unit, i.e. 0·8 units. In other words, in a gas mixture such as air the gases act independently of each other. They each produce only part of the total pressure. This part is known as partial pressure (P_p). The partial pressures always add up to give the total pressure. This is Dalton's Law. In the example above, the partial pressure of oxygen (P_pO_2) plus the partial pressure of nitrogen (P_pN_2) equals the total pressure of air,

$$\text{i.e. } TP_{air} = P_pO_2 + P_pN_2$$
$$= 0{\cdot}2 + 0{\cdot}8$$
$$= 1$$

When air at one atmosphere absolute (sea level) is now considered, it can be seen that:

$$TP_{air} = P_p0_2 + P_pN_2 = 1 \text{ ata}$$

The partial pressure of oxygen is equal to approximately 20% of the total pressure because air is 20% (1/5) oxygen.

Therefore $P_pO_2 = 1/5 \times 1 = 0{\cdot}2$ ata.

The partial pressure of nitrogen is equal to 80% (4/5) of the total pressure because air is 80% (4/5) nitrogen.

Therefore $P_pN_2 = 4/5 \times 1 = 0{\cdot}8$ ata.

To check, add up all the partial pressures. They should equal the total pressure.

If the total pressure in our lungs is now doubled, for example by diving to 10 metres, the percentage of each gas will remain the same but the partial pressures will double.

i.e. Total Pressure at 10 metres = 2 ata.

The partial pressure of oxygen is equal to 20% or 1/5 of the total pressure therefore partial pressure of oxygen at 10 metres is 1/5 of 2 = 0·4.

As the overall pressure increases, the partial pressures of constituent gases also increases.

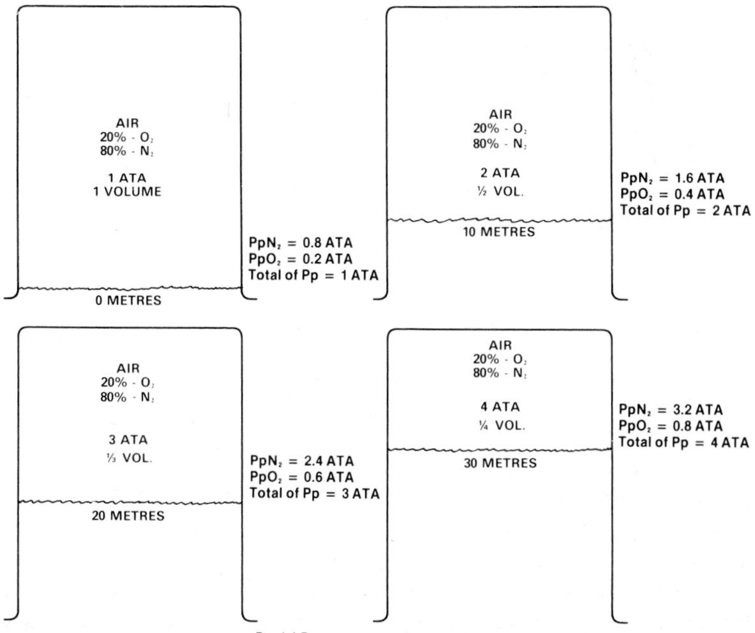

Boyle's Law will result in a reduction in volume and an increase in Pressure within the open-ended containers.

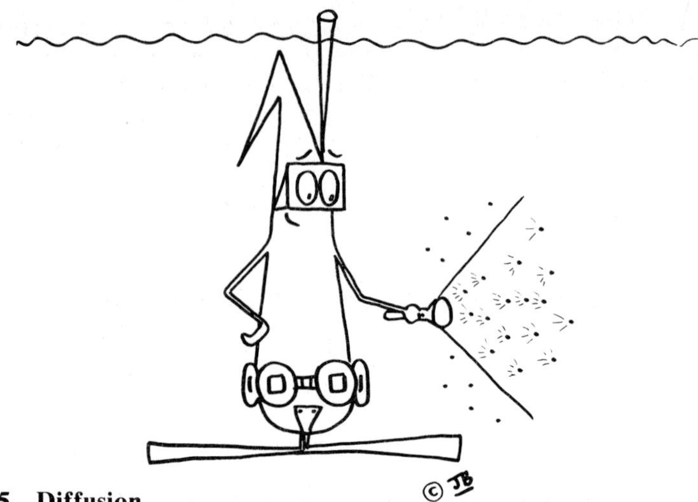

1B: 5 Diffusion

The movement of molecules is totally random and given sufficient time they will eventually spread out evenly to completely occupy the container which confines them. An example often experienced is of a bottle of perfume being opened in a closed room. The scent can rapidly be detected in all parts of the room as the molecules achieve even distribution.

(DIFFUSION)
Opened bottle of perfume.

This movement of molecules is referred to as diffusion. If two different gases were placed on either side of a perforated partition then they would eventually intermingle. However, the molecules don't travel at the same rate. The rate of diffusion depends on the weight of the molecule. The heavier the molecule, the slower it travels.

If we consider a bubble of nitrogen within a medium rich in oxygen, such as a nitrogen bubble in blood rich in oxygen, then the nitrogen which is lighter than oxygen will diffuse from the bubble faster than the oxygen can diffuse in. The result is that the bubble will decrease in volume. This is the reason that pure oxygen is administered to divers suffering from decompression sickness (see Section 3D).

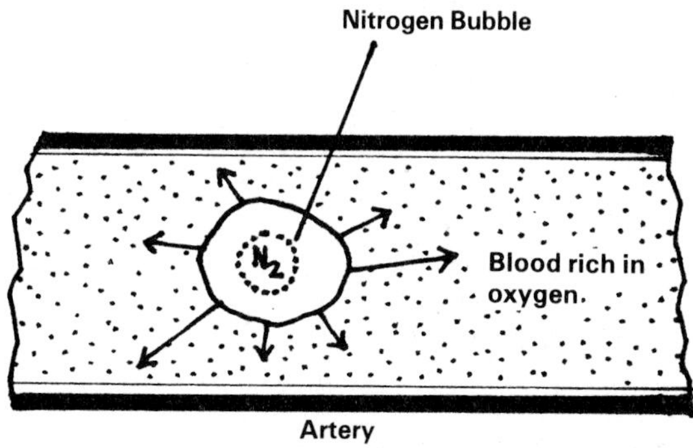

Nitrogen which is lighter than O_2 diffuses out of the bubble faster than the heavier O_2 can diffuse in.

1B: 6 Henry's Law

Gas diffusion need not only occur in air. Gases also diffuse into and out of liquids. This process, more commonly termed dissolving, is usually applied to solids dissolving in a liquid. A similar process allows gases to diffuse into a liquid. The nett result is the same. Given sufficient time a gas will diffuse into a liquid to a point where equilibrium or **saturation** occurs. That is, the amount of gas going into the liquid will equal the amount leaving.

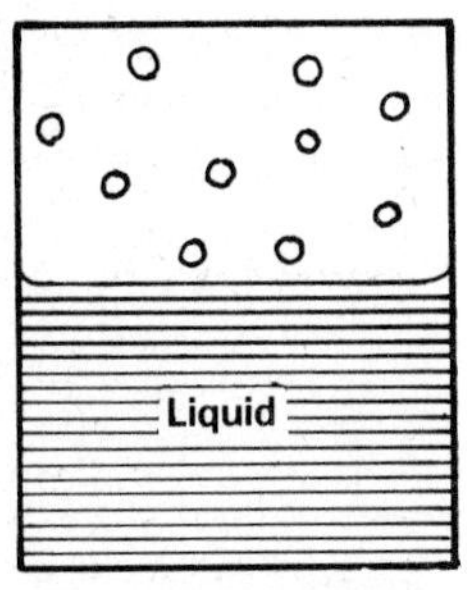

Gas molecules introduced above a liquid.

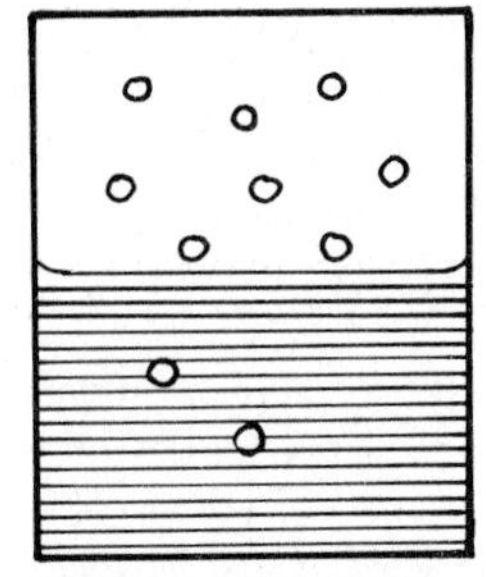

After a period of time molecules will dissolve into liquid.

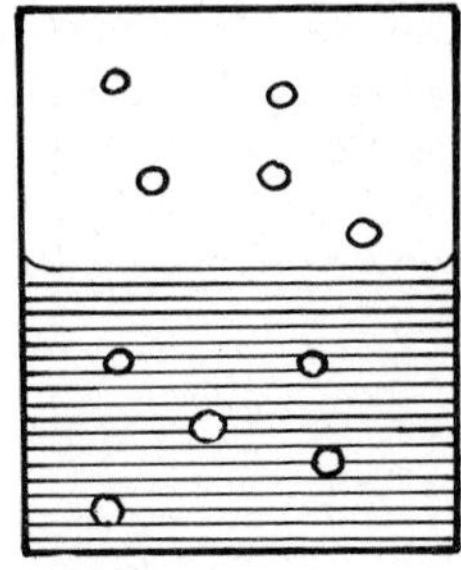

Eventually the gas pressure above and in the liquid equalize.

If the partial pressure of the gas over a liquid is increased then the amount of gas going into solution will exceed that coming out and after a period of time a new equilibrium will be established.

HENRY'S LAW

1 A.T.A.

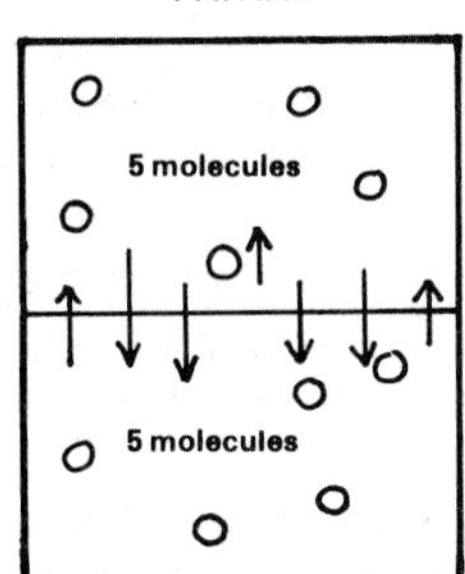

2 A.T.A.

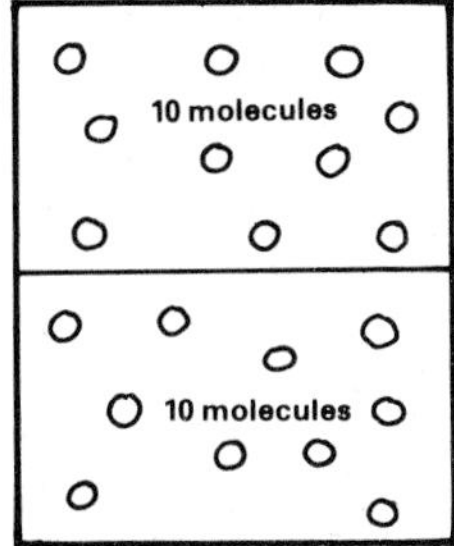

Conversely, when the partial pressure of a gas over a liquid drops, the amount of molecules coming out of solution will exceed the number going in. Therefore, a new equlibrium will be achieved after a period of time.

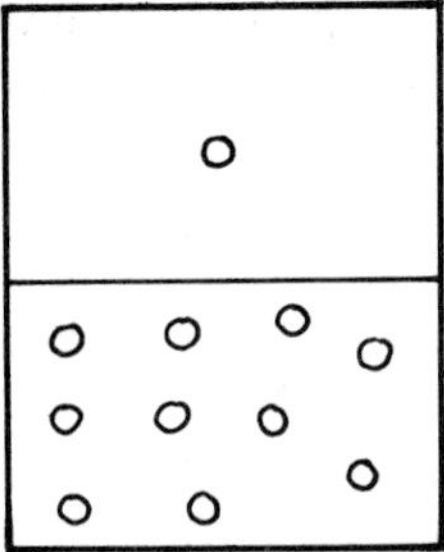

Pressure above the liquid drops.

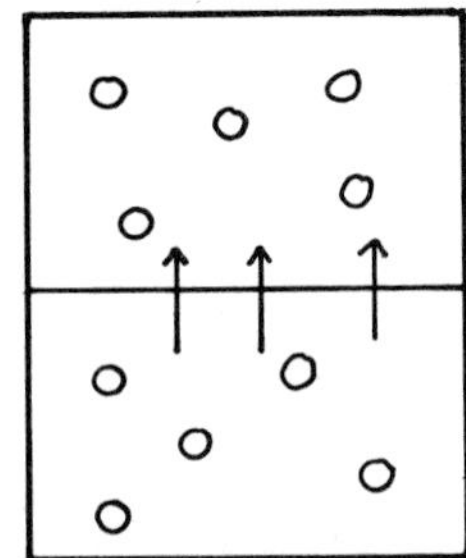

Molecules come out of solution until equilibrium is reached.

However, if the pressure drop is too rapid, molecules will come out of solution forming a bubble within the solution.

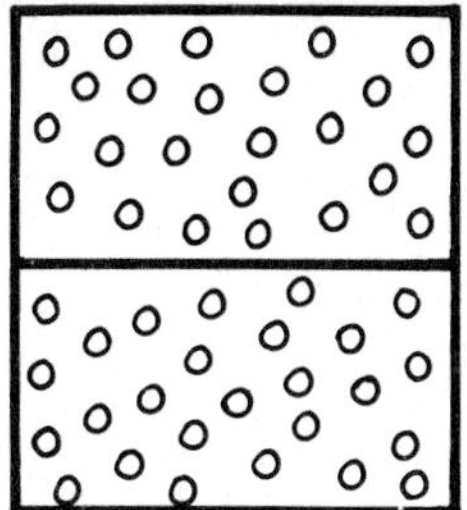
Gas Equilibrium

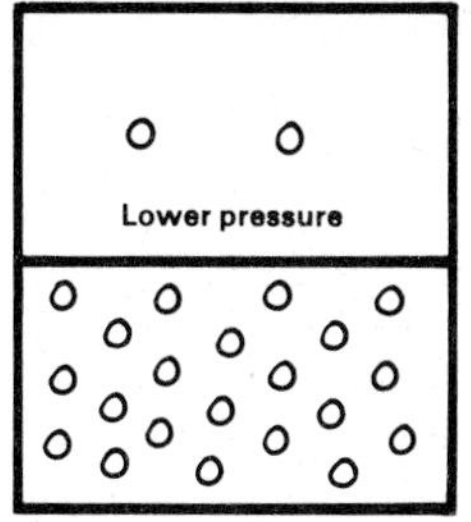

Pressure above liquid drops.

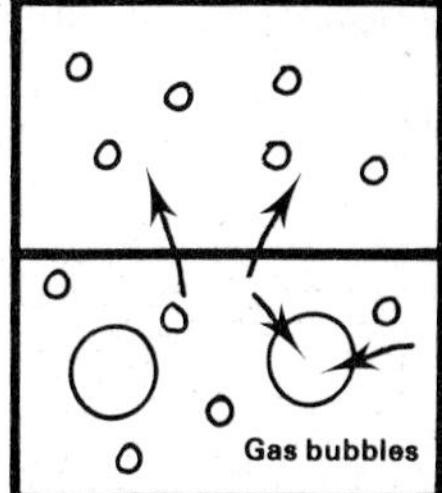

Molecules move out of solution and sometimes form bubbles.

This process can also occur in the human body. The lungs act as the gas space and the tissues of the body will receive the dissolved gases via the blood. The time for equilibrium to be achieved will depend on the solubility of the gas in the particular type of tissue and the rate at which the gas is supplied to the tissue via the blood stream. As a diver descends, the air he breathes is at a higher pressure therefore gases dissolve in his tissues until a new equilibrium is reached. This new equilibrium may take up to 12 hours to be reached depending upon the tissue. For instance, blood will achieve a new equilibrium almost instantaneously while bone tissue, because of its poor blood supply, will take up to 12 hours to equilibrate.

As the diver surfaces the partial pressures of the gases he breathes decreases and dissolved gases move out of the tissues until equilibrium is reached. This is known as **desaturation**. Blood will become desaturated rather rapidly while bone tissue will take a long time.

If a large amount of gas dissolves over a period of time then a similar period of time is required to eliminate the gas from the tissues. If insufficient time is allowed then the dissolved gas will come out of solution as bubbles. This principle can be demonstrated very readily when the top of a bottle of soft drink is removed. Gas, in this case carbon dioxide, has been held in solution by the pressure in the gas space between the liquid and the cap. Once the cap is removed, the amount of gas dissolved is too great to diffuse passively from the solution but instead forms bubbles.

Removing top slowly few bubbles form.

Removing top fast gas bubbles escape everywhere.

The clinical consequences of Henry's Law in conjunction with Dalton's Law of Partial Pressures and the principle of gas diffusion can be seen in the diving ailments known as decompression sickness, nitrogen narcosis and gas poisoning.

Section 2: EQUIPMENT

2A: Skindiving Equipment

1. Mask
2. Snorkel
3. Fins
4. Wet Suit
5. Weight Belt
6. Knife

2B: Buoyancy Compensators

1. Function
2. Essential Features
3. Recommended Features
4. Types of Buoyancy Compensators

2C: The Scuba Unit

1. Scuba Cylinders
2. Valves
3. Back Packs
4. Regulators
5. Submersible Contents Gauges

2D: Diver's Accessories

1. Depth Gauges
2. Octopus Regulators
3. Decompression Meters
4. Watches
5. Compasses
6. Torches
7. Divers' Flag
8. Surface Supplied Breathing Apparatus (Hookah)
9. Sport Divers' Spare Parts and Repair Kit

2E: Care and Maintenance

Section 2: EQUIPMENT

2A: Skindiving Equipment

1. Mask
2. Snorkel
3. Fins
4. Wet Suit
5. Weight Belt
6. Knife

Section 2 EQUIPMENT

2A Skindiving Equipment

The basic equipment of the snorkel diver is mask, fins, snorkel, wet suit, weight belt and knife.

With the correct use of this equipment, many hours of enjoyment can be expected without great expense. However, the physical effort required to become a safe and competent snorkel diver is such that proper selection of equipment suited to the task is essential.

2A: 1 Mask

Function: The mask is the most important item of diving equipment, and yet very little thought or effort goes into its selection. Its function is to provide an air space between the eyes and the water to allow correct focusing underwater (see page 13 and 14). If the mask leaks water, this function will not be achieved.

Essential Features: It is imperative that the mask be made of material which is soft enough to produce a complete seal on the face. This seal can be achieved by utilizing either a single edge of rubber or a double feathered edge of rubber on the mask. A proper sealing mask can be found by placing the mask to the face (hair must not interfere with seal) and breathing inwards through the nose. The mask should stay in place without the aid of hands or mask straps. To avoid eye damage should the mask break, the face plate must be made of tempered or safety glass. Indication of this is printed on the face plate, usually near the top of the mask. Provision of two indents in the lower surround of the mask must be present to allow equilization of the pressure in the middle ear (see Section 3B). The nose should be readily accessible through these indents, preferably with one hand.

Recommended Features: The above features are essential. However, before making the final selection of your mask the following points should be considered. The face plate should be easily removable and the clip holding it in place should be either plastic or stainless steel to avoid corrosion. Avoid selecting a mask with exposed nuts and bolts as they can catch hair or equipment. Black rubber is recommended as it is generally stronger, more resistant to perishing and less expensive than coloured rubber. The strap should be split at the back with a strong positive locking system, which is easily adjustable. Purge valves are a potential source of leakage and should be avoided.

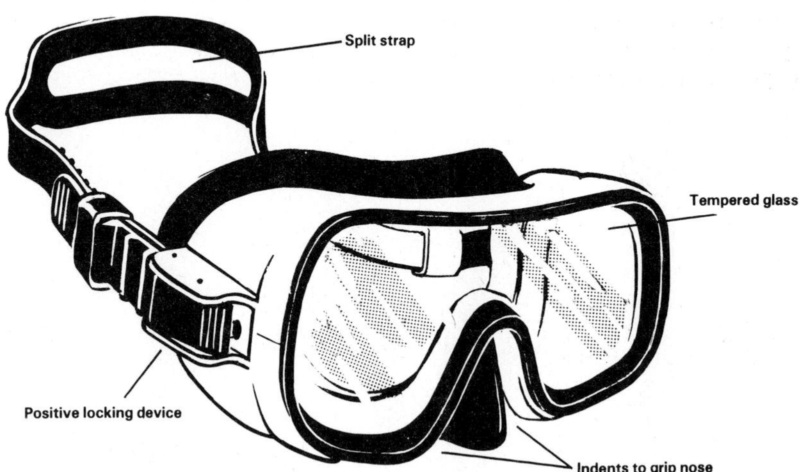

If the diver wears corrective lenses for normal vision, the problem can be overcome by one of three methods. The most common approach is to bond optically corrected lenses directly to the face plate. An alternative is to procure a set of frames which clip onto the face plate and hang free within the mask. This method is not recommended as fogging may become a problem. Some manufacturers market masks with individual lenses which can be removed and replaced with prescription lenses. These masks generally have a narrow field of vision.

Mask with optically corrected lenses

2A: 2 Snorkel

Function: The snorkel allows the diver to swim and breathe on the surface without having to lift his face out of the water. As such, the snorkel must fulfill certain requirements.

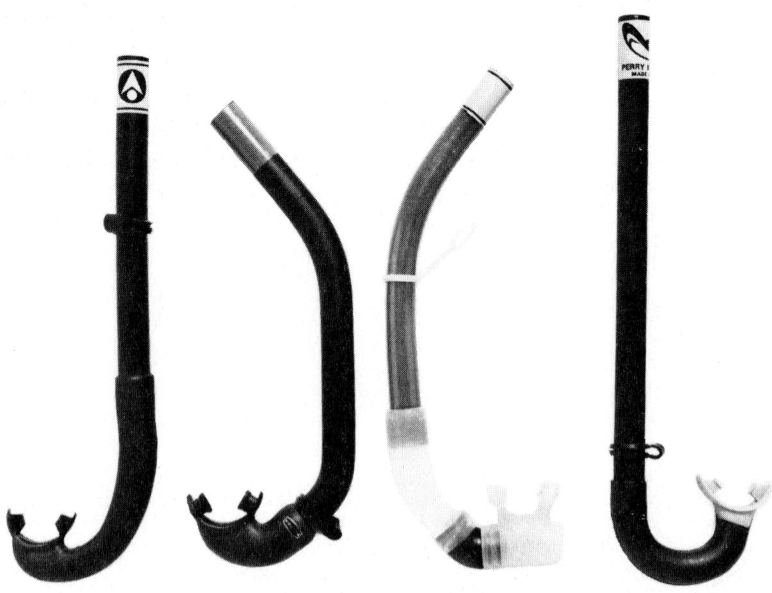

Essential Features: The snorkel needs to be an open ended J shaped tube 15-20 mm in diameter. The tube or barrel should be approximately 30-40 mm above mouth level while at the same time being constructed of flexible rubber. Avoid hard plastic tubes which may cause injury and mask flooding if caught while submerged.

Recommended Features: The choice of snorkel mainly depends on comfort. The mouthpiece should be soft, smooth and easily gripped. Corrugations, sharp angles and sharp edges all increase breathing resistance and should be avoided. Similarly, purge valves should be avoided as they are a source of leakage.

At all times, the snorkel should be attached to the left hand side of the mask strap to avoid loss and entanglement with scuba regulator hoses.

2A: 3 Fins

The sole purpose of fins is to propel the diver. They are designed for swimming — not walking. Walking in fins can often result in loss of balance, and injury to the diver.

Types of Fins: There are basically three types of fins:

a. Full foot type which are not adjustable but provide protection to heels from cuts and abrasions.
b. Open heel type which are adjustable but do not provide protection to heels from cuts and abrasions, unless neoprene booties are worn.
c. Fins are now available with rubber foot and various types of plastic forming the blades. Although expensive they give good performance.

Features: Black rubber should be used in all rubber products, particularly fins, as it is stronger, more durable, less flexible, and does not float. When beginning, choose fins which are of normal size and construction. Large stiff blades are more powerful, but require stronger leg muscles. Blades with vents or slots provide questionable increase in performance, and usually prove costly to purchase.

When choosing fins, select a pair which are not too tight. Though loose fins can cause problems, tight fins will cramp the muscles of the foot and leg. Loose fins can be held in place using triangular rubber straps known as fin grips or fix-palms.

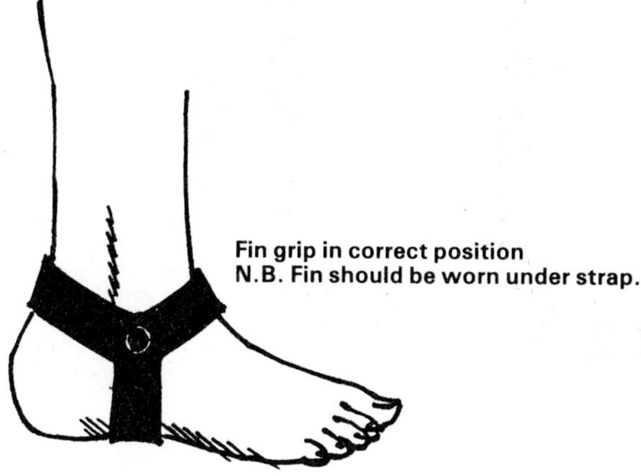

Fin grip in correct position
N.B. Fin should be worn under strap.

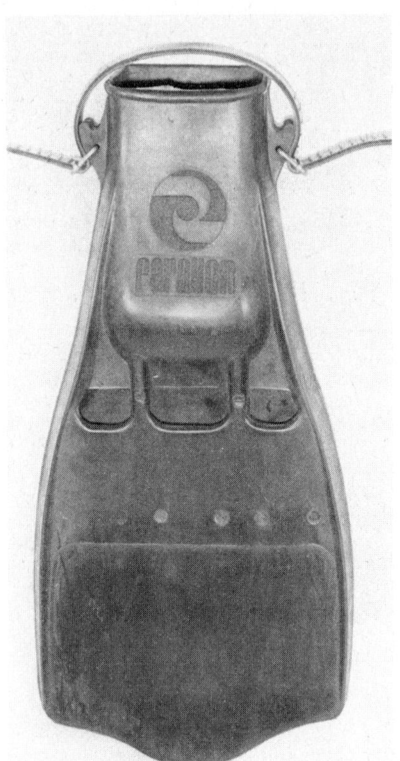

Open heel fin with slots.

Open heel fin without slots.

2A: 4 Wet Suits

Function: The majòr function of the wet suit is to minimize heat loss and therefore prevent the diver from getting too cold. Wet suit material, rubber neoprene, provides an insulating layer of tiny air bubbles between the diver's skin and the water. Neoprene also provides some physical protection against the sun, cuts, abrasions, stings and bruises. Wet suits also have limited reserve buoyancy in the advent of the weight belt being dropped, but they will not suport an unconscious diver face up.

Types of Suit: The choice of suit will depend on the diver's financial state and the proposed type of diving.

Obviously, the more rubber covering the body the warmer the suit will be. Emphasis should be placed on keeping the upper body and head warm.

The two types of suits generally used for diving are:

a. The standard dive suit; jacket, trousers and hood usually made from 5 mm thick material.
b. The professional dive suit; jacket with attached hood and farmer-john (long-john) type trousers usually 7 mm thick.

Both types of suits can be purchased in either single-lined (nylon on inside only) or in double-lined (nylon on both inside and outside surfaces) material. Double-lined material is more expensive but more resistant to wear and tear.

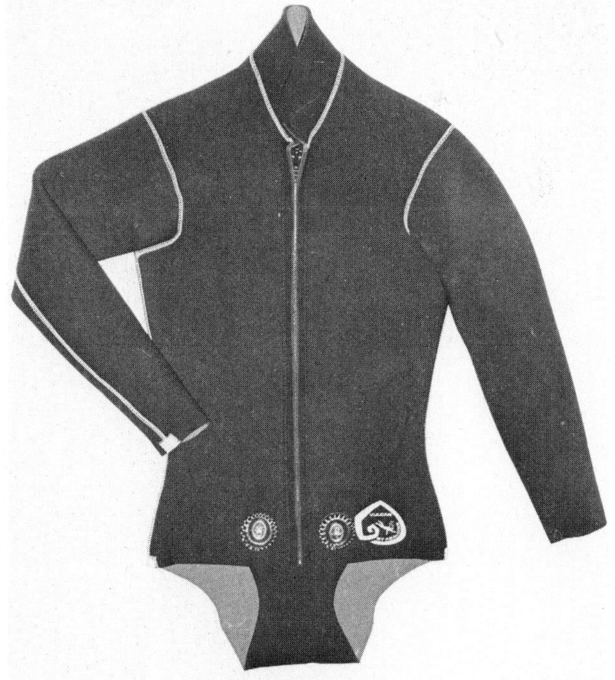

Standard dive suit coat.

Essential Features: The suit should have an all over snug fit without cramping or pinching. Spaces under the arms, at the neck or crotch should be avoided. Calves should be firm enough to prevent water flow but loose enough to allow free blood circulation in the extremities. A wet suit can be purchased directly off the rack or if an adequate fit cannot be obtained the suit can be tailor made.

Recommended Features: Most suits now come standard with glued and sewed seams. Gluing minimizes water leakage while sewing strengthens seams. If possible, suits should be worn with knee pads and perhaps elbow pads as well. These will increase the life of knee and elbow areas. Zippers in arms and legs may allow water leakage but do make dressing and undressing easier. If possible, avoid zippers.

Pro dive suit coat.

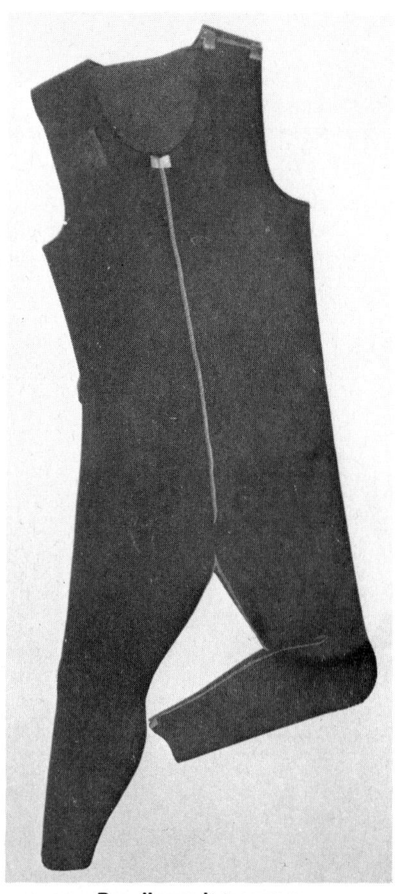

Pro dive suit trousers.

2A: 5 Weight Belts

Function: The weight belt (along with the lead weights) is carried to counter the increased buoyancy caused by the wet suit.

Essential Features: Most weight belts are constructed from 50 cm (2 inch) wide nylon webbing with one of two types of quick release buckles. Nylon webbing is durable and inexpensive but does allow the weights to slip from the belt. The most commonly used buckle is the flat lever type. This belt is easily adjusted and allows for quick removal and addition of weights.

The wire buckles are more difficult to adjust.

The overall concept of a quick release buckle is a buckle which can be opened with a clenched fist. It should be clear of all other straps and harness to ensure ease of removal.

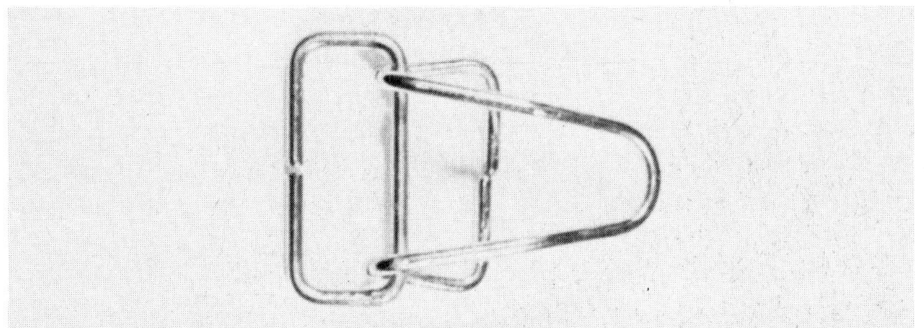

Wire weight belt buckle.

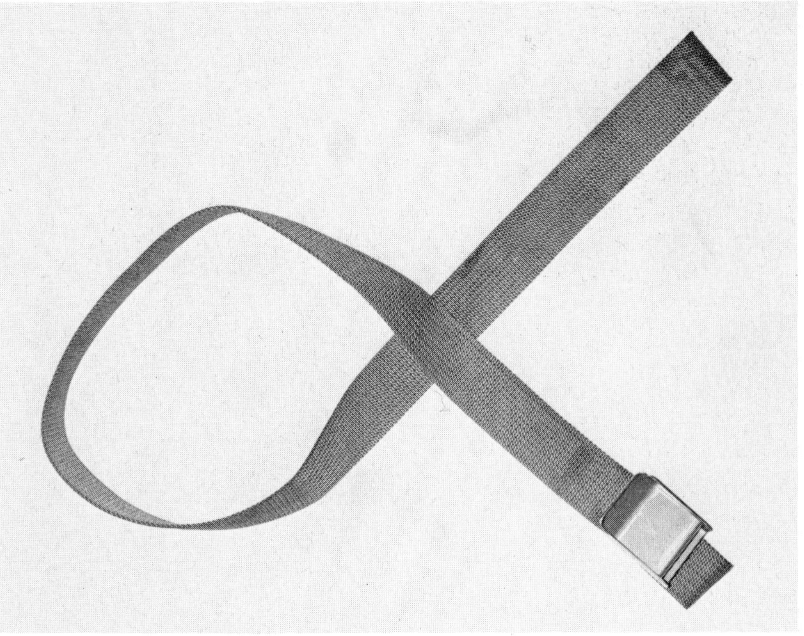

Modern weight belt with flat lever buckle.

2A: 6 Knife

Function: The function of the knife varies according to the diver wearing it. Its prime function should be for cutting but knives may be called upon to act as levers, hammers, prodders, or merely for the security they give the owner. Unfortunately, most knives on the market fall short of being useful as cutting instruments as they are generally made of stainless steel which is too soft.

Essential Features: A knife should have a handle which feels comfortable when held. The blade should be sharp and part of it should be serrated for better cutting.

If the owner wishes to use the knife as a lever for removing abalone shells, then the end should be wedge shaped and thickened. The sheath should be strong with a rubber loop device for holding the knife in place. The straps which hold the sheath to the arm or leg should be rubber to allow for wet suit compression while underwater.

If the knife is to be a useful cutting instrument it will have a dull (not chrome) blade and usually will show signs of rust very soon after use. This will indicate a higher carbon content and therefore a stronger blade. In order to keep the knife in usable condition, a small amount of silicone grease should be wiped over the blade after each use.

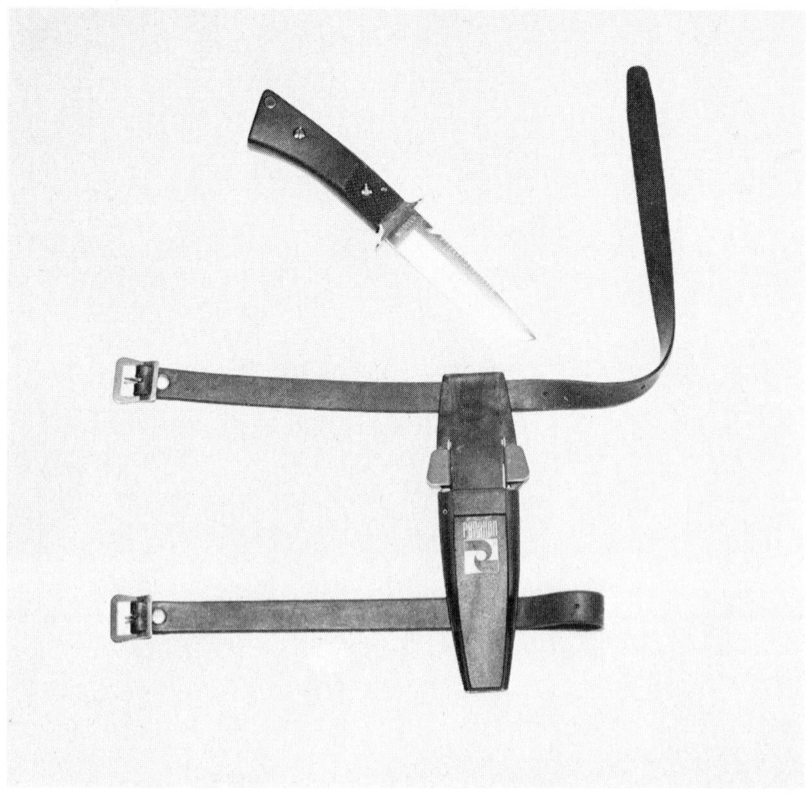

Section 2: EQUIPMENT

2B: Buoyancy Compensators

1. Function
2. Essential Features
3. Recommended Features
4. Types of Buoyancy Compensators

Section 2B BUOYANCY COMPENSATORS

2B: 1 Function

As the name implies, the major function of a buoyancy compensator is to help the diver compensate for buoyancy changes which occur during diving. Wet suit compression and the collection of artifacts will cause buoyancy changes during the dive. However, due to the potentially hazardous environment, a good compensator has many other functions as well. Probably the most obvious of these functions is an ascent and flotation aid. If a diver gets into trouble on the surface, or needs to make a rapid ascent (which should be avoided), then most compensators have some means whereby an emergency supply of compressed gas can be injected into them to rapidly increase the volume.

Once the surface is reached the compensator can be used to either aid in surface snorkelling or as a floating device for administering expired air respiration to an unconscious diver. A properly designed buoyancy compensator should float an unconscious diver face upwards at all times. Most boating authorities will not allow a buoyancy compensator to be worn in place of a life jacket while in a boat as they have to be manually inflated which is impossible if the wearer is knocked unconscious and they may also puncture if the wearer is washed onto sharp rocks.

2B: 2 Essential Features

Most compensators which are now produced have some method of emergency inflation, either by a carbon dioxide (CO_2) charged cartridge or a high pressure air filled bottle. If inflated while at depth the resulting expansion of gas on ascent necessitates that an over inflation pressure relief valve be incorporated into the vest to avoid bursting.

To avoid losing control of ascent it is essential to be able to dump excess gas quickly. To facilitate this a good compensator should have the oral inflation hose attached high on the collar or have a special dump valve. It is most important that a hose for oral inflation is included and that it is large in diameter and flexible so as to ensure that inflation is as easy as possible.

All straps included with the vest should be at least 25 mm to 35 mm wide with easy attachments. The inclusion of a crutch strap aids in keeping the vest held snugly to the body.

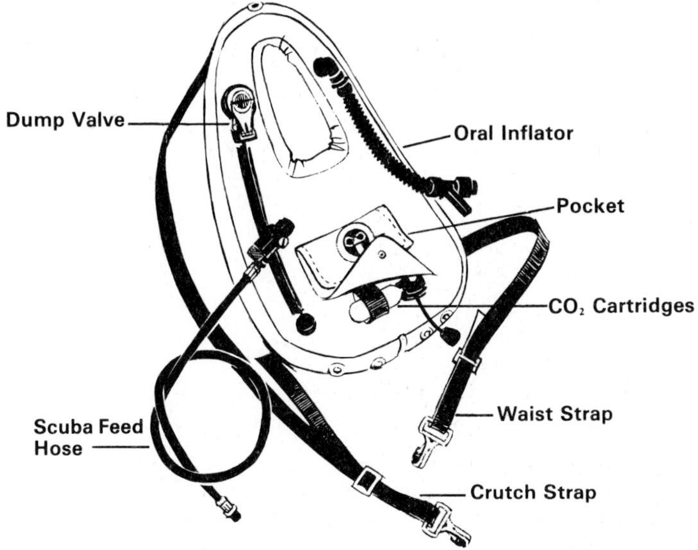

A Scuba Fed Buoyancy Compensator

2B: 3 Recommended Features:

Many vests are manufactured in brightly coloured materials for easy sighting and supplied with a whistle to attract attention on the surface. The vest should also have sufficient volume to keep a heavily laden diver clear of the water. As inflation occurs the volume increase should be away from the body without tightening the securing straps.

2B: 4 Types of Buoyancy Compensators:

Over the past few years buoyancy compensator design has markedly improved, not only in the quality of the material and workmanship but also in versatility. Most compensators can be grouped into one of four general designs. They are:

a. Carbon dioxide cartridge supply
b. Independent air supply
c. Scuba feed air supply
d. Stabilizer jacket

a. Carbon Dioxide Cartridge Supply: These are usually the cheapest and simplest to use. Most have all the above "essential features" but that is all. They have no emergency air supply and are generally small in volume. This type of compensator is ideal for snorkeling but rather limited in its use with scuba equipment. However, any type of compensator is better than none and so, because of cheapness, a considerable number are still sold to scuba divers. Most can be converted to scuba feed later on.

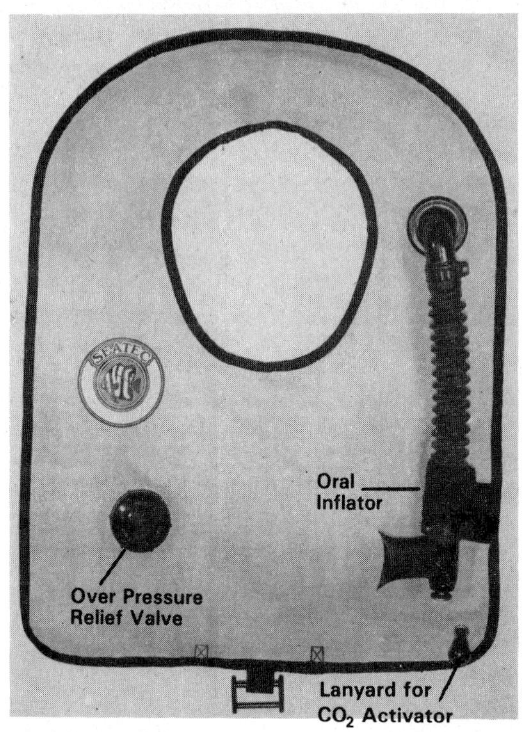
SEATEC
Oral Inflator
Over Pressure Relief Valve
Lanyard for CO_2 Activator

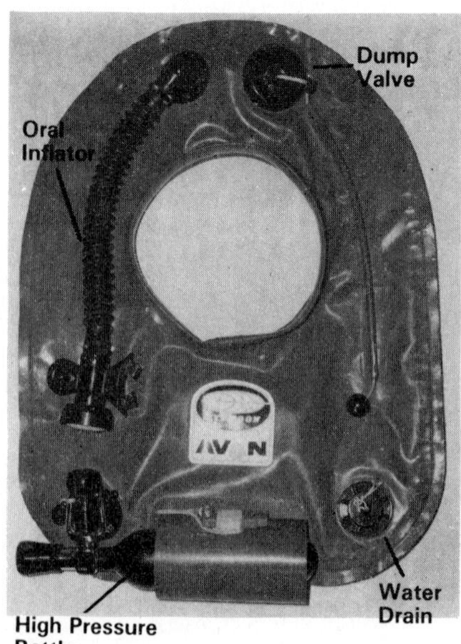
Dump Valve
Oral Inflator
Water Drain
High Pressure Bottle

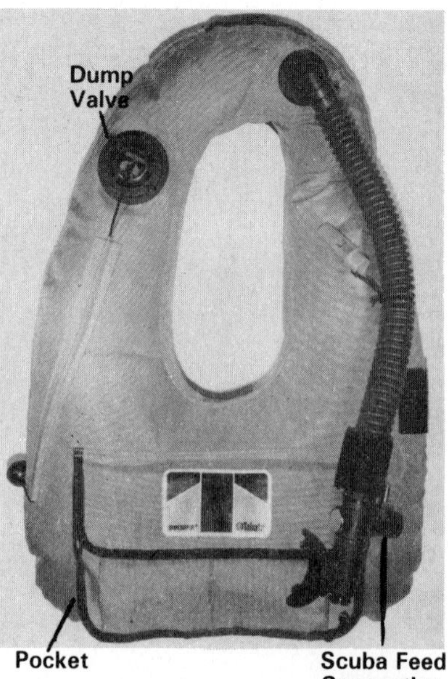
Dump Valve
Pocket
Scuba Feed Connection

b. Independent Air Supply: The major advantage of this type of compensator is that they have an independent air supply which can be breathed should the diver's main supply fail. All independent air supply compensators have a high pressure bottle which is filled from the scuba cylinder prior to the dive. They have all of the above essential features and have a large volume. However, they have many disadvantages. They are heavy and bulky as well as expensive and if the bag ruptures they are difficult to repair. There is also some difficulty getting the high pressure bottle tested for safety and most compensators of this type have no pocket for accessories.

c. Scuba Fed Air Supply: These compensators are similar to CO_2 cartridge supply compensators but have the inclusion of a hose and filling attachment from the first stage of the scuba regulator. Most have a large volume and many have accessory pockets as well. They usually have an inner bladder which is accessible through a zip surrounding the neck area of the compensator. If they become punctured they can be easily repaired using a swimming pool liner repair kit. Although they tend to be expensive they combine the best of both types above without most of the disadvantages of the independent air supply type. If the scuba cylinder needs to be ditched then a quick release fitting on the vest allows for rapid removal of the inflator hose from the compensator.

d. Stabilizer Jacket: These vests have all of the advantages of the scuba fed air supply type compensator and incorporate a back pack into the design. They are designed to be worn surrounding the chest to give maximum support and comfort. In general, provided that they in fact float the diver face upwards, they are very comfortable but expensive. Some varieties require considerable skill and practice to achieve the results advertised by the manufacturer.

In general compensators should be put on immediately after the wetsuit unless they are the stabilizing type. Once purchased, the diver should familiarize himself with the vest in a pool or enclosed water before venturing into the ocean. Buoyancy control, rescue and resuscitation techniques should be practised regularly.

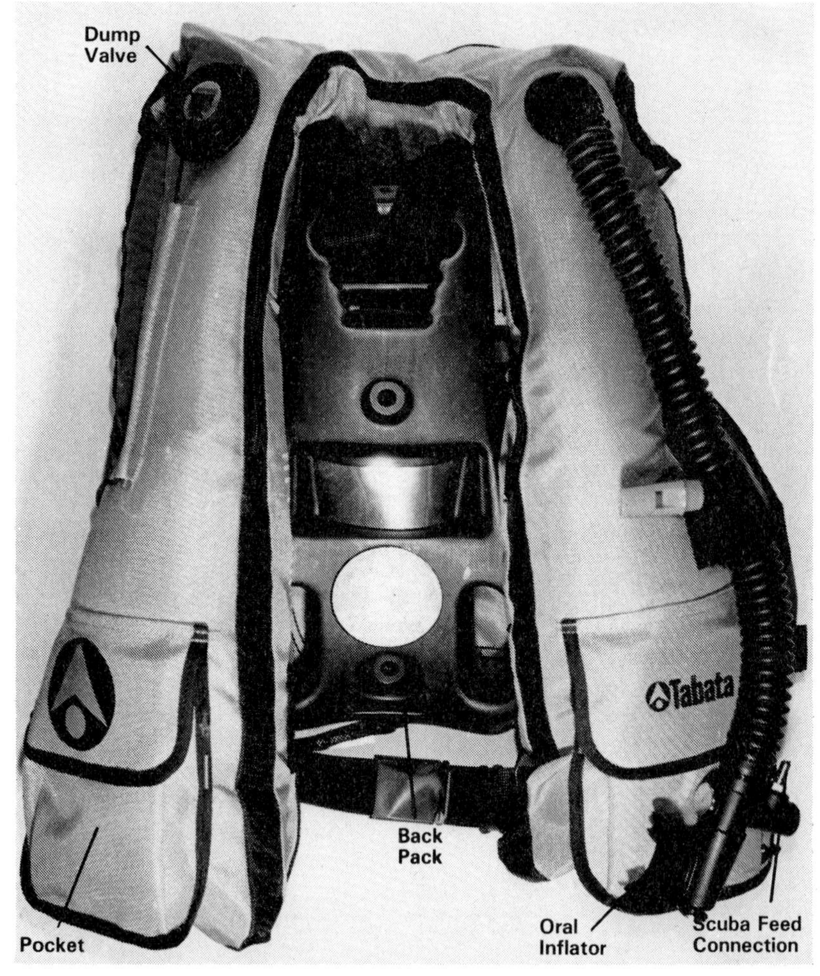

STABILIZER JACKET

Section 2: EQUIPMENT

2C: The Scuba Unit

1. Scuba Cylinders
2. Valves
3. Back Packs
4. Regulators
   a. Function
   b. Design principles of the regulator
   c. The first stage or reduction valve
   d. The second stage or demand valve
   e. Fault finding
5. Submersible Contents Gauges

Section 2C THE SCUBA UNIT

Man has been endeavouring, for one reason or another, to be able to extend his time under water for the past two thousand years. However, diving as we know it today really began after 1943 when Cousteau and Gagnon developed the forerunner to the modern SCUBA demand valve.

The term SCUBA refers to Self Contained Underwater Breathing Aparatus which, as the name implies, refers to the ability of the diver to breathe from a unit which is completely self contained. Nowadays the term "scuba" has become a word in itself and refers to diving with scuba equipment.

It is intended to cover those items of equipment being used by sport divers today. The true scuba unit consists of a metal cylinder filled with high pressure air, a valve which allows filling and emptying of the cylinder, a regulator comprising a reducing valve and a demand valve, a back pack to allow ease of carrying and a contents gauge to monitor the air supply.

2C: 1 Scuba Cylinders

Function: The basic function of the scuba cylinder, or tank, is to store high pressure air. Most cylinders on the market today are either steel alloy or aluminium alloy and have filling or working pressures (W.P. or C.P.) in the order of 150-300 atmospheres. Due to the extreme working conditions of scuba cylinders, they must be manufactured to very high standards and maintained to precise requirements as there is a remote possibility of explosion.

Essential Features: It is imperative that the cylinder first of all be manufactured to an acceptable specification.

SOME ACCEPTABLE SPECIFICATIONS

Australian Standards:

AS 1777	Seamless Aluminium Cylinders for compressed gases (0.10 to 130 litres)
AS B113	High Tensile Carbon-Manganese Steel Cylinders for the Storage and Transport of Permanent Gases and High Pressure Liquefiable Gases
AS B114	Alloy Steel Cylinders for the Storage and Transport of Permanent Gases and High-Pressure Liquefiable Gases.

British Home Office Specifications:

Steel Alloy	Aluminium Alloy	
HOS	HOAL 1	HOAL 3
HOT	HOAL 2	HOAL 4

Canadian Specifications:

BTC 3AA Steel Alloy

United States of America: (Department of Transport)

Steel Alloy	Aluminium Alloy	
ICC 3AA	DOT SP6498	DOT 3 AL
DOT 3AA	DOT E 6498	

In order to be acceptable the cylinder must have one of the codes shown in the above table stamped on the thick metal of the neck. If in doubt check with your local professional dive store.

However, knowing that the cylinder was originally acceptable does not mean that it is still in usable condition. To ensure that cylinders remain in a safe condition, a cylinder must be visually inspected annually and hydrostatically test regularly. For instance, in Australia the hydrostatic test (hydro meaning water and static meaning pressure) is required annually whereas in U.S.A. it is every five years. Check your country's requirements with your local professional dive store. Only certain test stations are authorised to act as inspection or test stations and it is important that the diver ascertains the authenticity of the station. An unauthorised station can damage a cylinder beyond repair.

When the cylinder is brought in for testing it is emptied and the valve removed. The only part of the valve which is checked is the threads. If the threads of the valve are damaged, then it will not be replaced if the cylinder itself passes. The cylinder is then inspected externally for signs of rust, pits, dents, gouges, and heat affected areas. The threads in the neck are then inspected, followed by a visual examination of the inside walls using a bright light lowered into the cylinder. If at this stage the cylinder has failed to meet the requirements, then it is cut into at least two pieces. Some steel cylinders will have rust which coats the inner walls obscuring the pits below. This superficial rust is removed by a process known as 'rumbling', where steel pellets are placed in the cylinder and rotated for up to twenty-four hours. After this process has been completed the internal walls are again inspected.

Once the cylinder has passed these initial requirements it is weighed and checked against the original tare weight (TW) of the cylinder, stamped in the neck, to give an indication of loss of metal due to corrosion and rumbling.

The cylinder is now filled with water and connected to a high pressure water pump. Water is used for two reasons.

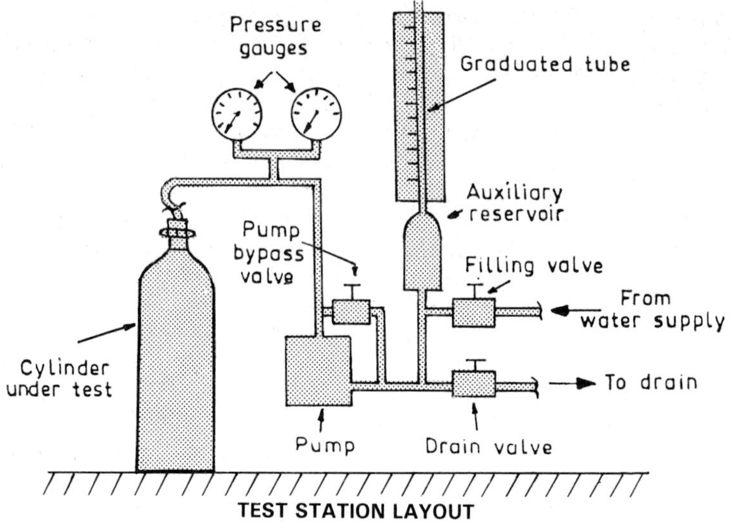

TEST STATION LAYOUT

Firstly, water is incompressible so if the cylinder fails the test it doesn't explode. Second, water will give a visual indication of any permanent stretching of the cylinder walls by the drop in level of water in the measuring equipment. The cylinder is now pressurised to its test pressure (T or TP) and held at that pressure for thirty seconds. During this time the walls of the cylinder will stretch and the water level in the capillary tube will drop. The pressure is then released and the water will move back up the tube as the cylinder walls contract again. If any permanent stretch has occurred it will be indicated by a drop in water level in the capillary tube. This test is the only way of ascertaining the strength of the cylinder and it is important that it is carried out accurately.

Once the cylinder has passed the test it is dried using hot air and the stamp of the test station and the date of test is placed on the metal of the neck.

The valve is now replaced and the cylinder is filled. It is essential that a cylinder not be bought if it does not have a test stamp within the previous twelve months.

Other information which can be found on the neck of the cylinder includes:

Serial number — important for cylinder identification.

Year of manufacture.

Water capacity — useful when testing cylinder for identification of permanent stretch and for calculating volume of usable air.

Dates of previous inspections.

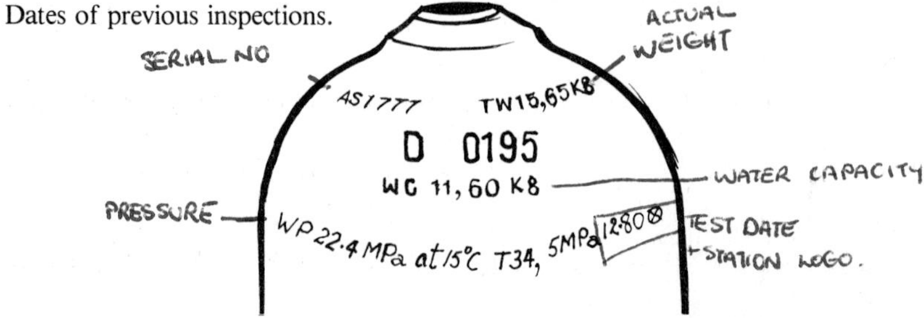

The capacity of the cylinder can vary considerably according to the volume of the cylinder (water capacity) and filling pressure. These two items together will give the number of litres of usable air. Most steel cylinders are approximately 1800 litres. Aluminium cylinders are manufactured in various litre capacities because their appropriate capacity and working pressures vary. The practice of over-filling a cylinder to gain more time under water should be avoided as it weakens and shortens the life expectancy of the cylinder.

Long term storage of cylinders poses a problem in that unless correct procedures are followed a steel cylinder may corrode to a point where it becomes unsafe within six to eight weeks. For periods of time longer than two months cylinders should be emptied down to the last 2 to 2·5 megapascals (20 to 25 atmospheres) of pressure. This is to ensure that the valve is left closed. Cylinders should be stood on end, in a cool, dry place, so that any corrosion which may occur does so in the base where the cylinder is at its thickest. The back pack and boot should be removed regularly to ensure that no corrosion is present under them.

Once the cylinder is to be used again it should be completely emptied and internally inspected then refilled.

2C: 2 Valves

The valves currently being used in most cylinders are of two basic designs. They are either referred to as the K valve, a valve with no reserve mechanism, or the J valve with a reserve mechanism.

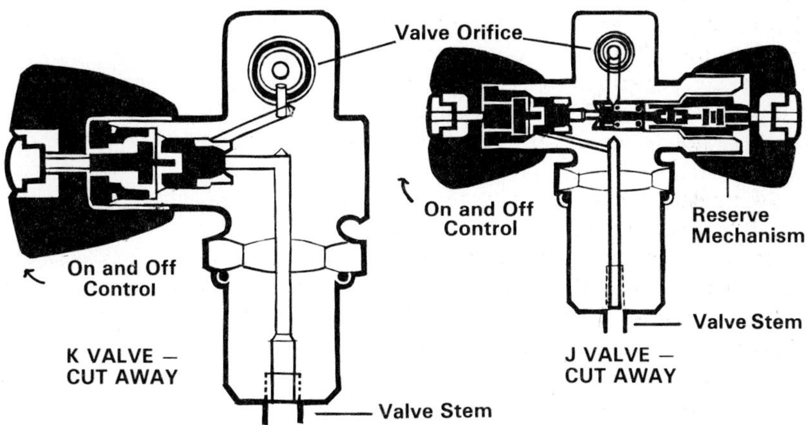

The J valve is easily remembered as it has a J-shaped piece of rod to pull the reserve mechanism on and off.

Function: The cylinder valve controls entry and exit of high pressure air into and out of the cylinder. Those valves with a built in reserve (J valves) also act as an emergency device in that they warn the diver when he is low on air.

Basic Valve Components:

a. On and off control — a brass plug with a teflon insert that screws onto the valve seat.

b. Valve orifice — O ring sealed opening which directs air flow into the scuba regulator.
c. Burst disc — older valves are equipped with a pressure relief valve which is designed to rupture when cylinder pressure exceeds a set safety margin. They consist of a brass plug held in place with a hollow screw. If the pressure of the cylinder exceeds the rating of the brass disc, its centre blows out through the centre of the screw, therefore releasing the cylinder contents. A new brass disc is then inserted and the cylinder refilled.
d. Cylinder O ring — creates an air tight seal between the cylinder and the valve. Valves need only be gently tightened into place by hand as the O ring forms an efficient seal.
e. Safety hole — located in the thread area of some valves so that excess air escapes if the valve is unscrewed while there is still positive pressure in the cylinder.
f. Valve stem — a protruding hollow rod which hangs down into the cylinder to stop contaminants inside the cylinder from clogging up the valve and the regulator.
g. High pressure outlet — optional orifice found on some valves for attachment of accessories such as submersible contents gauges.

J Valve versus K Valve

The K valve is a simple on and off type tap. There is very little that can actually go wrong, provided they are serviced annually.

The J valve, on the other hand, has the basic K valve components but also allows air to travel to the reverse side of the valve, where a teflon block is held in place by a spring with a tension equivalent to 20 atmospheres. While the cylinder contents are higher than 20 atmospheres the block and spring are pushed out of the way and air travels up to the regulator. Once the cylinder pressure drops to below 20 atmospheres the block shuts off the orifice and the diver's supply of air. By pulling the reserve lever down, the block is mechanically withdrawn, releasing the final 20 atmospheres to the diver.

In theory, the J valve is an excellent idea. However, they are only as efficient as the spring and teflon block will allow them to be. In fact, many things can and do go wrong with the J valve. The lever can be either lost or inadvertently knocked downwards during the dive so that when the diver goes to turn on the reserve it is already on. Another problem is that the spring will fatigue or the teflon block will become scarred, allowing the last 20 atmospheres to leak past.

Perhaps the most difficult problem to overcome is that 20 atmospheres of air is not enough to have as a reserve if something goes wrong or the dive is a particularly deep one. There are far better ways of regulating the dive so that adequate air is left for emergency purposes.

2C: 3 Back Packs

The back pack is a device for holding the cylinder securely and comfortably on the back of the diver. As such it needs to be robust in construction with a secure method of fastening the cylinder in place. The use of a "quick release" or "cam action" band allows easy removal of cylinders for washing or storing purposes.

The plate of the back pack should have solid handles on both sides at the base as well as one at the top. Cylinders should not be carried by their valves but by the handle at the top of the back pack.

Straps and buckles should be easily adjusted and be readily accessible at all times. Do not be tempted to buy a back pack unless it has a shoulder, as well as a waist, quick release buckle.

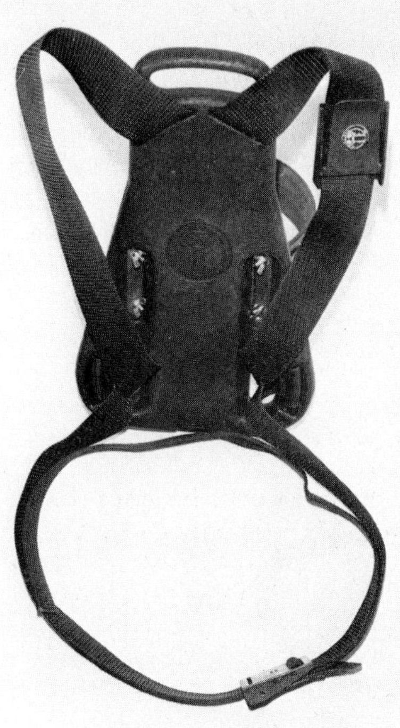

BACK PACK
Front View

BACK PACK
Back View

2C: 4 Regulators

Since the development of the modern regulator in 1943 there have been two major outward design principles involved. Though outwardly different in appearance, both types have very similar arrangements of parts and working principles. The original type of regulator was known as a twin hose regulator. It had either one or two stages of pressure reduction to reduce air to ambient pressure.

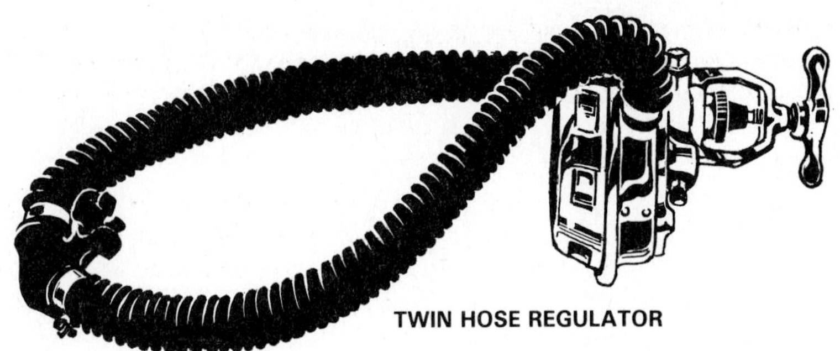
TWIN HOSE REGULATOR

Later, this type of regulator was modified to what is now referred to as the two stage single hose regulator.

Parts availability, performance, ease of use and many other factors all prevent the twin hose regulator being used extensively today. The single hose regulator has virtually captured the majority of the market and so it is intended to deal only with the single hose regulator here.

a. Function:

The function of the regulator is twofold. The first function is to reduce the tank pressure (which is variable) down to a line pressure (which is constant). This constant line pressure, usually about 6-9 atmospheres above ambient pressure, is further reduced to slightly above ambient. Since reduction of tank pressure is carried out in two stages by different mechanisms the regulator is referred to as a two stage single hose regulator.

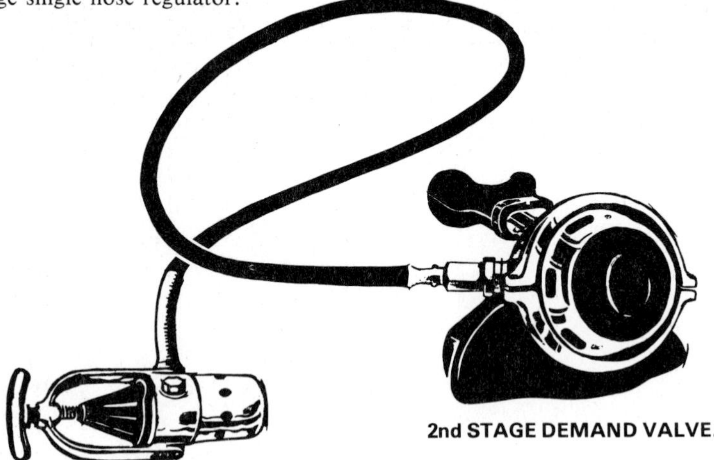
2nd STAGE DEMAND VALVE.

1st STAGE REDUCING VALVE.

b. Design Principle of the Regulator:

To become fully conversant with the design and function of a regulator would take a manual by itself and many hours of practical work. This level of understanding is not required. However, the diver should have some idea of what is available in regulator design and the relative merits of each type.

c. *First Stage or Reducing Valve*

All first stage designs require water pressure to act on them to ensure line pressure is always above ambient. Line pressure is achieved in one of four basic designs.

(i) Diaphragm First Stage

The diaphragm first stage is the offshoot from the older twin hose regulator. They are generally the cheapest of the regulators on the market but this may not always be the case. In the diaphragm first stage the diaphragm acts as a seal and protects the moving parts from the water. However, corrosion can still occur if the dust cap is not promptly replaced after a dive.

The disadvantages far outweigh the advantages. As well as poor airflow, the diaphragm first stage does not give rise to constant line pressure and free flow of the demand valve may occur as the cylinder pressure drops.

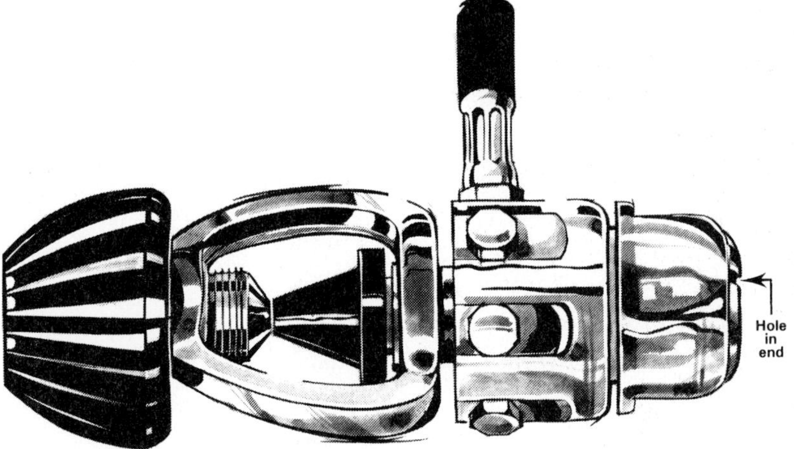

DIAPHRAM 1st STAGE

(ii) Piston First Stage

This type of first stage has many advantages over the diaphragm first stage. The major advantage is the improved air flow which can be achieved with such a design. Also, maintenance and repair is far easier due to simple design and only two moving parts which generally require no fine adjustments.

The major disadvantage is that the moving parts are exposed to the water and therefore sand and grit may cause wear and tear. This can be avoided by thoroughly washing the regulator after each use.

Like the diaphragm first stage the piston first stage does not provide a constant line pressure. In this case the line pressure falls as cylinder pressure drops, therefore making it harder to breathe towards the end of the dive.

In order to overcome two major problems, that is air flow and line pressure, the first stage design was improved and "balanced" regulators evolved. Balanced first stages have good air flow at a greater range of depth. They also deliver air at a constant line pressure no matter what the cylinder pressure is, which ensures consistent demand valve function.

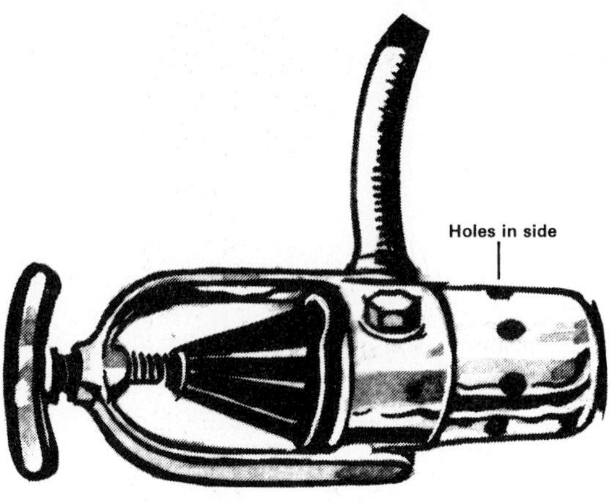

PISTON 1st STAGE

(iii) Balanced Diaphragm First Stage

The advantages of the balanced diaphragm are the same as for the diaphragm as well as having an improved air flow rating. They also deliver a constant line pressure, therefore improving the performance of the demand valve. The main disadvantages of the balanced diaphragm first stage is its expense, and more complicated workings increasing the maintenance required.

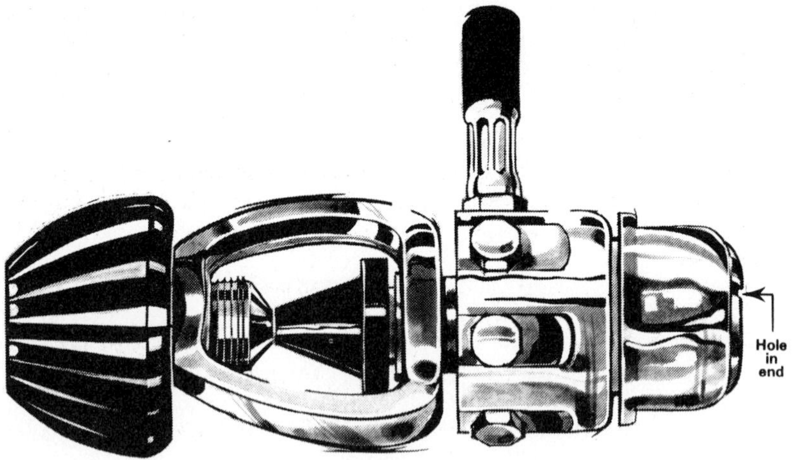

BALANCED DIAPHRAM 1st STAGE

(iv) Balanced Piston First Stage

This is generally the "Rolls Royce" of regulators in that it has all the advantages of the piston with even better flow characteristics, and it delivers a constant line pressure to improve demand valve performance. Once again, corrosion problems are the major concern. Expense can also be prohibitive.

The first stage or reduction valve is connected by a low pressure hose to the second stage or demand valve. The hose requires protection at the first and second stage junction points. To achieve this, hose protectors can be purchased at most dive stores.

d. Second Stage or Demand Valve

The function of the second stage is to reduce the line pressure to ambient pressure so that it can be breathed comfortably by the diver. There are basically two types of second stage valve mechanisms in use today. They are known as the upstream (tilt) valve and downstream (lever) valve.

(i) Upstream or Tilt Valve

Tilt valves were the first type of valve developed for use in demand valves and were mainly used in twin hose regulators. They are opened by a force tilting the rod and allowing air to escape past the seal. The valve opens into, or upstream of, the air flow.

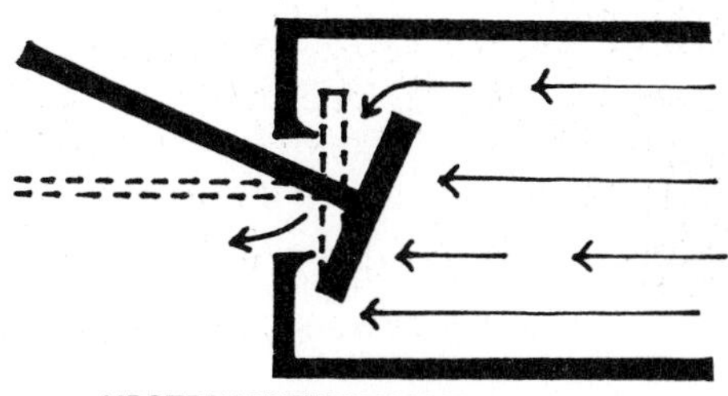

UPSTREAM TILT VALVE

The main advantages are that they function relatively well regardless of the line pressure. They are also cheap to manufacture and easy to maintain.

A pressure relief valve is required on the first stage in case the first stage malfunctions and delivers higher pressure air to the second stage. If this were to occur then the upstream valve would be forced closed until the hose ruptured.

Perhaps the greatest disadvantage is the relative inefficiency of the valve. The flow rate is very low. Its main use is with surface supplied equipment known as Hookah, because the compressor delivering the air does not sustain a constant line pressure. The tilt valve is able to handle varying line pressures, but must be supplied with a non-return valve, fitted close to the demand valve. Otherwise, if the hose, which may be at a shallower depth and therefore a lower pressure, bursts, the air within the remaining line attached to the diver will rapidly flow out, creating a suction effect in the mouthpiece that can be dangerous.

The Hookah system must also have a pressure relief valve.

(ii) Downstream or Lever Valve

The downstream or lever valve was developed exclusively for use with scuba demand valves. The demand valve diaphragm pushes the lever, therefore opening the valve downstream or with the air flow. Lever valves can be finely adjusted for easier breathing (particularly at depth), and automatically free flow if the first stage over-pressurise the hose.

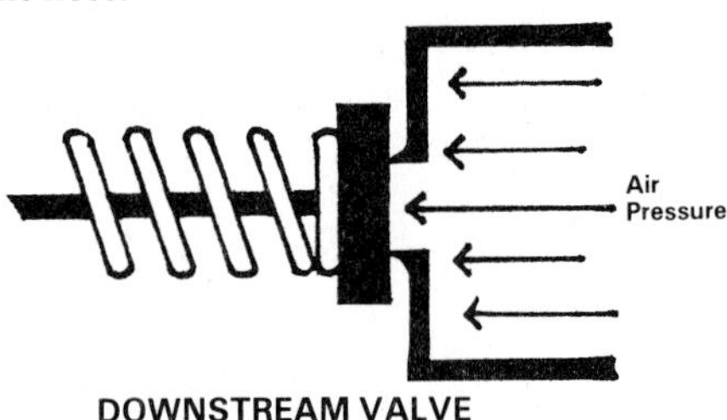

DOWNSTREAM VALVE

The great advantage of the downstream is the size of the orifice which can now be used, therefore increasing the air flow.

The main disadvantages are that they are expensive to manufacture and require a little more maintenance. They cannot handle varying line pressure and so are unsuited for Hookahs.

(iii) Second Stage Function

As the diver breathes inwards he will reduce the pressure inside the demand valve therefore causing the diaphragm to bow inwards. As the diaphragm bows inwards it causes the valve to be opened and allows air from the first stage to fill the demand valve and hence the diver's lungs. As soon as the pressure within the lungs and the demand valve chamber reaches the ambient pressure the diaphragm moves back out, therefore shutting off the delivery valve.

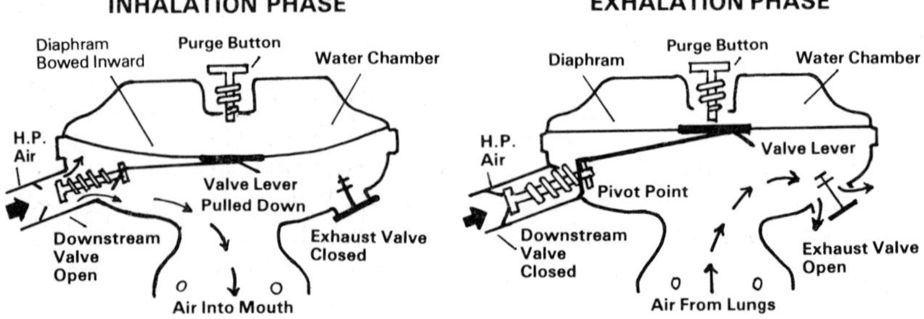

As the diver exhales, the air is forced out of the exhaust valve, which consists of a lightweight rubber flap over a hole in the base of the mouthpiece.

e. Fault Finding

Generally problems arising with regulators require the expert attention of the professional dive shop proprietor. However, there are some things which can be fixed at the dive site.

Problem: Air fails to enter regulator.

Possible Solution: Tank valve is off
Tank empty.
Regulator malfunction, therefore dive shop attention is required.

Problem: Water entering second stage.

Possible Solution: Foreign matter holding exhaust port open or exhaust port inverted, or holed.
Mouth piece perished and holed.
Diaphragm with a hole therefore dive shop attention required.

Problem: Air leakage between regulator and tank valve.

Possible Solution: Damaged tank valve O ring (replace O ring).

Problem: Can't breathe out.

Possible Solution: Exhaust valve stuck closed (perished).
Blow hard to clear, check for tears before proceeding.

Most other problems require dive shop attention.

2C: 5 Submersible Contents Gauges

A submersible contents gauge is as essential to the diver as a fuel gauge is to the automobile owner. They allow the diver to continually monitor his air supply and so ensure the dive will be concluded safely. They are attached to the high pressure port, usually marked HP, on the first stage of the regulator. Once the regulator is attached to the tank and turned on, the contents gauge will automatically show tank contents.

Most submersible contents gauges have an oil or air filled chamber. Generally oil filled gauges are more reliable though more expensive. Mechanisms used to calibrate the gauge vary but generally the more expensive models tend to be more reliable and accurate.

In order for submersible contents gauges to be useful, they need to be checked regularly during the dive. It is a habit which needs to be developed and one which must be kept in mind at all times.

A less expensive version of the submersible contents gauge is the tactile gauge. These gauges are designed to be felt, hence the name tactile gauge. However, they are very inaccurate. In fact, with most models, the last 15 atmospheres of air is not recorded because the needle disappears back into the housing. They are also prone to water penetration and corrosion.

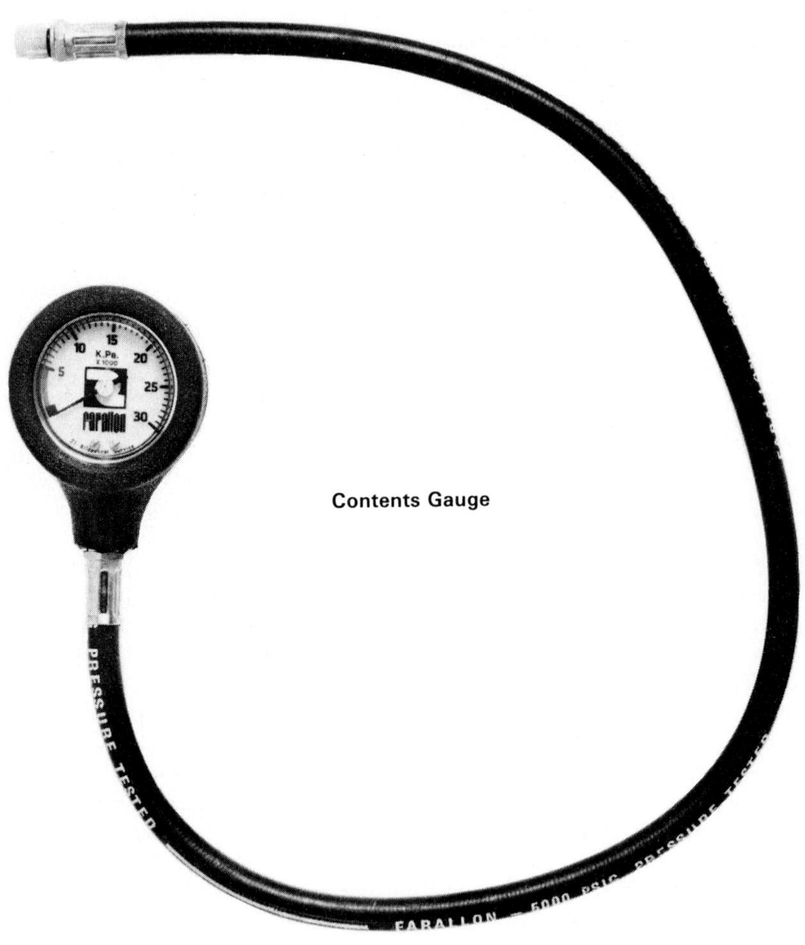

Contents Gauge

Section 2: EQUIPMENT

2D: Diver's Accessories

1. Depth Gauges
2. Octopus Regulators
3. Decompression Meters
4. Watches
5. Compasses
6. Torches
7. Divers' Flag
8. Surface Supplied Breathing Apparatus (Hookah)
9. Sport Divers' Spare Parts and Repair Kit

Section 2D DIVERS ACCESSORIES

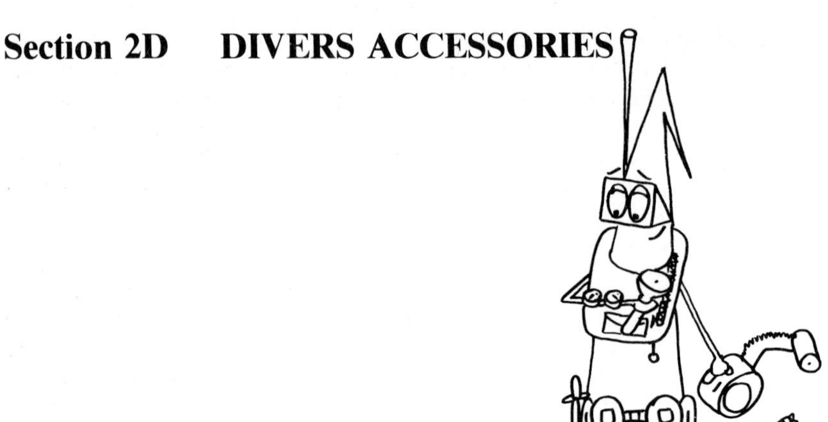

2D: 1 Depth Gauges

A depth gauge is an essential piece of equipment as it is the only way of determining the depth once the surface has been left. In order to be able to plan a dive adequately, and therefore avoid the problems associated with depth, the diver will require a depth gauge which can be read in conditions of low light and visibility. Generally there are three types of depth gauges.

Depth Gauge

a. Capillary Tube

As the diver descends, water enters the tube and compresses the remaining air volume. According to Boyle's Law, half the gauge will be used for the first ten metres followed by half the remainder for the next twenty metres, and so on. The result is that they are very accurate while at shallow depths but become progressively harder to read at deeper depths. They are accurate and inexpensive but difficult to read.

b. Bourdon Tube

As the diver descends, pressure is transmitted into a curved metal tube which will straighten as pressure increases. The best example of this physical action can be seen with a child's party whistle. These devices uncurl as the child blows into the mouth piece. As the metal tube uncurls, the needle moves around the gauge. These are more expensive than capillary gauges and require more attention and care, but are easier to read regardless of depth.

c. Oil Filled Gauges

In oil filled gauges the mechanism within the gauge is sealed from the water. This prevents the working parts from becoming encrusted with salt as well as protecting them from corrosion. Oil filled gauges are more accurate and less easily knocked out of calibration.

Generally, capillary gauges are adeqate for very shallow dives but one of the other two types is essential when diving deeper than twenty metres. Price and need determine the diver's choice.

2D: 2 Octopus Regulators

One of the latest developments regarding sport diver safety is the use of a second demand valve or octopus regulator. Due to the inefficiency of buddy

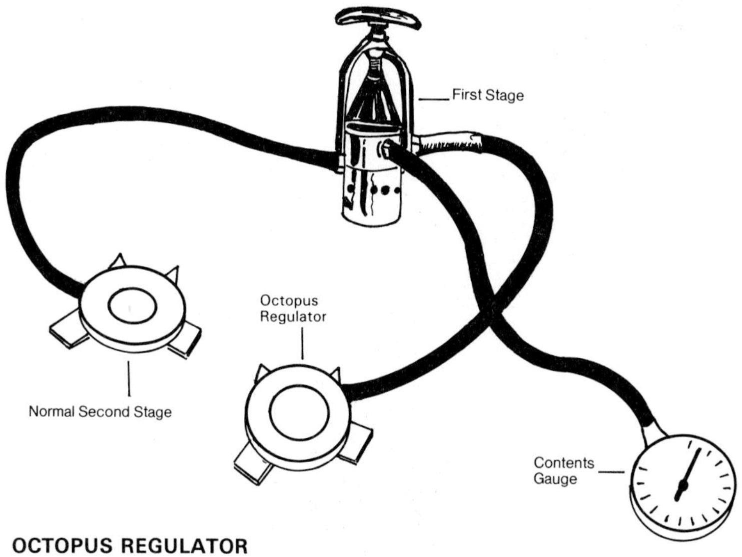

OCTOPUS REGULATOR

breathing, many instructors and sports divers have adopted the use of this device to be used in the advent of their own second stage malfunctioning or the loss of air supply to a buddy.

The octopus regulator is a second demand valve with a long hose which is screwed into a second low pressure outlet port on the first stage. Many divers carry this spare second stage in the pocket of the buoyancy compensator, or at least secure it in such a way that it is kept free of silt and sand. If a neckstrap is used be sure that it is "quick release". The advantages of the octopus regulator are obvious. It is an alternative back-up system and can be used instead of buddy breathing.

2D: 3 Decompression Meters

Decompression meters are mechanical instruments which try to approximate the body's absorption of gases, in particular nitrogen. They then indicate the rate of ascent which can be tolerated in order to prevent bubbles forming. The overall aim of the decompression meter is to prevent decompression sickness (see section 3D).

As they are calibrated on the average tissue absorption rate and do not take into account exercise, fitness, age, or any of the other predisposing factors of decompression sickness, decompression meters are definitely not recommended for the sports diver. The only way to avoid decompression sickness is to understand the problem itself and plan the dive adequately. Usually, the only time the diver finds that his decompression meter has been knocked out of calibration or is not working correctly is when he suffers from decompression sickness (bends).

2D: 4 Watches

Watches are an essential piece of equipment if the sports diver is intending to dive deeper than ten metres. Over this depth time becomes an important factor with regard to decompression sickness and so the watch needs to be pressure resistant, waterproof, easily read, and have a rotating outer bezel for quick reference to time elapsed. It is preferable that the bezel rotate anticlockwise so that time cannot be accidently subtracted. Within the next decade the diver could see more and more elaborate digital watches incorporating depth and time elapse functions as well. However, at this stage the diver is advised to choose from better known brands and to avoid less expensive watches.

2D: 5 Compasses

Once initial training has been completed and the diver ventures into the ocean, occasions will arise when visibility will be less than ideal. Diver location then becomes of considerable importance and the use of a compass is recommended. A good diving compass must be oil filled and include a rotating bezel, luminous dial and needle, and the ability to move if the compass is off the horizontal.

Proficient use of the compass requires practice and this should be done in enclosed water where the diver has a limited area in which to become disorientated.

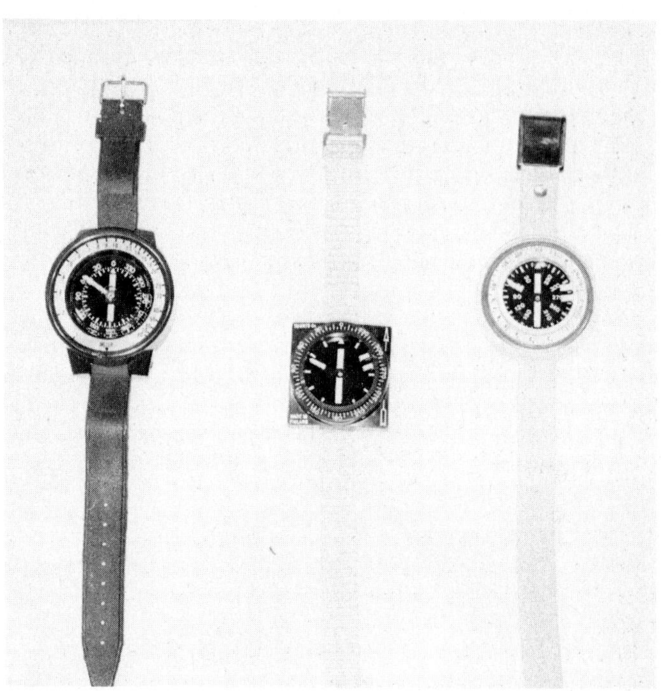

Compasses

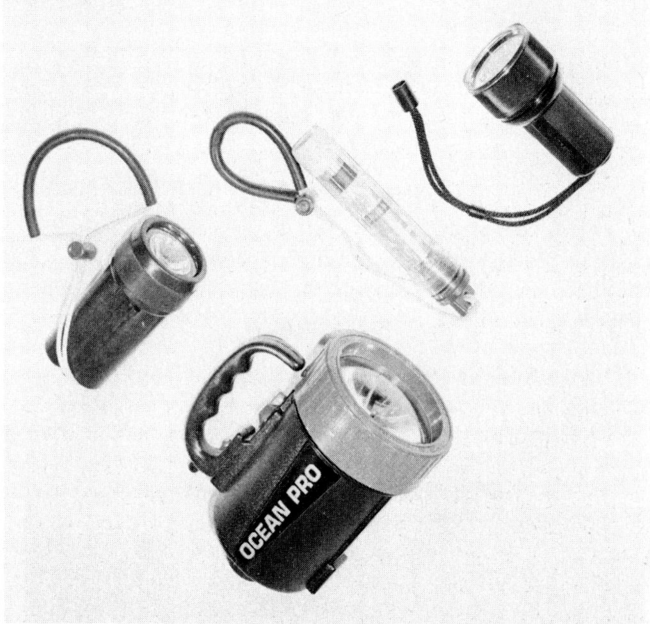

Torches

2D: 6 Torches

With the reduced light available under water, torches are often useful particularly when investigating ledges and caves as well as for night diving. Most torches on the market today can be termed either rechargeable torches or dry cell torches. Both have advantages as well as disadvantages and the final choice will depend to some extent on the price, and type of diving being considered.

The modern trend is towards smaller, more compact torches, but regardless of size and power, ensure that the torch finally purchased has a flat lens in contact with the water to ensure the most concentrated beam.

2D: 7 Diving Flag

The *internationally* recognised symbol of a diver's presence is the International Code Flag A (Flag Alpha). It comprises a white flag with a blue swallow's tail and must be flown above any location where divers are present. The size of the flag will depend on whether it is flown from a boat or a personal float towed by the diver. The boat flag needs to be 75 cm by 60 cm. The float flag needs to be 30 cm by 20 cm and must be 20 cm above the water.

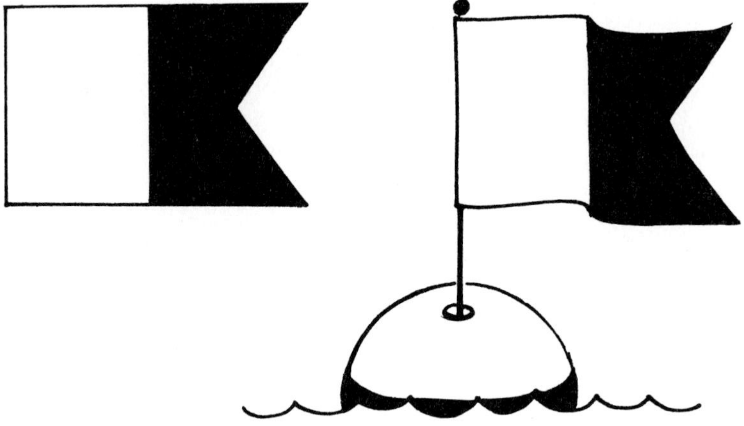

Divers' floats can be used to mark a single position or can be towed behind the diver. They have a multitude of uses, as they can also be used to carry items such as fish, cameras, and tools.

2D: 8 Surface Supplied Breathing Apparatus (Hookah)

The hookah unit comprises a low pressure compressor driven by a petrol motor. Most units deliver up to 200 litres of air per minute at approximately 8 atmospheres pressure. They usually have up to 100 metres of hose which is attached to the diver so that the demand valve cannot be pulled out of the diver's mouthpiece. The demand valve is usually upstream and has a non-return valve fitted (see section 2C). A reserve air supply should also be fitted to the unit.

All physiological problems associated with compressed air diving are relevant to hookah divers, but special emphasis needs to be given to gas toxicity, especially carbon monoxide poisoning (see section 3C).

It is essential that an attendant be present at the surface to monitor the hookah for wind changes and mechanical failure.

2D: 9 Sport Diver's Spare Parts & Repair Kit

Generally diving equipment deteriorates slowly and gives the diver adequate warning of impending failure. Plenty of time is usually available to ensure repairs are carried out before an item fails if regular inspection is carried out.

Occasionally, some items of equipment will be lost or broken at the dive site. It is important that a repair kit be taken to each dive to ensure that annoying last minute failures do not mean cancellation of the dive.

Such a repair kit would include:

Wet Suit	Turn buckle for jacket Zipper slide Wetsuit glue Needle and thread
Mask	Strap and buckle
Snorkel	Holder
Fins	Fin strap, buckle, and fix palm if required.
Back Pack	quick release buckle for harness as well as for weight belt.
Buoyancy Compensator	CO_2 cartridge
Knife	Sheath retainer ring Sheath straps
Weight belt	extra weights
Regulator	Dust cap Diaphragm Exhaust port
Cylinder	O ring O ring retainer Burst disc
Torch	O ring Silicon grease Beam or globe, batteries
Tools	Phillips head and flat screwdriver Two adjustable spanners Pliers Dentist pick

As well as the above a diver should also carry an adequate first aid kit suitable for the location being dived, a set of plastic decompression tables (usually carried in the pocket of the buoyancy compensator) and a list of emergency numbers.

Section 2: EQUIPMENT

2E: Care and Maintenance

Section 2E CARE AND MAINTENANCE

The maintenance of diving equipment falls into three major categories: rubber goods, the scuba unit, and nylon and plastic goods.

Rubber goods such as mask, fins, and snorkel need thorough washing in fresh water, and drying away from the sun. An occasional spray with a protective substance such as 'armorol' keeps the surface looking good.

The wet suit must also be thoroughly washed in fresh water after use. An occasional, gentle wash in a washing machine will not harm a wet suit. To prevent the neoprene cells from collapsing it is important to allow the wet suit to dry. Avoid drying the wet suit in direct sunlight, and hanging it on a coat-hanger will minimise the formation of creases which weaken a wet suit.

The scuba unit should also be washed in fresh water after every use. When washing the cylinder ensure that the valve is off (a cylinder should always have air in it), and remove the back pack and boot.

A regulator requires thorough washing in warm, fresh water to remove salt and to avoid corrosion. Ensure that the dust cap is in place. Another alternative is to wash the regulator while it is on the tank with high pressure air in it. The purge button can then be pressed to ensure all working parts are washed thoroughly.

To guarantee correct functioning of the scuba unit it is important that preventative maintenance is carried out at least annually. Do not wait for something to go wrong before repair work is instigated. The cylinder needs an annual inspection and the valve should be serviced at the same time.

A regulator should be serviced before each diving season to ensure correct lubrication and function of all working parts. Servicing should only be performed by a reputable pro-dive shop. To prevent corrosion during storage periods, the regulator should be regreased and checked at the end of the period.

Contents gauges need to have O-rings replaced annually.

Nylon products deteriorate rapidly in ultra-violet light, so it is important to wash, dry and store the buoyancy compensator, weight belt and other nylon products away from direct sunlight.

The buoyancy compensator needs special attention. Bacterial growth can occur inside the buoyancy compensator and therefore it should be disinfected periodically. Mild disinfectant will do the job but ensure that it is diluted or the material of the compensator may be affected. The CO_2 cartridge needs to be removed periodically and the mechanism greased and checked for correct function. O-rings should be replaced annually. When storing a buoyancy compensator it should be partially inflated to prevent the inner bag from perishing or becoming glued to itself.

Metal goods such as knives should be washed and coated with silicone jelly to prevent rusting during storage.

Torches should be stored with batteries removed. A battery will break down during storage and the acid produced will generally corrode the metal parts of the torch.

All delicate instruments such as depth gauges, watches and contents gauges should be washed, stored and transported carefully as they are easily bumped out of calibration.

In general, equipment which is maintained in good order should last a lifetime and give accurate, reliable service.

Section 3: MEDICAL CONSIDERATIONS

3A: Respiration and Circulation

1. The Respiratory System
2. The Circulatory System
3. Gas Exchange and Transport
4. Control of Breathing

3B: Barotrauma

1. Ears and Ear Barotrauma
2. Pulmonary Barotrauma
3. Sinus Barotrauma
4. Mask Barotrauma
5. Tooth Barotrauma
6. Gastro-intestinal Barotrauma

3C: Gas Poisoning

1. Oxygen
2. Carbon Dioxide
3. Hyperventilation
4. Latent Anoxia
5. Nitrogen
6. Carbon Monoxide Poisoning

3D: Decompression Sickness

1. Decompression Sickness
2. Aseptic Bone Necrosis
3. Use of Air Decompression Tables

3E: Hypothermia

1. Mild Hypothermia
2. Severe Hypothermia
3. General Prevention

3F: Miscellaneous Complaints

1. Salt Water Aspiration Syndrome
2. Outer Ear Infection
3. Sunburn
4. Heat Exhaustion
5. Sea Sickness

3G: First Aid

1. Massive Bleeding
2. Respiratory Arrest
3. Cardiac Arrest
4. Shock

3H: Resuscitation

1. Expired Air Resuscitation
2. External Cardiac Compression
3. Cardio-Pulmonary Resuscitation

Section 3 MEDICAL CONSIDERATIONS

This section deals with the many diving ailments which can affect the sport diver. Each topic is dealt with in a similar way — cause, signs and symptoms, first aid, and prevention are all discussed.

The student scuba diver must have a basic knowledge of the cause of an ailment, how to recognise it, how to treat it, and more importantly, how to prevent it.

The causes of diving accidents are many and varied but can generally be categorised into direct effects of pressure (Boyle's Law), indirect effects of pressure (Dalton's Law and Henry's Law) and exposure.

Signs which the first aider can see, such as bleeding, and symptoms which the victim feels, such as pain, are grouped together to avoid confusion.

First aid is important. If properly administered first aid will prevent further damage and can save a life. Obviously, the need for first aid will be avoided if the ailment can be prevented. Prevention will result from knowledge and sound dive planning.

Section 3: MEDICAL CONSIDERATIONS

3A: Respiration and Circulation

1. The Respiratory System
2. The Circulatory System
3. Gas Exchange and Transport
4. Control of Breathing

Section 3 MEDICAL CONSIDERATIONS

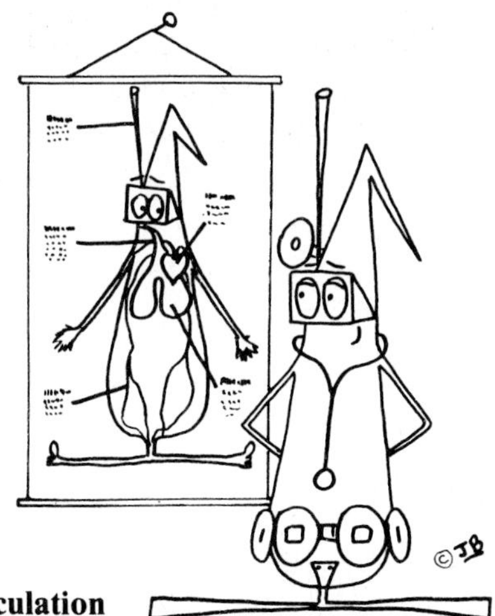

3A Respiration and Circulation

The understanding of many diving ailments discussed throughout the text is dependent upon knowledge of the basic anatomy and function of the respiratory system (lungs) and the circulatory system (heart).

The circulatory and respiratory systems of the human body are closely integrated. Breathing provides oxygen and rids the body of carbon dioxide, a waste product produced during respiration. The circulatory system transports oxygen and carbon dioxide throughout the body via the blood.

Respiration at cellular level utilises oxygen in the blood to produce energy.

3A: 1 The Respiratory System

The respiratory system begins in the mouth and nasal passages where air is filtered, humidified and warmed before passing into the lungs. Air then passes down the trachea (wind pipe) into the lung passages. The base of the trachea

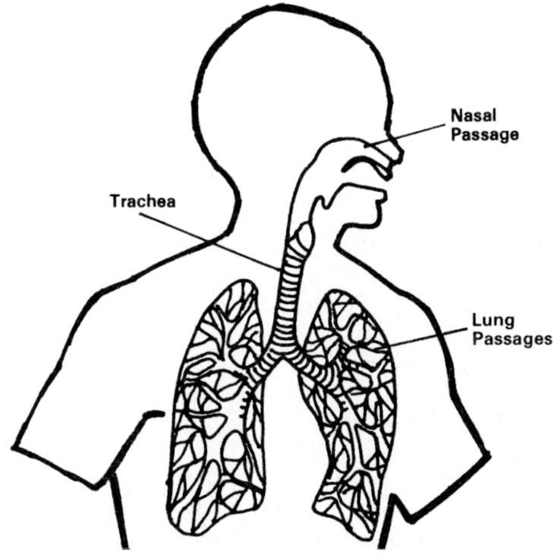

branches into the left and right lung. The bronchial tubes branch into smaller and smaller branches, the bronchi, and then into bronchioles, and terminate in tiny microscopic air sacs, the alveoli. There are in excess of 300 million alveoli in the human lungs. It is in the alveoli that gas exchange takes place. The respiratory passages are referred to as "dead space" since gas exchange does not occur in these passages. Breathing apparatus, such as a snorkel, increases dead space by artificially extending the length of the trachea. If dead space is too great proper ventilation will not occur and carbon dioxide excess can result (see section 3B). The alveoli are surrounded by a vast bed of capillaries. It is in this area that gas exchange occurs. Carbon dioxide diffuses from the carbon dioxide rich blood into the alveoli, while simultaneously, oxygen diffuses into the blood from the alveoli.

ALVEOLI

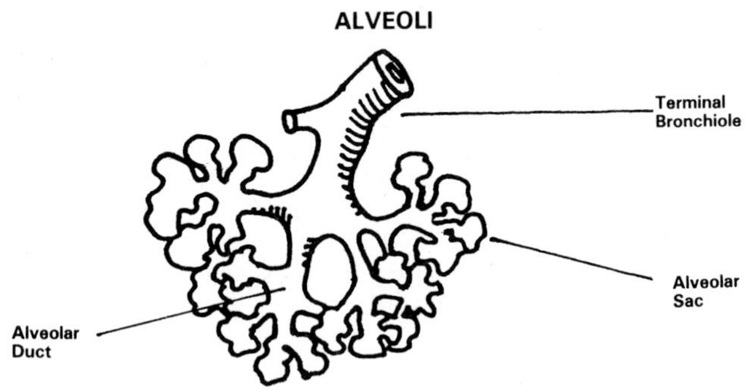

Each lung is surrounded by a pair of membranes, each consisting of thin layers of cells. These membranes are referred to as the pleura. Normally the pleura, separated by a thin fluid layer, sit on top of each other to help reduce friction between the lung and the chest wall during inspiration and expiration.

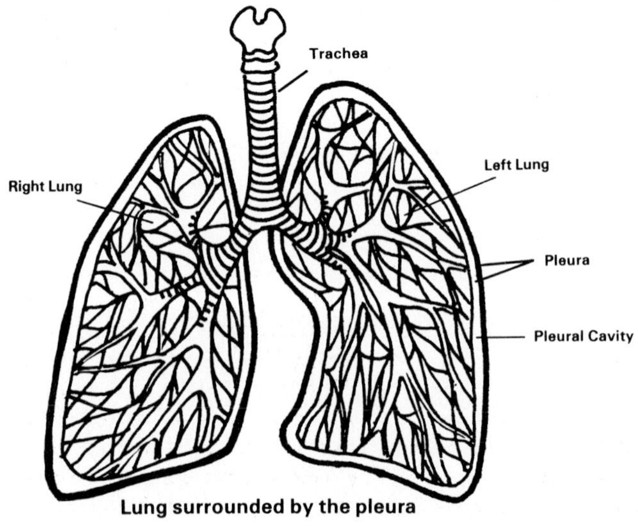

Lung surrounded by the pleura

The lungs, located in the thorax, are separated from the abdomen by the diaphragm. Inspiration (breathing in) is achieved by contraction of the chest wall muscles and the diaphragm. Reduced pressure caused by this contraction creates an inflow of air. Expiration (breathing out), is due to the elastic recoil of the lungs, forces an outflow of gases into the atmosphere.

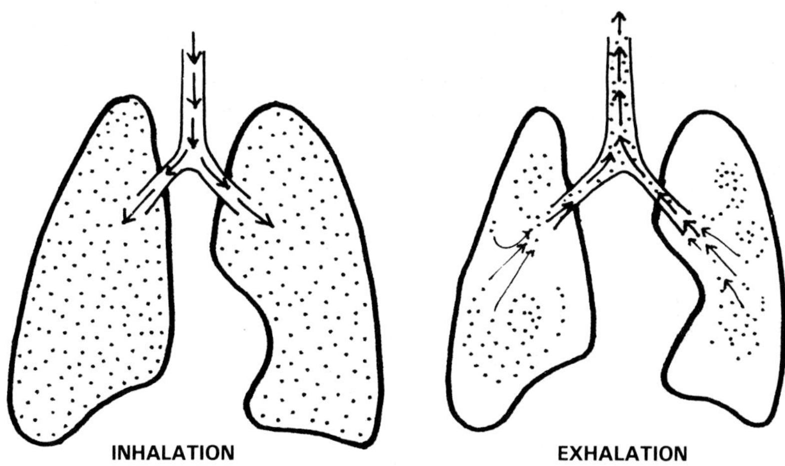

There are a number of functional terms associated with breathing with which the diver should be familiar.

(1) Total Lung Volume (TLC): The amount of air contained by the lungs when they are inflated from total collapse to maximum inflation. The average is 6 litres.

(2) Vital Capacity (VC): The amount of air which can be inhaled after maximal expiration. The average is 4·5 litres.

(3) Residual Volume (RV): The amount of air remaining in the lungs after maximal expiration. It is usually 25% of the total lung volume. The average is 1·5 litres.
NB: TLC = VC + RV

(4) Respiratory Minute Volume (RMV): The amount of air breathed in one minute. The average is 25-30 litres per minute for moderate work.

3A: 2 The Circulatory System

The circulatory system consists of the heart, arteries, veins and capillaries and this system transports oxygen and carbon dioxide around the body.

Veins carrying oxygen depleted blood enter the right atrium of the heart. Blood is then passed into the right ventricle of the heart and is pumped via the pulmonary artery to the lungs. This artery branches into smaller and smaller vessels to form the pulmonary capillaries which surround the alveoli. After gas exchange, oxygen rich blood flows from the capillaries into the pulmonary vein which empties into the left atrium. This oxygen rich blood flows into the left ventricle and is pumped via the aorta to the general body arteries where oxygen is

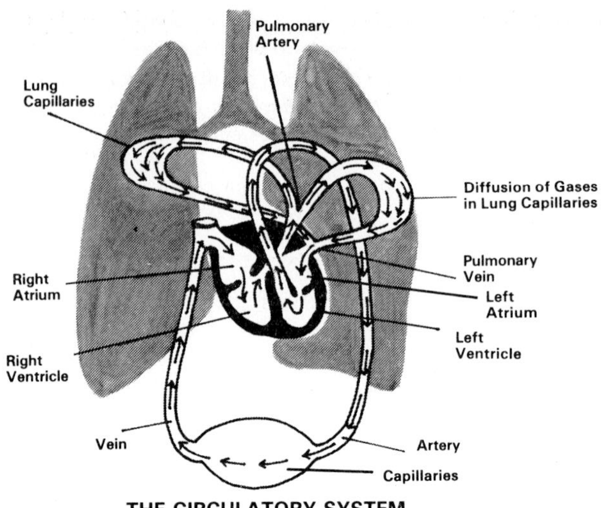

THE CIRCULATORY SYSTEM

removed from the capillaries by various tissues and replaced by carbon dioxide. The oxygen depleted blood is returned via the veins to the right atrium and the sequence is repeated.

3A: 3 Gas Exchange and Transport

Gas exchange in the lungs and tissues occurs by diffusion. In the lungs carbon dioxide diffuses from the blood into the alveoli and oxygen diffuses into the blood from the alveoli. In the tissues the gas movements are reversed.

Oxygen is primarily carried by the red blood cells and has a low solubility in blood fluids (plasma). There is very little variation in oxygen blood levels because the red blood cells are nearly 100% saturated at an oxygen partial pressure of 0·2 atmospheres. Carbon dioxide is transported mainly as a dissolved gas in the blood plasma. As such the level of carbon dioxide in the blood can vary significantly. Overbreathing (hyperventilation) can produce dangerously low levels of carbon dioxide in the blood (see section 3C).

3A:4 Control of Breathing

Although we can voluntarily control our breathing to a small degree, for example during a breath-hold dive, the desire to breathe is regulated primarily by the concentration of carbon dioxide in the blood, and this desire cannot be overcome — eventually a breath will take place in water or air.

There are carbon dioxide sensors in the aorta and the carotid arteries (arteries which supply the brain) called chemoreceptors. The chemoreceptors can monitor the level of carbon dioxide in the blood and can relay a message to the brain. If the level of carbon dioxide is too high breathing will be stimulated.

The elasticity of the alveoli also plays a minor role in breathing control. If the alveoli have expanded too much a signal will be sent to the respiratory centre for exhalation to occur. However, this signal is weak and can be easily overcome voluntarily.

Section 3: MEDICAL CONSIDERATIONS

3B: Barotrauma

1. Ears and Ear Barotrauma
2. Pulmonary Barotrauma
3. Sinus Barotrauma
4. Mask Barotrauma
5. Tooth Barotrauma
6. Gastro-intestinal Barotrauma

Section 3 MEDICAL CONSIDERATIONS

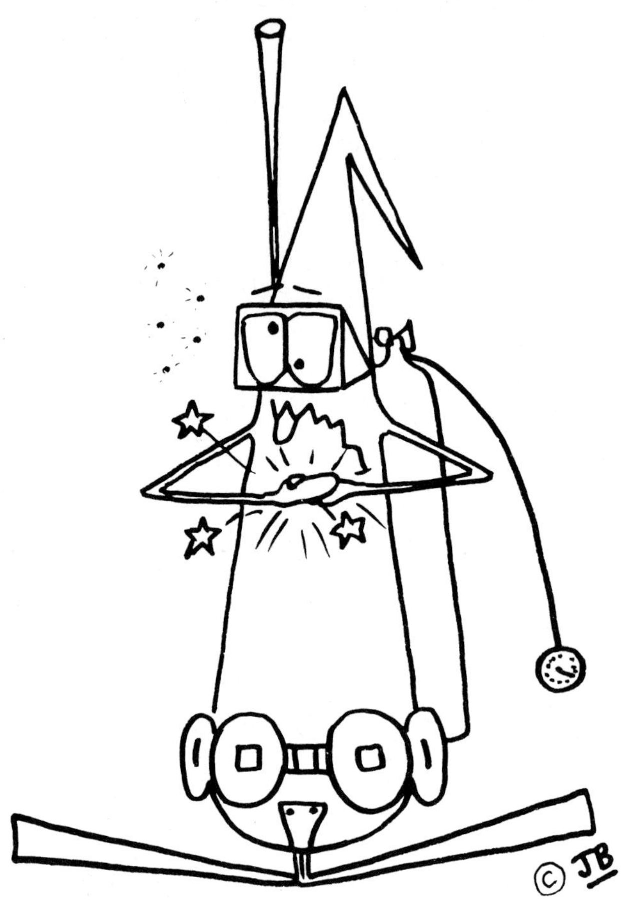

3B Barotrauma

Barotrauma is the medical term used to describe pressure injuries. The word is derived from *baro* meaning pressure and *trauma* referring to injury.

A barotrauma or pressure injury results from failure to equalise a differing pressure within the body's gas spaces and the surrounding environment.

The body's gas spaces are surrounded by incompressible watery tissues and usually automatically equalise to the ambient pressure through the airways.

During descent, volume will decrease (according to Boyle's Law) and a descent barotrauma will result if equalisation does not occur. If the volume decrease is not equalised by gas entering the space, pain will be felt due to the swelling of the surrounding tissues as they attempt to move into the space to equalize the pressure. When a further decrease in volume occurs, tiny blood vessels may rupture. Resultant bleeding will reduce the volume and therefore relieve pain.

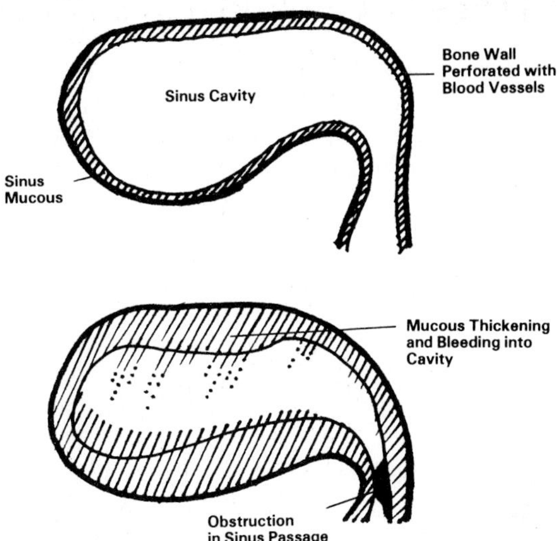

During ascent if equalisation does not occur gas will expand (according to Boyle's Law) and an ascent barotrauma will result if the increased volume is not released via normal passages. This condition is often referred to as a reverse squeeze.

REVERSE SQUEEZE

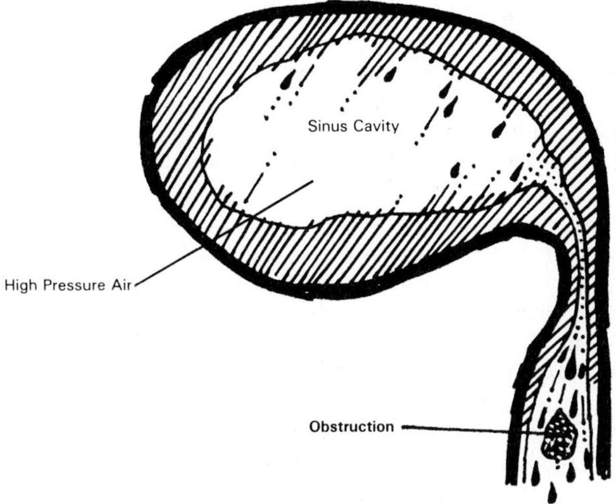

Gas expands and expels obstruction during ascent causing bleeding.

3B: 1 Ears and Barotrauma

a. The Ear

The ear is physically divided into three major areas all of which are subject to injury.

The ear drum separates the air filled external ear and middle ear. The fluid filled inner ear, containing the balance and hearing organs, is surrounded by bone and therefore is not subject to volume changes.

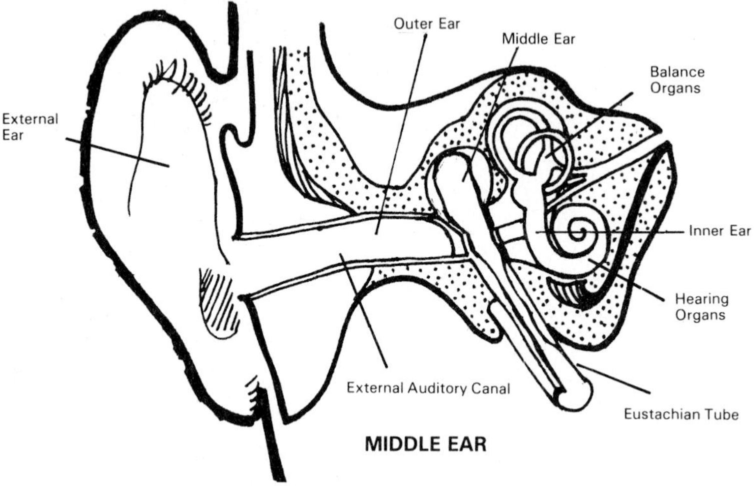

MIDDLE EAR

The outer ear collects sound waves and directs them down the ear canal to the ear drum, a thin, elastic membrane, which then vibrates. The vibrations are then transmitted across the three conduction bones to the hearing organs in the inner ear, converted into nerve impulses and hence a sound is registered.

The narrow Eustachian tube connects the middle ear to the back of the throat, allowing air to flow into and out of the middle ear to ensure that pressure remains equal.

It is important that equalisation of pressure be achieved before pain is felt. Equalisation can be achieved in a variety of ways: by swallowing, wriggling the lower jaw, a yawn, or by sealing the nostrils and gently blowing (the Valsalva Manoeuvre). A charateristic pop, similar to that experienced when driving up a mountain, may be heard when equalisation has been achieved. Equalisation is usually easier if carried out in a head up, feet down position, while descending.

Any conditions which hinder equalisation, such as colds, flu, allergies, growths, ear infections or cigarette smoking automatically exclude persons from diving until successfully treated.

b. Middle Ear Barotrauma of Descent (Middle Ear Squeeze)

Cause: This is the most common barotrauma in sport divers. The primary cause is failure to equalise pressure in the middle ear during descent.

Signs and Symptoms: Descent should not be continued if pain is felt. Pain indicates abnormal inward bulging of the ear drum and swelling of tissue lining in the

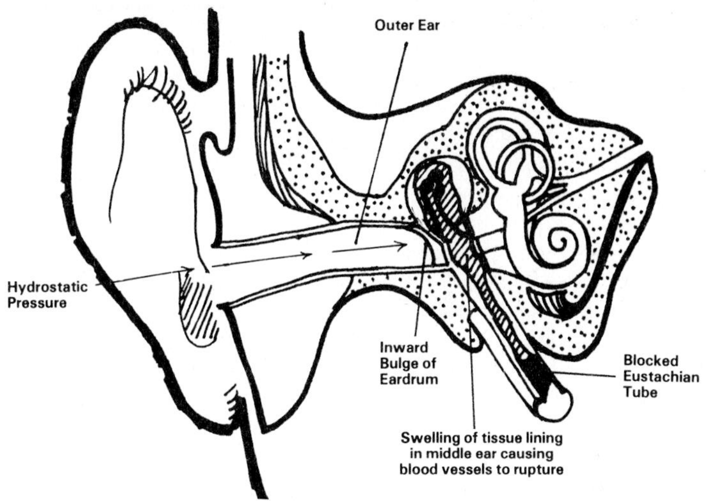

middle ear. Pain is experienced by most people at depths greater than 1·5 metres when equalisation has not occurred. If descent is continued, blood vessels will burst in an effort to fill the gap left by compressed air in the middle ear. Bleeding will cause a feeling of fullness in the ear and may also impair hearing.

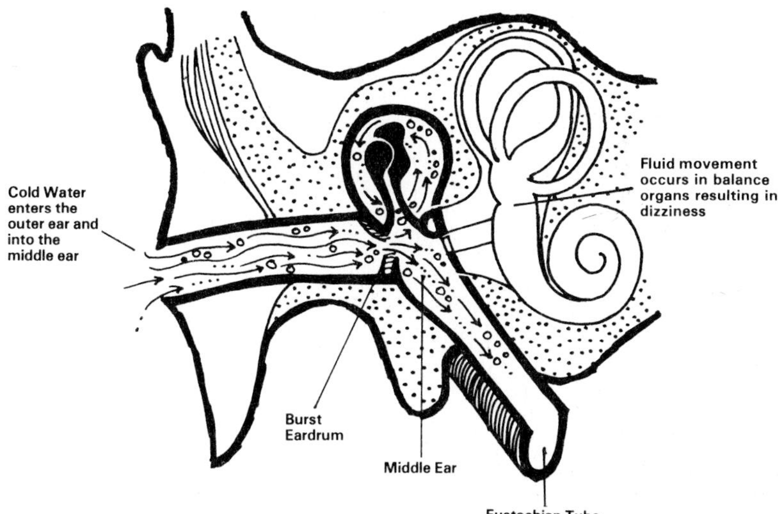

Should a rapid descent continue without equalisation the ear drum may burst (rupture), thus immediately relieving any pain or feeling of pressure and allowing cold water to enter the middle ear. If the cold water comes in contact with the inner ear the temperature difference may cause a movement of fluid in the balance organs, causing dizziness (vertigo) and sometimes nausea. Bleeding from the ear canal may indicate a burst ear drum.

It should be noted that not all signs and symptoms occur together, nor do they occur immediately. They may take several minutes to manifest themselves.

First Aid: Should a ruptured ear drum or middle ear barotrauma be suspected a hand should be placed over the ear (both if you are unsure which is affected), to minimise the entry of water which will cause dizziness. If dizziness occurs, positive buoyancy must be achieved by inflating the buoyancy compensator or by ditching the weight belt. Dizziness usually lasts until the temperature of the water inside the middle ear equalises with that in the inner ear. This may take about thirty seconds. Hold onto something solid until dizziness subsides.

The diver must then immediately surface, dry the area around the ear and cover it with a clean cloth (e.g. a towel). Nothing should be placed in the ear canal. It is advisable not to equalise on the surface as this may worsen any small perforation which has occurred. A suspected middle ear barotrauma or ruptured ear drum requires medical attention. Consultation with a **diving** doctor is highly recommended.

Treatment: Treatment requires that the patient does not dive, swim, or fly for at least six weeks. Antibiotics may help avoid infection, and decongestants will help reduce excessive fluid.

Prevention: To prevent middle ear barotrauma of descent make sure equalisation occurs before pressure is felt. If ears do not clear easily on the surface, or if you are suffering from a cold, flu, allergies or you're a heavy smoker, **do not dive**.

c. Inner Ear Barotrauma (Inner Ear Rupture)

Cause: Sometimes difficulty in equalising may be experienced. Should this occur, forceful equalisation must not be attempted as serious, permanent damage to the inner ear can occur.

During descent, if equalisation is not achieved, the ear drum bulges inwards, therefore pushing the conducting bones out of position. Should equalisation be achieved suddenly, the conducting bones will rush back into position, thereby causing a movement of inner ear fluid which may rupture one of the small membranes dividing the middle ear from the inner ear.

Signs and Symptoms: Should a rupture occur, inner ear fluid will leak out, resulting in mild to severe deafness. Deafness may be permanent if treatment is not sought immediately. Other signs and symptoms include ringing or buzzing noises, dizziness and disturbed balance.

Treatment: A diver suspecting this injury must seek medical advice immediately. Treatment will involve surgical repair, bed rest and the cessation of further diving or flying.

Prevention: Rapid descents and forceful equalisations must be avoided. It is quite common, particularly on second dives the same day, that difficulty in clearing the ears is experienced. If ears do not clear easily on the surface, **do not dive**.

d. Reverse Ear Barotrauma (Reverse Ear Squeeze)

If air pressure in the middle ear area exceeds the pressure in the external ear the ear drum will bulge outwards and may ultimately rupture.

Cause: The outward bulging may be caused in one of two ways. The first is blockage of the Eustachian tube before ascent. This is usually a result of tissue swelling around the opening of the Eustachian tube in the back of the throat. Swelling can occur after the effects of a decongestant have worn off. It is essential to avoid diving while taking **any** medication.

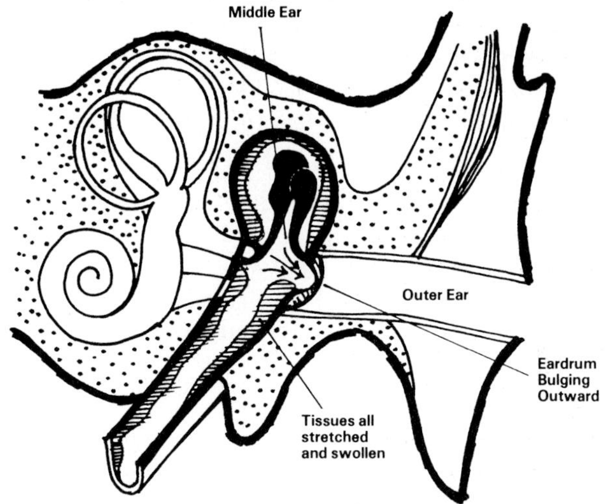

Pressure in middle ear exceeds pressure in outer ear and equalisation can only occur after eardrum ruptures.

The second is blockage of the outer ear canal which occurs due to ear plugs, excessive wax, or a tight fitting hood while descending. It can be seen in the diagram that equalisation cannot occur without ear drum rupture.

Signs and Symptoms: Signs and symptoms may include difficulty in clearing ears, pain and bleeding from the ear.

First Aid: The ear must be kept dry and a doctor's opinion must be sought.

Prevention: To prevent reverse ear squeeze the diver must ensure that the ear canals are clear. Avoid the use of ear plugs. If a tight hood is the problem, small holes about three to four millimetres in diameter may be cut in the hood near the ears, to allow free flow of water. Diving with colds, allergies, ear infections, or after excessive smoking must be avoided.

e. Alternobaric Vertigo (Different Pressure Dizziness)

Cause: During descent or ascent the ears may not equalise simultaneously with the changing water pressure. The result is varying pressures within the middle ears.

Signs and Symptoms: The delicate balance organs are therefore stimulated to a varying extent resulting in vertigo (dizziness) and occasionally nausea.

First Aid: Should alternobaric vertigo occur on descent your course of action should be to stop, hang on to something solid such as a rock, anchor, rope or buddy, and wait until the discomfort passes. Then proceed slowly ensuring that adequate equalisation of both ears occurs. If the problem persists, surface immediately and seek medical advise. If dizziness occurs while ascending, once again stop and grasp something solid until the symptoms abate.

This condition can occur at any time to anyone. The need for a buddy system so that assistance can be rendered is apparent.

Alternobaric vertigo is generally a condition which occurs when inflamation of the Eustachian tube is present, particularly after having had a cold.

3B: 2 Pulmonary Barotrauma

a. Pulmonary Barotrauma of Descent (Lung Squeeze)

Cause: During a breath-hold dive the lungs become compressed with increasing depth. (Boyle's Law). If the lung volume is reduced to a volume below the residual volume, tissue damage may occur. Residual volume is the volume of air left in the lungs after a complete exhalation. The average human lung capacity is 6 litres and the average residual volume is 1·5 litres. If an average breath-hold diver descends to thirty metres then his lung volume becomes 1·5 litres which is equal to the residual volume. Beyond thirty metres his lung volume is less than the residual volume and he may suffer pulmonary barotrauma (lung pressure injury) of descent.

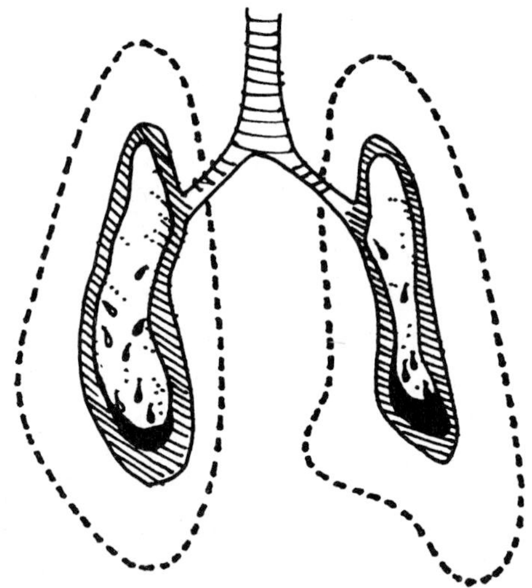

Lung volume reduced to below residual volume. Lungs will squeeze inwards and tissues will bleed in an effort to equalise pressure.

Signs and Symptoms: Signs and symptoms include chest pain, coughing up blood and even death. Infection may follow due to lung tissue damage.

First Aid: The victim should be treated for shock including administration of 100% oxygen if available. Medical assistance must be sought.

Prevention: Avoid breath-hold dives to excessive depths.

b. Pulmonary Barotrauma of Ascent

Pulmonary barotrauma (lung pressure injury) of ascent is the most serious of all diving ailments. As such any suspected pulmonary barotrauma requires urgent treatment.

Cause: If a scuba diver holds his breath during ascent, expanding gases in the lungs cannot excape and tissue damage will result. The damage may vary from a small pinhole rupture of an alveolus to a larger tear in the lung tissue.

Signs and Symptoms: The onset of signs and symptoms is almost immediate. Most develop within five minutes. Immediate onset is a result of escaped gas expanding rapidly during ascent (Boyle's Law). A diver suffering from pulmonary barotrauma may, upon surfacing, release a sudden characteristic cry caused by rapid release of expanding gases through the vocal chords. Severe shortness of breath, chest pain, and coughing may quickly follow. Often coughing may produce pink frothy blood, a sure sign of lung tissue damage. If the barotrauma is severe, shock, cyanosis (blueness), unconsciousness, and even death could follow.

In addition to the general signs and symptoms of pulmonary tissue damage there may be four specific types of barotrauma. All result from a burst lung with air escaping and entering various areas of the body. These four conditions may occur singly or in any combination.

PULMONARY BAROTRAUMA

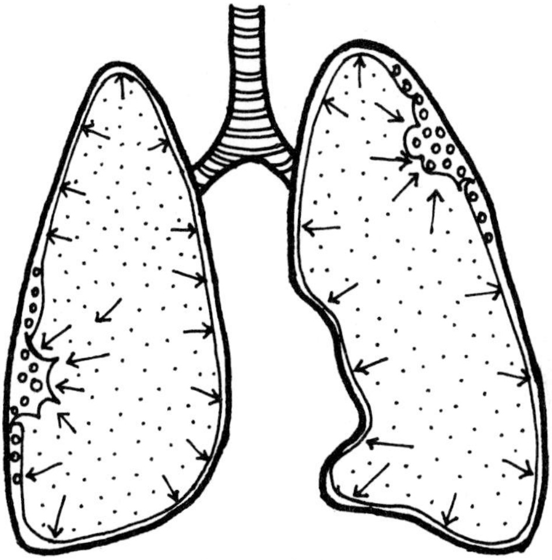

**Holding breath during ascent.
Air in lungs cannot escape and will rupture lung tissue, allowing bubbles to escape.**

(i) Air Embolism

Air embolism literally means a blockage of the blood stream by an air bubble.

The alveolus, a thin air sac embedded in a mass of capillaries, is where gas exchange takes place.

Should a small tear in the alveolus occur, air can escape directly into the blood stream and be transported around the body. A small tear can occur from a pressure change as little as 0·1 atmosphere absolute (i.e. from one metre in depth to the surface). Of course, as the diver ascends the bubble will increase in size (according to Boyle's Law).

A bubble in the blood stream will travel until it becomes lodged in a vessel of

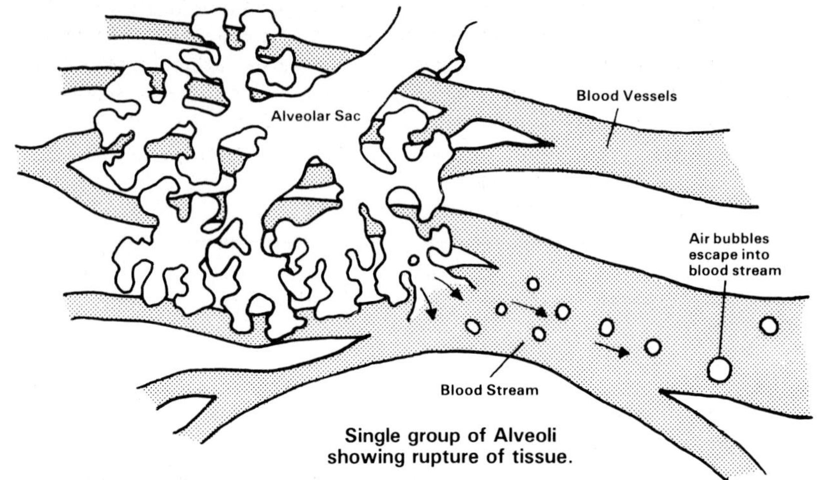

Single group of Alveoli showing rupture of tissue.

equal diameter. All tissues beyond the blockage will then be deprived of oxygen and other nutrients necessary to maintain function. Hence the signs and symptoms of air embolism will be determined by the location of the blockage. If the rupture occurs near the surface only a small vessel may become blocked. Therefore, the outcome may not be as serious. However, if the rupture should occur at depth, during ascent the bubble volume will increase and blockage of a major vessel may result, in which case the resultant signs and symptoms would be dramatic.

Signs and Symptoms: A blockage can obviously occur anywhere throughout the body. The most serious are blockages occurring in the brain and heart. If the brain is involved, then as well as general burst lung symptoms, more serious signs and symptoms may occur. These include confusion, visual disturbances, dizziness, convulsions, paralysis, unconsciousness, and death. Since any trauma is dependent on where bubbles lodge, any function of the body can be affected.

Should an artery supplying the heart become blocked the signs and symptoms will be similar to a heart attack. These include severe chest pains, shock, unconsciousness, and death.

First Aid: The prime consideration in treatment of air embolism is to reduce the size of the bubble. The only way this can be achieved is by recompression in an air filled chamber. This procedure is known as therapeutic recompression.

While arranging recompression the patient is placed in the coma position. To help reduce bubble size pure oxygen at atmospheric pressure should be administered as this will encourage diffusion of nitrogen gas out of the bubble. Resuscitators, such as the oxy-viva that deliver oxygen under pressure, should be avoided as they may aggravate lung tissue damage. (See Appendix G.)

Should the patient require resuscitation, apply expired air resuscitation (EAR) and external cardiac compression (ECC). Transport to the chamber should be by road, by a low flying aircraft or by an aircraft capable of pressurisation to sea level. (Most commercial aircraft pressurize to approximately 2000 m). High flying or unpressurised aircraft will increase the bubble size and aggravate the injury.

Treatment: Immediate recompression in a recompression chamber to fifty metres under medical supervision is required. Recompression reduces the size of the bubble in two ways: direct volume reduction (Boyle's Law) and increased gas solubility (Henry's Law), thereby relieving the signs and symptoms. However, death or serious brain damage is the most likely outcome of air embolism.

Recompression in water is not recommended for the following reasons:

1. Depth required for treatment.
2. Difficulty in finding depth and maintaining it.
3. Hypothermia.
4. Length of time required for treatment.
5. Unconscious victims cannot be medically treated in water.
6. Air supply required for treatment.
7. Danger to assistants.
8. Sea sickness.
9. Hunger.
10. Risk of shark attack.

Prevention: Prevention is simple. Do not hold your breath on ascent; always breathe normally. Diving with a cold, hay fever, asthma, or if you are a heavy smoker may cause blockage of the alveoli, due to excessive mucus or inflamation, therefore even though you may be breathing normally a rupture can occur on ascent. Be sure to avoid diving until the condition has cleared up completely.

(ii) Mediastinal Emphysema

If air passes out of the alveoli it can travel through the passages between the lung tissue and lodge in the mediastinum. The mediastinum is the area in the middle of the chest where the heart lies. If air is in this area the condition is known as mediastinal emphysema. Emphysema refers to air in the tissues.

Because of the air pressure against the heart, chest pain, breathing difficulties, and shock are all signs and symptoms of mediastinal emphysema.

If any pulmonary barotrauma is suspected **assume air embolism** and treat as such. Do not try to recompress the victim in the water. Give pure oxygen.

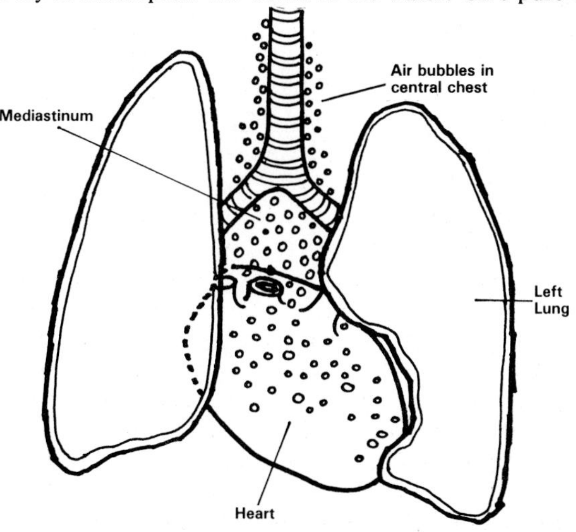

(iii) Subcutaneous Emphysema.

From the central chest area, air bubbles can travel into the upper chest cavity and lodge under the skin in the neck region. The word subcutaneous is derived from *sub* meaning under and *cutaneous* meaning skin. Subcutaneous emphysema is the medical term for air in the tissue under the skin. Signs and symptoms include breathing difficulties, swelling in the lower neck region, crackling skin and voice changes.

If any pulmonary barotrauma is suspected **assume air embolism** and treat as such. Do not try to recompress the victim in the water. Give pure oxygen.

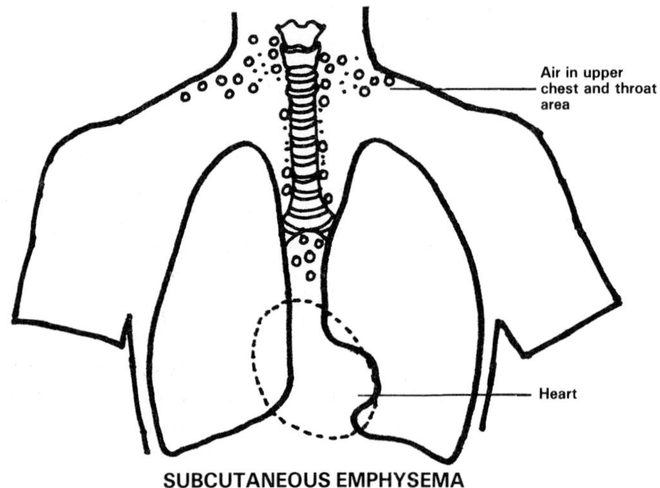

SUBCUTANEOUS EMPHYSEMA

(iv) Pneumothorax

Surrounding each lung is a pair of thin, moist membranes called pleura. The area between these membranes is called pleural cavity.

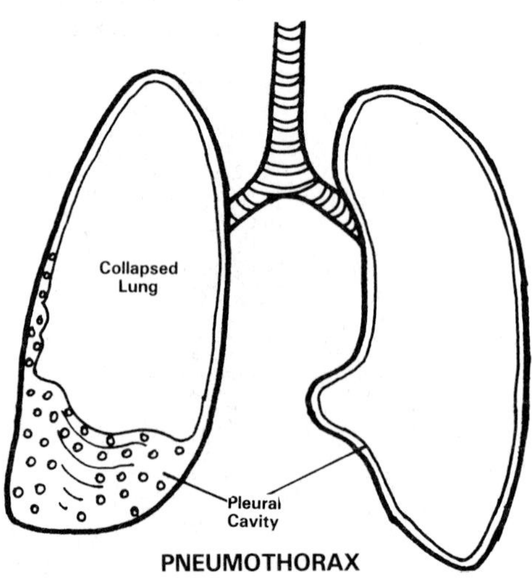

PNEUMOTHORAX

If an alveolus near the pleural lining ruptures a tear may also occur in one of the membranes. If air escapes into the pleural space it will cause the lung or lungs to collapse. This condition is known as pneumothorax, meaning air in the chest. The word is derived from *pneumo* pertaining to air, and *thorax* referring to the chest.

Expanding air in the pleural spaces can also affect circulation. Chest pain, breathing difficulty, reduced chest movements, shock and cyanosis (blueness) all indicate pneumothorax.

If any pulmonary barotrauma is suspected **assume air embolism** and treat as such. Do not try to recompress the victim in the water. Give pure oxygen.

Remember, prevention is always better than cure. Therefore never hold your breath on ascent. Breathe normally at all times.

3B: 3 Sinus Barotrauma (Sinus Squeeze)

Cause: Normally sinuses (hollow areas in the skull opening into the nasal passages) are clear and equalisation occurs automatically. However, when a person is suffering from cold, flu, sinus infection, or allergy, blockages can occur thus trapping pockets of air. If diving is attempted trapped air will expand and compress during ascent and descent respectively, thereby causing sinus barotrauma.

Signs and Symptoms: During descent the volume of air inside the sinuses will decrease. In an effort to equalise, the tissue lining in the sinus will swell, causing pain which will worsen on further descent. If descent is continued bleeding into the sinus will occur so as to equalise the pressure. On ascent air will expand and force blood and mucus out of the sinus into the face mask. Pain may persist for hours.

First Aid: Aspirin will relieve pain and no further treatment may be required. However, if pain or condition persists medical advice must be sought.

Prevention: Sinus barotrauma may be avoided by not diving with a cold, flu or sinus infection, and by descending slowly.

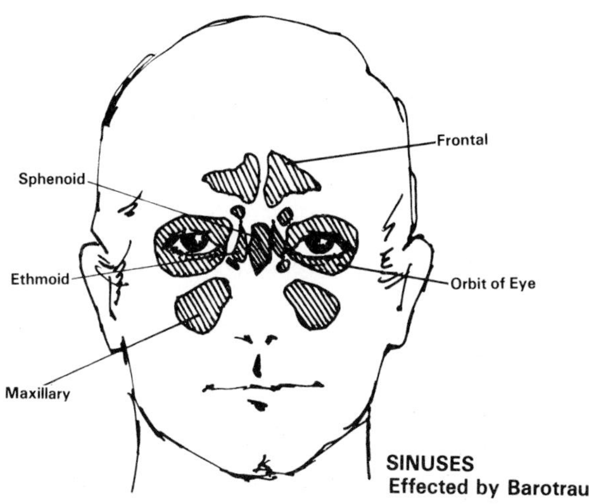

SINUSES
Effected by Barotrauma

3B: 4 Mask Barotrauma (Mask Squeeze)

To enable in focus vision underwater a face mask must be worn. The mask provides an air space which is subject to volume changes during ascent and descent.

Cause: During descent if the pressure between the face and the face mask is not equalised by blowing high pressure air through the nose, swelling of facial tissues and even the eye will occur.

Signs and Symptoms: The first symptom of mask squeeze is a feeling of tightness on the face. If ascent is continued the face may redden or bruise and the eyelids become puffy. Red eyes may also result from capillary rupture.

First Aid: Mask barotrauma is generally self-healing but diving must be terminated until recovery. If the eye is damaged seek medical advice.

Prevention: When pressure is felt exhale into the face mask. Avoid the use of goggles that do not allow equalisation.

3B: 5 Tooth Barotrauma (Tooth Squeeze)

Cause: Tooth decay, the most common disease in our society, can cause small air spaces. Dental repair usually eliminates the air space in most cases. However, should a small volume of air be present between a tooth and filling, a barotrauma can occur during a dive.

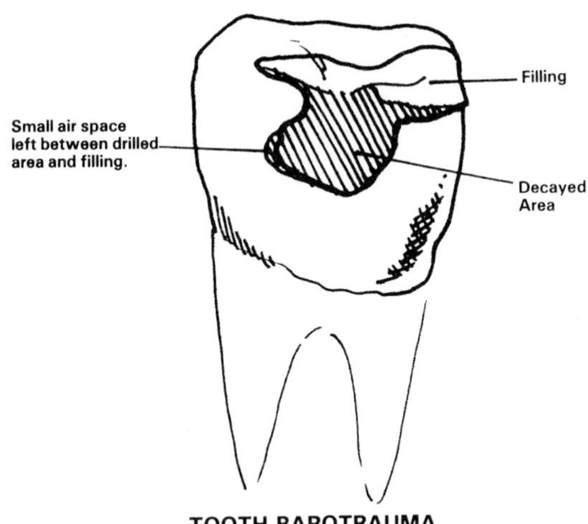

TOOTH BAROTRAUMA

Signs and Symptoms: Swelling of the tissue and bleeding into the air space will occur during descent as gas volume decreases.

Upon ascent the compressed air in the tooth will expand causing mild to severe pain. In some cases the tooth may break due to increased internal pressure.

First Aid: Aspirin will help ease the pain until the dentist can repair the affected tooth. Regular visits to the dentist will help eliminate the chance of suffering tooth barotrauma.

3B: 6 Gastro-intestinal Barotrauma (Gut Squeeze)

Cause: Foods which produce gas during the digestive process can cause discomfort to the diver. Gas spaces produced in the stomach or intestines expand and compress during ascent and descent respectively.

Signs and Symptoms: Gastro-intestinal barotrauma will cause belching or burping, abdominal discomfort and colicky pains. If severe, fainting and shock may occur.

First Aid: Divers experiencing gastro-intestinal barotrauma should decrease rate of ascent, stop ascent until pain subsides, or descend to relieve pain. The diver can then slowly ascend.

On the surface, to ease the condition, release any tight fitting gear.

Prevention: Avoid carbonated beverages and heavy meals before diving.

Section 3: MEDICAL CONSIDERATIONS

3C: Gas Poisoning

1. Oxygen
2. Carbon Dioxide
3. Hyperventilation
4. Latent Anoxia
5. Nitrogen
6. Carbon Monoxide Poisoning

Section 3 MEDICAL CONSIDERATIONS

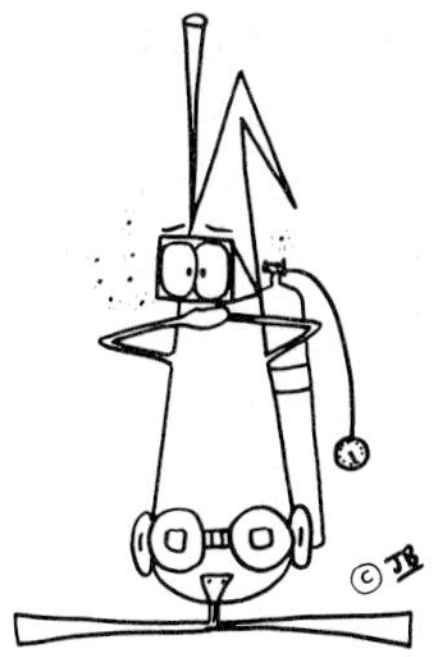

3C Gas Poisoning

The earth's atmosphere is a mixture of many gases, most of which are poisonous at various concentrations. Oxygen (O_2), nitrogen (N_2), carbon dioxide (CO_2) and carbon monoxide (CO) are the four most important gases affecting the sport diver. The effect of various concentrations of these gases must be understood to avoid adverse physiological reactions.

3C: 1 Oxygen

Approximately 20% of the air we breathe is oxygen (O_2). Oxygen produced in plants by photosynthesis is essential for maintenance of life. The human body requires a partial pressure of oxygen between 0·19 and 0·21 atmospheres absolute for normal function. Oxygen poisoning will occur if oxygen is breathed at partial pressures greater than 0·6 atmospheres absolute. Hypoxia, (low oxygen level), occurs when the partial pressure of oxygen breathed is below 0·16 atmospheres absolute. Hypoxia is derived from *hypo* meaning low and *oxia* referring to oxygen.

a. Oxygen Poisoning.

The degree of poisoning by high pressure oxygen depends on the partial pressure of oxygen breathed and exposure time.

A high partial pressure of oxygen can be achieved in two ways: breathing air at depths greater than 20 metres or breathing pure oxygen at any depth.

(i) Low Pressure Oxygen Poisoning (Chronic Oxygen Poisoning)

Progressive breakdown of lung tissue occurs if oxygen is breathed at partial pressures greater than 0·6 atmospheres absolute for extended periods. Breathing pure oxygen on the surface or air at depths greater than 20 metres will achieve such partial pressures.

Signs and symptoms of low pressure oxygen poisoning occur after exposure for several hours to days, depending on individual susceptibility. Low pressure oxygen poisoning is generally a problem in sub-aquatic habitats, and in recompression chambers. Prolonged periods of breathing pure oxygen should be avoided.

(ii) High Pressure Oxygen Poisoning (Acute Oxygen Poisoning)

Cause: High pressure oxygen poisoning will occur in most individuals when the partial pressure of oxygen breathed exceeds 2 atmospheres absolute. Diving, using air to depths in excess of 90 metres, or diving in excess of 10 metres using pure oxygen will achieve an oxygen partial pressure greater than 2 atmospheres absolute.

Signs and Symptoms: The onset of high pressure oxygen poisoning is usually rapid. Early warning signs and symptoms such as nausea, dizziness, incoordination, muscular twitching (particularly of facial muscles), may not even be noticed. The most obvious sign is usually convulsion.

First Aid: A reduction of oxygen partial pressure must be achieved by ascent. To avoid pulmonary barotrauma of ascent it is important to maintain depth until the convulsion which may cause blockage of the airway ceases and the victim is relaxed. This usually takes up to 30 seconds.

Recovery will be rapid unless some water aspiration occurs (see section 3F). In all cases, medical attention is required.

Prevention: It is important to ensure that all scuba cylinders are filled only with pure breathing air, **not** oxygen, and excessive depths on scuba are avoided.

b. Hypoxia

Maintenance of normal levels of oxygen is important for normal function of the human body. Under water, if the level drops below 0·16 atmospheres absolute (i.e. the diver becomes hypoxic), results may be fatal.

Cause: The individual causes of hypoxia are many and varied. Generally, there are two major categories:

1. Failure of sufficient oxygen reaching the lungs, e.g. equipment failure, exhaustion of air supply, contamination, and drowning.
2. Failure of sufficient oxygen reaching the tissues, e.g. cardiac arrest, air embolism, and carbon monoxide poisoning.

Individual discussion on each cause will be dealt with throughout the text.

Signs and Symptoms: When the partial pressure of oxygen in the body falls an oxygen debt is incurred; the amount of oxygen required exceeds the amount available.

As this debt increases a feeling of fatigue may be replaced by confusion, incoordination and panic, while in very rare cases of hypoxia, a final stage of euphoria (a feeling of well being) may be reached, followed by unconsciousness.

First Aid: It is imperative to remove the unconscious diver from the water to avoid drowning. Upon reaching the surface administer 100% oxygen if available. Should respiratory or cardiac failure occur resuscitation must be commenced immediately and medical aid sought.

Prevention: Regular equipment servicing and the use of a contents gauge should eliminate the failure of air supply. Contamination will be avoided by getting scuba cylinders recharged at a reputable dive shop. Correct training in the practical aspects of diving, good dive planning and maintenance of good physical condition will ensure that a situation involving hypoxia will not occur.

If the total supply of oxygen to the diver is removed, a condition known as anoxia will result. Anoxia is a state of no oxygen as opposed to hypoxia which is a state of low oxygen.

3C: 2 Carbon Dioxide

Carbon Dioxide (CO_2) is produced by combustion and respiration. Consequently the concentration of carbon dioxide in the atmosphere varies. In heavily industrialised areas the level of carbon dioxide would be high compared to the open ocean. Carbon dioxide is also produced as a waste product of respiration in animals. In mammals, carbon dioxide is exhaled via the lungs. If proper ventilation does not occur, a build-up of carbon dioxide in the respiratory system follows and will eventually cause carbon dioxide poisoning.

Physiologically, carbon dioxide is very important since it is the primary stimulant of the respiratory system. Chemoreceptors located in the major arteries monitor the level of carbon dioxide in the blood and send information to the respiratory centre located in the brain. If the concentration of carbon dioxide is high the respiratory centre stimulates breathing. The depth and rate of breathing will be increased in an effort to rid the system of excess carbon dioxide.

a. Carbon Dioxide Poisoning

Carbon dioxide can be blamed for one of the most common complaints in sport diving — headache.

Cause: Although contamination and poor regulator function can be blamed for carbon dioxide poisoning, the main cause lies with the diver.

Poor ventilation resulting from "skip breathing" or diving too deep will cause carbon dioxide build-up in the system. Skip breathing is the act of infrequent or shallow breathing during a scuba dive.

Signs and Symptoms: Generally a build-up of carbon dioxide will result in a stimulus to breathe. The most noticeable symptom of carbon dioxide poisoning may be a slight increase in breathing rate during the dive. Upon reaching the surface the diver may suffer a throbbing headache with associated nausea, vomiting and confusion.

First Aid: If loss of breathing control should occur during the dive it is important to try to restore a normal breathing pattern by ceasing all muscular activity. If normal breathing is not restored, ascend and breathe fresh air. In severe cases, administer 100% oxygen if available.

Prevention: Skip breathing in an effort to conserve air is false economy and should be avoided. When diving deep avoid the use of poor quality equipment, and remember to breathe out fully.

3C: 3 Hyperventilation

Hyperventilation (*hyper* refers to over and *ventilation* means breathing) is most dangerous when combined with breath-hold diving. Taking more than three or four breaths before a breath-hold dive constitutes dangerous hyperventilation (over breathing). Traditionally, hyperventilation has been practised by spearfishermen in an effort to prolong the time of a breath-hold dive. By hyperventilating, the partial pressure of carbon dioxide in the blood is lowered leading to a delayed urge to breathe. Although the carbon dioxide level is lowered, oxygen levels are not significantly increased. This is because most oxygen is carried by red blood cells which are normally 97% saturated.

It is because the oxygen levels do not increase as the carbon dioxide levels decrease that makes the practice of hyperventilation dangerous.

3C: 4 Hyperventilation anoxia (Latent Anoxia, Shallow Water Blackout)

Hyperventilation is not restricted to spearfishermen. Many underwater swimmers have fallen victim to it.

Cause: Primarily, hyperventilation is the cause. During a breath-hold dive, without hyperventilation, the urge to breathe occurs normally, allowing enough time to reach the surface safely. It the breath-hold diver hyperventilates, although the urge to breathe is delayed, oxygen consumption remains the same. Upon ascent, as total pressure lowers, the oxygen partial pressure drops to below the level required to sustain consciousness.

Signs and Symptoms: Unconsciousness usually occurs without any warning while the diver is ascending.

First Aid: Drowning is obviously inevitable unless the victim is quickly recovered. Expired air resuscitation (EAR) should be commenced immediately to aid re-establishment of normal carbon dioxide levels. When breathing has stabilised administer 100% oxygen for treatment of possible salt water aspiration. It is essential to continue observation of the patient as respiratory failure may recur due to the low level of carbon dioxide in the system. Medical advice and observation for at least 24 hours is required.

Prevention: Hyperventilation, whether intentional or unintentional, is a very dangerous practice and should always be avoided. The need for a good buddy system (see section 4C) is once again emphasised.

3C: 5 Nitrogen

Nitrogen, approximately 80% of the atmosphere, is not used by the body. However, when breathed at high partial pressures, it has a narcotic effect on the diver.

Nitrogen Narcosis (Narcs; Rapture of the deep; Inert gas narcosis)

Nitrogen narcosis, although in itself not physiologically damaging, has been the indirect cause of many diving fatalities.

Cause: The reasons why breathing high partial pressure nitrogen causes nitrogen narcosis are still not completely understood. However, it can be clinically detected in all divers at 30 metres. Beyond this depth the influence of nitrogen will worsen, depending on individual susceptibility. It becomes hazardous at depths beyond 40 metres.

Signs and Symptoms: Although narcosis will occur within minutes of reaching a particular depth, continued descent will worsen the effect. Regular exposure appears to develop some degree of resistance.

Lack of co-ordination and concentration are the most obvious signs and symptoms. Should descent be continued, a state of mental confusion and even unconsciousness may result.

First Aid: If nitrogen narcosis is evident, immediate **ascent** to shallower depths will eliminate its effects. It should be noted that both divers in a buddy system may be affected. Therefore the symptoms may pass unnoticed and no attempt may be made to remedy the situation.

Prevention: By restricting sport divers to above 40 metres, nitrogen narcosis should not be a problem. Constant assessment during any dive below 30 metres is essential.

Predisposing Factors: Any factors that will increase the likelihood of nitrogen narcosis are termed predisposing factors. Increased carbon dioxide retention resulting from rapid descent or hard work at depth will increase the effects of narcosis until proper ventilation is re-established. Inexperience will develop anxiety which, combined with dives greater than 30 metres, will result in greater susceptibility to nitrogen narcosis. The chances of a diver experiencing narcosis are markedly increased by hypothermia, hangover, alcohol and other drugs. Individual susceptibility and low intelligence are other predisposing factors. Strong motivation and will-power are marginally beneficial in overcoming narcosis.

3C: 6 Carbon Monoxide Poisoning

Carbon monoxide is produced in the combustion process when the supply of oxygen is limited (such as in an automobile engine). The capacity of carbon monoxide to bind with red blood cells is 200-300 times greater than with oxygen. As a result quite small amounts of carbon monoxide will successfully replace oxygen. The red blood cell/carbon monoxide combination serves no useful purpose and only acts to reduce the blood's oxygen carrying capacity. This reduced number of red blood cells able to carry oxygen leads to hypoxia.

Cause: Breathing air can become contaminated by poor positioning of a compressor hose.

Even though an intake hose is correctly positioned carbon monoxide contamination can still occur if the compressor is poorly maintained. In a well maintained compressor the cylinder rings will prevent oil from entering the head area. If the rings become worn, oil will be left on the cylinder wall during the piston's downstroke. When the piston comes up the oil will be in a high pressure area and can spontaneously ignite ('flash') producing carbon monoxide.

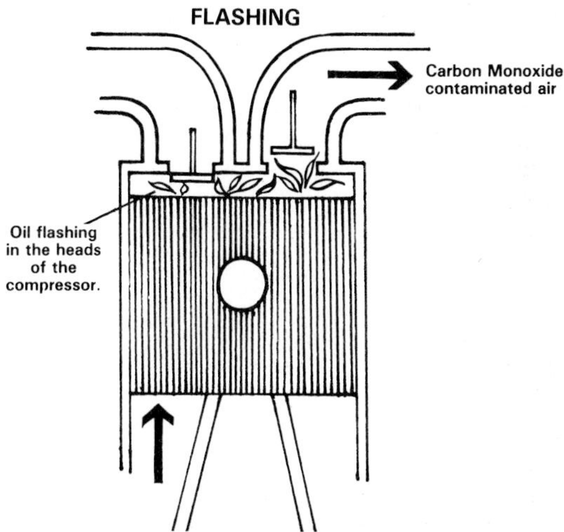

FLASHING IN THE HEADS OF A COMPRESSOR

Most compressor filtration systems do not filter out carbon monoxide, therefore contamination of the scuba air supply will occur even though pure air is entering the compressor.

Signs and Symptoms: Carbon monoxide poisoning will resemble hypoxia, in that headaches, dizziness, shortness of breath, nausea, vomiting, weak pulse, and unconsciousness may be apparent. The most distinguishing feature of carbon monoxide poisoning is the cherry red appearance of lips and finger nail beds. This arises because the red blood cell/carbon monoxide combination results in a bright red colour. Therefore areas close to the surface of the body appear flushed. Unfortunately, this symptom usually manifests itself after death because a high level of contamination is needed.

It is worth noting that the effects of carbon monoxide poisoning will decrease with increasing depth. More oxygen will dissolve in the blood plasma and transport of oxygen to tissues can be maintained.

First Aid: Removal of the victim from the source of contamination is vital. Signs and symptoms will be relieved by exposure to fresh air or by breathing 100% oxygen. In severe cases where the patient is not breathing resuscitation may be necessary and medical aid must be sought.

Treatment: Hyperbaric (high pressure) oxygen in a hospital will aid recovery of a severely affected diver.

Prevention: It is important to ensure a clean air supply by taking care in positioning the air intake hose of a compressor and to keep the compressor well maintained.

Air that has an oily odour or taste may be contaminated with carbon monoxide and should not be used.

Section 3: MEDICAL CONSIDERATIONS

3D: Decompression Sickness

1. Decompression Sickness
2. Aseptic Bone Necrosis
3. Use of Air Decompression Tables

Section 3 MEDICAL CONSIDERATIONS

3D: 1 Decompression Sickness (Bends, Caisson's Disease, Itches, Niggles, Chokes, Staggers)

Every time a diver descends under water the increase in ambient pressure will cause more air to dissolve in the blood stream (Henry's Law). The increased levels of oxygen and carbon dioxide in the blood will pose very little problem because they are consumed via the body's normal physiological processes. Nitrogen is not used by the body and increased levels will be distributed by the blood throughout the body. Different tissues will absorb nitrogen at different rates. For instance, bone tissue will absorb nitrogen slowly due to its poor blood supply whereas brain tissue will absorb nitrogen more readily due to its prolific blood supply. As dive time progresses, more and more nitrogen will diffuse from the lungs into the blood stream and hence into various tissues. Saturation of tissues can take up to twelve hours.

Cause: **Depth** and **time** will determine how much nitrogen will actually dissolve in the tissues. During ascent from depths greater than 9 metres, time must be allowed so that excess nitrogen can be eliminated via the lungs. If ascent is too rapid, and the pressure drop is too great, nitrogen molecules will form bubbles in the tissues.

Signs and Symptoms: It is the formation of nitrogen bubbles in the tissues as a result of rapid ascent that determines the signs and symptoms of decompression sickness. Decompression sickness will usually manifest itself within a few hours of completion of the dive. Signs and symptoms usually occur within five minutes to six hours after surfacing, although in some cases divers have gone to bed quite normal and awoken suffering from decompression sickness up to twelve hours later. Any complaint, however vague or unusual, following exposure to pressure, should be regarded and treated as decompression sickness unless proved otherwise.

The signs and symptoms can be broken into four major categories:

(1) ***Skin and general body involvement: 'Itches'***

If decompression is too rapid small bubbles may form under the skin. Small vessels may rupture and general red blotching of the skin will occur. The small bubbles may also stimulate the nerves under the skin causing an itching or burning sensation. This condition is commonly termed 'itches' and may be the only indication of decompression sickness. Although the condition usually passes off slowly, medical aid should still be obtained as 'itches' may be a warning of further problems.

(2) ***Joint involvement: 'Niggles' or 'Bends'***
After inadequate decompression, bubbles of nitrogen form in the joints,particularly in the shoulder. Other joints affected may include the elbow, wrist, hand, hip, knee and ankle. Numbness or discomfort around the joint — 'niggles' — may, after a period of time, develop into a mild to severe, deep boring pain — the 'bends'. Pain will usually be aggravated by movement of the limb.

The majority of sport diving decompression sickness causes fall into the above categories. The more serious forms of decompression sickness are usually the result of prolonged exposures beyond the sport diver range. However, serious cases can occur in sport divers, particularly from repetitive dives.

(3) ***Lung involvement: 'Chokes'***
Chokes or decompression sickness involving the lungs results from the accumulation of nitrogen bubbles in the lung tissue. Shortness of breath, chest pain, coughing, and unconsciousness all indicate 'chokes'. It is important that the possibility of lung damage due to pulmonary barotrauma be eliminated by a thorough check of the victim's dive details.

(4) ***Brain and spinal cord involvement: 'Staggers'***
The brain and spinal cord make up the central nervous system. Involvement of the central nervous system is the most serious level of decompression sickness. Any function of the human body can be affected. Nitrogen bubbles in the brain can cause headaches, confusion, convulsions, unconsciousness, visual disturbances, ringing in the ears, dizziness, general weakness, partial paralysis, nausea, vomiting, and stomach cramps. 'Staggers' — difficulty in co-ordination or partial paralysis — is usually the result of bubbles interfering with spinal cord function.

First Aid: Careful handling of the patient is imperative. If one can imagine the ready formation of bubbles when a bottle of carbonated beverage is agitated, the need for careful handling becomes obvious. The patient should be placed in the recovery position (see section 3G) and continually observed in case of respiratory or cardiac arrest. The patient should take 300 mg of aspirin to help minimise blood clotting in the vessels. Orange juice is recommended to help maintain the body fluids and salt balance. If available, 100% oxygen should be administered during transport to recompression facilities. The oxygen will help ease symptoms by speeding elimination of excess nitrogen from the body. Transport to a recompression chamber via road, by low flying aircraft or aircraft pressurized to sea level should be arranged immediately.

Treatment: Recompression in a chamber under medical supervision using therapeutic recompression tables is essential. Therapeutic tables are special treatment tables and must never be used for sport diving.

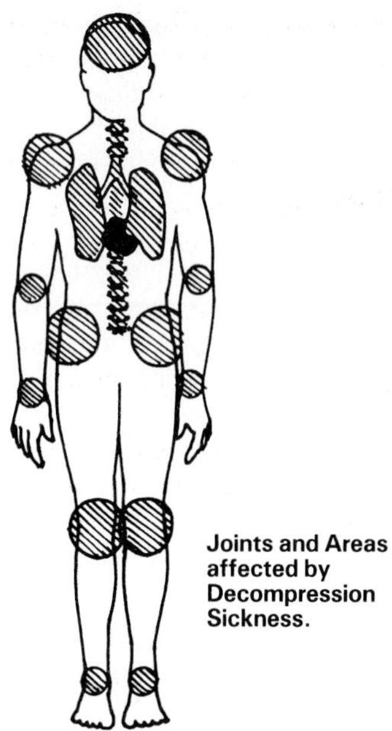

Joints and Areas affected by Decompression Sickness.

A list of recompression chambers at the time of printing is provided in the appendix. The nearest recompression facility should be contacted as soon as possible if there is any doubt regarding management of a case of decompression sickness. This number can be called 24 hours a day.

Prevention: Decompression sickness will only be avoided by the correct use of air decompression tables. It is absolutely essential that all scuba divers have an accurate working knowledge of the tables (see section 3D).

Predisposing Factors: Not only correct use of tables, but also an understanding of predisposing factors is necessary in prevention of decompression sickness. Although the tables may be correctly followed, there are many factors which will increase the chances of a diver suffering decompression sickness.

Divers over the age of 40, or those who are obese, have been shown to suffer an increased incidence of the bends. A history of decompression sickness or previous joint injury seem to predispose the diver to decompression sickness. Exertion at depth, maintenance of a cramped position, and fatigue are other factors which will increase the probability of decompression sickness, even if proper decompression has been performed. Cold, hangover, alcohol and other drugs affect the blood flow within the body and predispose decompression sickness. Even though the surface may be reached safely, bubbles can be induced by flying after diving or exercising after a dive. Both activities should be avoided for twelve hours after diving.

It should be noted that most air decompression tables are calculated to bring the diver safely to the surface at sea level. Therefore, altitude diving requires special consideration.

Decompression meters should be avoided, particularly for repetitive dives. They are unreliable and many divers have suffered decompression sickness when using them.

3D: 2 Aseptic Bone Necrosis (Dysbaric Osteonecrosis)

Cause: The cause of aseptic bone necrosis is not known. However, deep diving and untreated decompression sickness may cause the blood vessels supplying the bones to become blocked. Generally, the long bones of the upper arm and upper leg are most affected. If the blood supply to the bone tissue is blocked, oxygen and other essential nutrients will not be supplied and the bone tissue will die. This condition is known as aseptic (without infection) bone necrosis (death), i.e., non-infectious death of bone tissue.

Signs and Symptoms: Aseptic bone necrosis can only be detected by X-ray examination. Manifestation can take up to nine months. In more serious cases the joint will become immobile and limb movement will be severely hindered. Commonly affected joints are shoulder and hip.

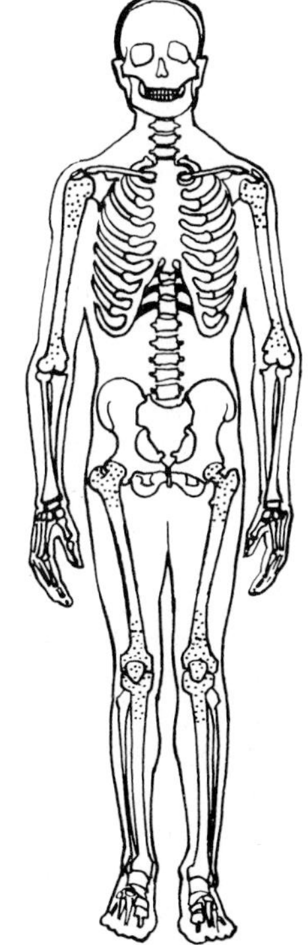

MAJOR SITES OF BONE NECROSIS

Treatment: In severe cases, very little can be done other than surgical joint replacement. If aseptic bone necrosis is detected it is advisable to cease all diving activities.

Prevention: The correct use of air decompression tables and avoiding deep or repetitive dives will help prevent the occurrence of aseptic bone necrosis. Early recognition of the condition is imperative so that further damage can be prevented by stopping diving activities. Long bone X-rays are recommended three to four months after any incidence of decompression sickness or if any minor joint pains persist for more than two or three days.

3D: 3 Use of Air Decompression Tables

To prevent the development of decompression sickness, special air decompression tables have to be used. Many Navies throughout the world have developed decompression tables. The Royal Navy (RN) and the United States Navy (USN) decompression tables are the most widely accepted tables in use today. Both tables are the result of many years of scientific study, experimentation, and extensive field studies. Both tables tend to become less accurate as depths and times increase. Therefore they require careful application. Even if the table is used correctly, a low incidence of decompression sickness may occur.

Due to different experimental criteria the Royal Navy (RN) table is more conservative. It can be presumed safer. However, there is no doubt that the USN table is more practical in some parts of Australia. Both tables can be used in three ways:

(1) For calculation of no decompression dives.
(2) For calculation of decompression stops.
(3) For calculation of repetitive dive procedures.

Each will be discussed in turn.

a. Definition of terms:

It is important that the sport diver becomes familiar with the following terms and definitions:

Depth — the maximum depth attained during the dive, measured in metres or feet of sea water, depending on which units the particular tables work in.

Bottom time — the total elapsed time, in minutes, from when the diver leaves the surface to the time (next whole minute) he begins his **final** ascent.

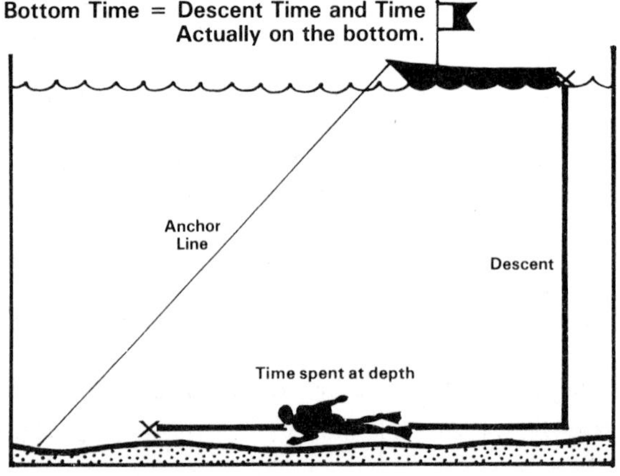

Rate of ascent — the recommended rate of ascent is twenty metres per minute (sixty feet per minute using U.S.N. tables). The best approximation of this in practical terms is the speed of the slowest visible exhaust bubbles.

Decompression stop — a specified depth at which a diver must remain for a specified length of time as designated by the decompression schedule, to allow liberation of nitrogen via the lungs.

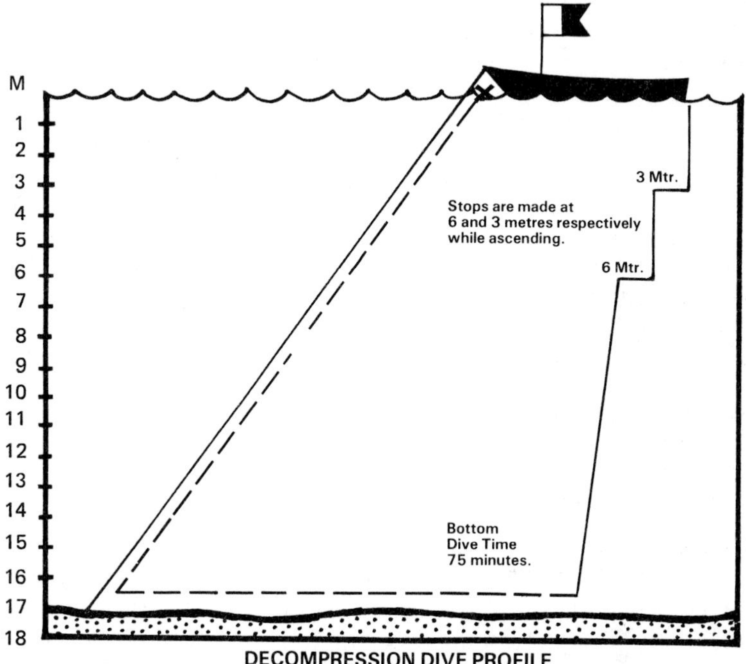

DECOMPRESSION DIVE PROFILE

Decompression schedule — specific decompression procedure for a given combination of depth and bottom time, as listed in a decompression table.

No decompression dive — a dive that does not require a decompression stop.

No decompression limit — maximum bottom time allowed for a specific depth to avoid a decompression stop.

Single dive — any dive conducted after a six hour surface interval. (12 hours using U.S.N. tables.)

Surface interval — the time a diver has spent on the surface following a dive; beginning as soon as the diver surfaces and ending as soon as he starts his next descent.

Repetitive dive — any dive conducted with less than a six hour surface interval. (12 hours using U.S.N. tables.)

Residual nitrogen — the amount of nitrogen in the tissues in excess of normal levels after completion of a dive.

Extra definitions for use of USN decompression table:

Repetitive group designation — a letter used to designate the amount of residual nitrogen in a diver's body.

Residual nitrogen time — an amount of time in minutes which must be **added** to the planned bottom time of a repetitive dive to compensate for the residual nitrogen from a previous dive.
Equivalent single dive — a dive for which the bottom time used to select the decompression schedule is the sum of the residual nitrogen time and the actual bottom time of the dive.

b. Selection of Decompression Schedule

When planning a dive the table must be consulted. The diver should plan his *maximum depth* and *bottom time* on the surface. When reading the table, if the maximum depth planned is not listed the next deepest depth should be used. Likewise for the bottom time, if the planned bottom time is not listed use the next longest time.

If the USN Standard Air Decompression Table was being used to select the correct schedules for a dive to 32 metres (105 feet) for a bottom time of 31 minutes, decompression would be carried out in accordance with the 33/40 (110/40) schedule.

The RN table is used in exactly the same way.

Never attempt to interpolate between decompression schedules.

If the diver were to be affected by any of the predisposing factors previously discussed the next longest and/or the next deepest decompression schedule than the one normally followed should be selected. The normal schedule for the 28 metres (91 feet) 31 minute dive is 30/40 (100/40). If a diver were exceptionally cold or fatigued he should decompress according to the 30/50 (100/50) or 33/40 (110/40) or better still, the 33/50 (110/50) schedule.

If a decompression stop has to be done the diver must maintain the scheduled depth at chest level. The only way to successfully achieve this is by using a weighted shot line marked at nine metre (30 feet), six metre (20 feet) and three metre (10 feet) intervals. During a decompression stop the diver must remain still. Swimming around using a depth gauge is not recommended as it will increase the likelihood of decompression sickness dramatically.

Basically both the USN and RN tables are used in the same way. The only difference lies in the time of the decompression stop. The USN table specifies the exact time to be spent at the decompression stop, whereas the RN table decompression stop time includes ascent time as well as time to be spent at the decompression stop.

A dive may require a five minute stop at 3 metres (10 feet). If using RN tables the time spent at three metres is actually four minutes; one minute is allowed for ascent. If using USN tables the time spent at three metres is five minutes.

c. No Decompression Dives

It is important in sport diving to avoid dives that require decompression stops. No decompression dives should always be planned, where practical. If decompression is required, a diver may risk decompression sickness by surfacing immediately. However, in an emergency, the surface must be reached as a matter of priority, as reluctance to surface **has** cost lives.

d. Repetitive Dive Procedure

Although the tables allow a diver to surface safely there is still excess nitrogen in the tissues. This is referred to as residual nitrogen and must be considered if further dives are planned with a 6 hour period (12 hours if U.S.N. tables). Both tables treat the problem differently.

(i) Royal Navy Repetitive Dive Procedure

When using the RN table the second dive must be combined with the first. The bottom times of all dives within a period of six hours must be added and the maximum depth obtained in any of the dives used.

Consider two dives, one to 18 metres (60 feet) for a bottom time of 40 minutes; the other to 12 metres (40 feet) with a 40 minute bottom time. If the surface interval exceeds six hours no decompression is required. If the dives are within six hours of each other the second dive becomes a repetitive dive. As such the decompression required for the second dive can be calculated by adding the bottom time (40 + 40 = 80 minutes) and using the deepest depth (18 metres). The appropriate decompression is: 5 minutes at 6 metres (20 feet) and 5 minutes at 3 metres (10 feet).

	Surface Interval (hrs:mins)	**Depth metres (feet)**	**Bottom Time (minutes)**
Dive 1			
Decompression schedule		18 (60)	40
No decompression is required			
Dive 2	Less than	12 (40)	40
	6 hours	18 (60)	80
Decompression schedule			

Decompression required: 5 minutes at 6 metres (20 feet)
5 minutes at 3 metres (10 feet)

Calculation of No Decompression Time for a Repetitive Dive Using RN Tables

In the above example, the diver wishes to make his second dive a no decompression dive. He has already had a bottom time of 40 minutes in the first dive. From the RN table the no decompression limit for 60 feet is 60 minutes; therefore, on the second dive he can only have a bottom time of 20 minutes (60 minus 40) at 12 metres (40 feet) to avoid the need for a decompression stop.

(ii) United States Navy Repetitive Dive Procedure

Upon the completion of a dive two important pieces of information must be recorded. The first is the beginning of the surface interval and, secondly, the repetitive group designation. The repetitive group designation can be found in two tables. If the first dive is a no decompression dive the No Decompression Limits and Repetitive Group Designation Tables for No-Decompression Air Dives (table 1-11) must be consulted.

Take a dive to 18 metres (60 feet) with a bottom time of 40 minutes, using table 1-11, the repetitive group designation is G.

If the first dive is a decompression dive the repetitive group designation will be found using the USN Standard Air Decompression Tables (table 1-10). Take a dive to 80 feet for a bottom time of 50 minutes, using table 1-10, the repetitive group designation is K.

Once the residual nitrogen designation has been determined the Surface Interval Credit Tables (table 1-12) can be consulted to obtain the new repetitive group designation. To do this enter table 1-12 on the left hand side and move horizontally to the right to the interval in which the diver's surface interval lies. The time spent on the surface must be between or equal to the limits of the selected interval. Now read vertically upwards to the new repetitive group designation.

If the residual nitrogen designation is K after a dive, and the surface interval is two hours and twenty minutes (2:20), the new residual nitrogen group is F. Dives following surface intervals of more than twelve hours are not repetitive dives.

The next step is to calculate the residual nitrogen time. To do this, consult the Repetitive Nitrogen Table for Air Dives (table 1-13). If the new repetitive group is F, and the second dive is to a depth of 50 feet then the residual nitrogen time is 47 minutes. This means that the diver must assume that he has already spent 47 minutes bottom time before he starts the repetitive (second) dive to this depth (50 feet). To find out how long he can stay at 50 feet to avoid a decompression stop he must consult either table 1-10 or table 1-11. The no decompression limit for 50 feet is 100 minutes. Therefore, he can spend 53 minutes (100 minus 47) minutes at 50 feet.

e. A Comparative Example of Repetitive Dive Procedures

Problem: A repetitive dive is to be made to 26 metres (85 feet) for an estimated bottom time of 20 minutes. The following dive is to a depth of 34 metres (112 feet) and had a bottom time of 15 minutes. The diver's surface interval is 5 hours and 28 minutes (5:28). What decompression schedule should be used for the repetitive dive?

Solution using RN tables:

	Surface Interval	Depth M.	Depth Ft.	Bottom Time Min.
Dive 1	**over six hours**	**26 metres (85 ft.)**		**20 minutes**
Decompression schedule		**27**	**(90)**	**20 minutes**
No decompression is needed				
Dive 2	5:28	34	(112)	15 minutes

This is a repetitive dive. Use maximum depth and total bottom time to determine decompression schedule.

Decompression schedule	34	(112)	20 and 15
Use	36	(120)	(35) minutes

Decompression required: 5 minutes at 6 metres (20 feet)
and: 20 minutes at 3 metres (10 feet)

Solution using USN Tables:

	Surface Interval over 12 hours	Depth m.	(ft)	Bottom Time min.	Repetitive Group Designation
Dive 1	over 12 hours	26	(85)	20	
Decompression schedule		27	(90)	20	F (from table 1-11)
		No decompression required			
	5:28				New repetitive dive group B (from table 1-12)

Residual nitrogen time for a dive to 112 feet (from table 1-13) is 6 minutes. This must be added to bottom time.

Dive 2		34	(112)	15 + 6 (21)
Decompression schedule		36	(120)	25
	Decompression required: 6 minutes at 10 feet			

If repetitive dives are planned, as a general rule **do the deepest dive first**. By doing the deepest dive first, the shallower second dive will aid the elimination of residual nitrogen. It is also wise to plan the second dive so decompression stops can be avoided. In a 6 hour period (12 hours if U.S.N. tables are used), any **final** dive to depths less than 9 metres will not require decompression because the final pressure change on ascent is not great enough for bubble formation.

Many modifications of both RN and USN repetitive dive procedures can be found. The most notable are the RNPL-BSAC table, a modification of the Royal Navy Table and the ''NU-way'' Repetitive Dives Table, a modification of the USN table.

Section 3: MEDICAL CONSIDERATIONS

3E: Hypothermia

1. Mild Hypothermia
2. Severe Hypothermia
3. General Prevention

Section 3 MEDICAL CONSIDERATIONS

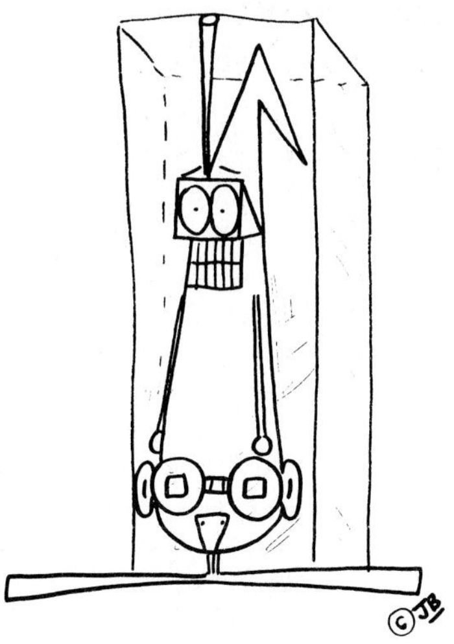

3E Hypothermia (Cold Water Exhaustion)

Hypothermia (loss of body heat to the surrounding environment) is derived from *hypo*, meaning low, and *thermia*, pertaining to temperature. Medically speaking, hypothermia is a condition where the body's core temperature drops below normal (37°C). The core temperature refers to the temperature of the vital organs such as brain, heart, and liver. It is essential that the core temperature be maintained. Should the body get too hot or too cold, function of the vital organs will be impaired.

Man has evolved different responses to hot or cold stimuli, so that the normal core temperature can be maintained.

For instance, when we get hot, the two most noticeable reactions are perspiration and a flushed appearance. Perspiring cools the body by evaporation. The flushed appearance, particularly noticeable after a hot shower, results from vasodilation. Vasodilation, opening of the surface blood vessels, allows excessive heat to escape from the body. Alcohol and other drugs will also cause vasodilation.

In response to cold stimuli, goose bumps, shivering and loss of colour occurs. Goose bumps result from erection of hairs on our skin. When man was a hairy animal, this hair would trap air and cause a layer of insulation over the skin, helping to prevent heat loss. It is quite obvious that this has little effect in modern man. Shivering, however, is quite effective as it generates the production of heat within our body. As we get colder, loss of colour occurs because the surface blood vessels are closed off in an effort to prevent heat loss via the skin. This is referred to as vasoconstriction.

Cause: If we become immersed, heat is rapidly lost to the water. Water has 25 times the thermal conductivity of air (see section 1A). As a result even mild water temperatures (18-22°C) can cause a dramatic drop in core temperature.

3E: 1 Mild Hypothermia

Signs and Symptoms: The body can tolerate a small drop in core temperature. In fact, in most places throughout Australia, a fall in core temperature can be expected during a dive. As the body cools, shivering will occur in an effort to replace lost heat. Unfortunately, the loss of body heat in water exceeds production of body heat, and core temperature will steadily drop. Progressive loss of colour occurs due to increased vasoconstriction of surface vessels. As the blood supply to the extremities is reduced, the ability to perform fine tasks, such as focusing a camera, becomes more difficult due to numbness combined with shivering. Further loss of heat to surrounding water stimulates the body to shut down larger vessels, particularly those in the limbs. Fatigue and inco-ordination will occur. Confusion is a sure sign of the cooler blood impairing brain function.

First Aid: Continued immersion beyond this level may result in death. Therefore, an early recognition of the onset of hypothermia is important. Divers suffering from mild hypothermia should leave the water. Further heat loss will be prevented by removing the wet suit and dressing the victim in warm, dry clothing. Remaining in a sodden wet suit after a dive does not aid rewarming because wind will cause evaporation and hence further heat loss. If possible, a warm shower will be of great benefit. Warm, sweet, non-alcoholic drinks will also aid rewarming. Alcohol only worsens the condition by causing vasodilation.

3E: 2 Severe Hypothermia

Early Warning Signs: There is a fine dividing line between mild and severe hypothermia. When a diver begins to show early warning signs, such as uncontrollable shivering, inco-ordination, and confusion, continued exposure will lessen the chances of recovery.

Signs and Symptoms: When the core temperature drops to below 34°C the patient can be regarded as severely cold. Shivering will be replaced by muscle rigidity. Therefore an unaided diver will drown. Unconsciousness and heart irregularities will occur, followed by death.

First Aid: Active rewarming, such as massage, hot bath or shower, placing the victim in front of an open fire should **never** be attempted. Active rewarming or external heat may cause death by causing peripheral vessels to dilate and hence a fall in blood pressure. Rewarming at the first aid level should only be attempted using body warmth by skin to skin contact with unaffected divers. If the victim is conscious, warm, sweet, non-alcoholic drinks will help. It is extremely important to get the victim to a hospital so the rewarming can be done under medical supervision. Resuscitation may be required.

3E: 3 General Prevention:

Although hypothermia is inevitable, its onset can be delayed by wearing a well manufactured wet suit designed for diving (see Section 2A). A good wet suit provides an insulating layer between the body and the surrounding water.

Regular exposures to cold water over long periods will aid acclimatisation, therefore reducing reaction to lower temperature.

Diet can also affect the onset of hypothermia. An increased deposit of body fat will aid insulation, but remember this will predispose you to decompression sickness. Eating a sensible high calorie meal one to two hours prior to exposure will provide reserve energy.

Heat loss can be minimised by reducing the amount of exercise in water. Although exercise does produce heat, the production of heat will not overcome the heat loss. Avoiding currents or excessive movement will enable flow of water over the body to be kept to a minimum.

Alcohol will reverse the body's normal reaction to the cold and worsen the effects of hypothermia. Alcohol must be avoided before and after a dive. Repetitive dives should not be performed until the diver's response to hot and cold are back to normal, i.e. do not return to the water until sweating has occurred. A snack and light exercise will achieve this.

The signs and symptoms of hypothermia are such that they will often mask signs of other diving related problems. The drowsiness and lack of response nor mally associated with carbon monoxide poisoning will be very hard to determine when in the presence of hypothermia. Similarly, mild symptoms of decompression sickness, such as skin rash and itchiness, can often be confused with the blotchy appearance and tingling of a cold diver. A thorough understanding of dive conditions and of any associated problems arising from the dive must be sought by thorough, careful cross-examination to eliminate the possibility of any ailments co-existing with hypothermia.

Section 3: MEDICAL CONSIDERATIONS

3F: Miscellaneous Complaints

1. Salt Water Aspiration Syndrome
2. Outer Ear Infection
3. Sunburn
4. Heat Exhaustion
5. Sea Sickness

Section 3 MEDICAL CONSIDERATIONS

3F: 1 Salt Water Aspiration Syndrome

Cause: Salt water aspiration syndrome (the inhalation of a fine mist of salt water) causes an acute inflammation of the alveoli.

The major cause of salt water aspiration syndrome is poor regulator condition. Regulators should be checked frequently to ensure breathing is moisture free. Moisture can enter a regulator through faulty exhaust valves, a hole in the diaphragm or a tear in the mouth piece. Other causes of inhalation include buddy breathing, inadequately cleared snorkels, continually leaking masks, free ascents, in fact any condition where the diver is forced to inhale fine droplets of water.

Free ascents involve a scuba diver surfacing without an air supply and expose the diver to the risk of inhaling as well as a grave risk of pulmonary barotrauma of ascent.

Signs and Symptoms: The first indication of salt water aspiration is coughing soon after surfacing. This may be followed one to two hours later by shortness of breath, pain in the chest, uncontrollable shivering, fever, loss of appetite, nausea and vomiting. There has been no report of any fatality.

First Aid: Mild cases may be treated by keeping the patient warm, bed rest, and 100% oxygen if available. Analgesics such as paracetamol will ease the condition. Medical advice must be sought to confirm diagnosis. The condition usually passes within 24 hours.

Prevention: Regular and proper maintenance of diving equipment and correct training procedures will minimise the occurrence of salt water aspiration syndrome.

3F: 2 Outer Ear Infection (Otitis Externa, Swimmer's or Tropical Ear)

Cause: Outer ear infection is common in swimmers and divers. Infection, usually caused by bacteria, results from not allowing the ear canal to dry.

Signs and Symptoms: Pain in the ear develops and the ear becomes sore to touch. Partial deafness and a feeling of fullness may result from a swollen ear canal.

First Aid: Very little can be done apart from taking aspirin to relieve the pain. A doctor should be consulted immediately and a swab taken to determine the causal organism and its sensitivity to antibiotics.

Treatment: Diving activities should be ceased until treatment with prescribed antibiotics is successful.

Prevention: Proper drying of the ear canal after diving is important. ''Aquaear'', a solution readily available at most pharmacies, should be applied as directed after diving, to dry the ear canal. A few drops of methylated spirits in each ear after a dive works just as well. Do not dry the ear canal by using a towel as this can cause infection.

Sunburn

Many divers are affected by sunburn, but very few appreciate the potential danger of serious sunburn. Sunburn (over exposure to the sun) is implicated in the cause of skin cancer.

First Aid: The casualty should rest in a cool area, and be given copious amounts of fluid to drink. Cool, moist compresses should be applied to the sunburnt areas. Suitable lotions from chemist shops should be applied to affected areas. If blistering has occurred a doctor should be consulted.

Prevention: When over exposure to the sun cannot be avoided, proper sunburn creams, such as UV cream or zinc cream should be used. Always carry a hat and shirt with you.

Heat Exhaustion

Cause: Heat exhaustion is the result of being in hot, humid conditions. Divers staying in wet suits on hot days, or on open boats for extended periods, will be likely victims of heat exhaustion.

Signs and Symptoms: A rapid pulse, headache, cramps, feeling faint, paleness of skin and excessive sweating all indicate heat exhaustion.

First Aid: A person suffering from heat exhaustion should be removed to cool surroundings, have clothes removed and should be sponged with cool water. If excessive sweating has occurred the patient should be given water with a teaspoon of common table salt in every 600 millilitres. The patient must be reassured and medical aid sought.

Prevention: Always get into the water before getting too hot.

Sea Sickness (Motion Sickness)

Sea sickness is an unpleasant hazard that has ruined many a good day's boat diving.

Cause: Movements of fluid in the balance mechanism of the inner ear (semicircular canals) out of phase with eye movements, will cause stimulation of the nausea centre in the brain of certain people.

Signs and Symptoms: Dizziness, thick dry tongue, nausea, vomiting and pallid complexion indicate sea sickness.

Diving should never be attempted when suffering from sea sickness. Vomiting under water into the regulator can be fatal. Vomitis can cause malfunction of the regulator as well as increase the probability of inhalation of water which may result in drowning.

First Aid: Very little can be done apart from fresh air or having feet firmly planted on solid ground. Lying down with head lower than the rest of the body may help.

Prevention: Many motion sickness tablets are available which will help alleviate sea sickness. However, most contain drugs that cause drowziness and predispose a diver to nitrogen narcosis. Motion sickness tablets for diving should only be taken under medical advice.

A strong mental attitude against being sick can help some people prevent sea sickness.

If you are prone to sea sickness enter the water as soon as possible before sea sickness takes over. However, abort the dive if there is no immediate improvement.

Section 3: MEDICAL CONSIDERATIONS

3G: First Aid

1. Massive Bleeding
2. Respiratory Arrest
3. Cardiac Arrest
4. Shock

Section 3 MEDICAL CONSIDERATIONS

3G First Aid

First aid is exactly what the term implies — first aid. As a diving buddy, if there is an accident, no matter how minor, you will be first to know about it, and as such should know how to deal with the situation. The aim of first aid is to sustain life and prevent further damage from occurring until proper medical aid is obtained. A calm approach is essential.

In many first aid situations a number of items need to be assessed immediately.

(1) Bleeding — any massive bleeding must be controlled immediately. Bleeding from an artery must be controlled before expired air resuscitation (EAR) is commenced. A person can bleed to death in two or three minutes, whereas he can survive without air for a slightly longer period.

(2) Breathing — a clear airway must be established and if breathing is absent expired air resuscitation (EAR) must be commenced. External cardiac compression (ECC) must also be commenced if there is a cardiac arrest.

(3) Shock — no matter how minor the accident, physiological shock can be a major problem. After any accident the patient must be observed and treated for shock.

After bleeding, breathing and shock have been treated, specific first aid can be administered. Medical advice should be sought promptly and the doctor provided with a record of events.

3G: 1 Massive Bleeding

Cause: Massive bleeding, bleeding from a severed artery, may result from a propellor accident or a shark attack.

Signs and Symptoms: Blood spurting from a wound may result in massive blood loss causing shock and death within two to three minutes unless controlled immediately.

First Aid: Pressure and elevation are key factors in control of bleeding. Direct pressure should be applied using a broad bandage. A towel wrapped tightly around the limb over the wound, or even a hand placed firmly on the wound would do, if a bandage is not available. Indirect pressure applied by pressing firmly on pressure points will also stop bleeding.

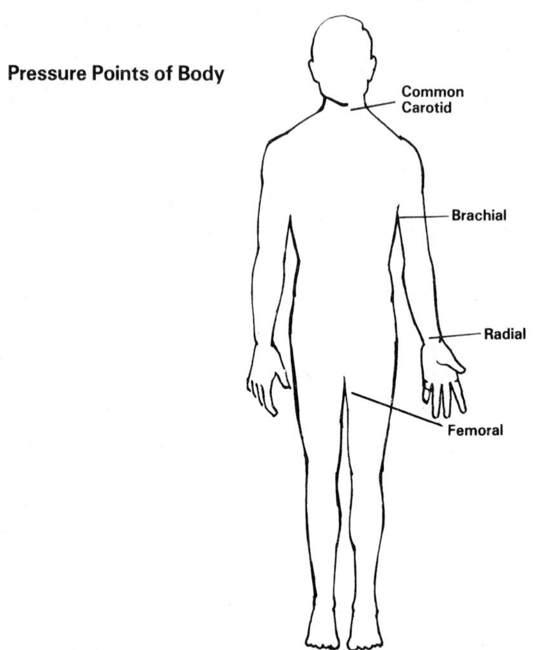

When pressure has been applied it is important to elevate the limb to reduce blood flow. Also maintain the recovery position keeping the head lower than the rest of the body.

If bleeding persists and the dressing saturated, reinforce the dressing by applying another. **Never** remove previous dressings.

Treat for shock, observe for respiratory and cardiac arrest and resuscitate as necessary.

It is important not to rush the victim off to hospital. Get on-site medical aid. Shock can be dramatically worsened by rushed transport. Do not move the victim until all visible signs of shock have abated or at least thirty minutes have elapsed.

3G: 2 Respiratory Arrest (Breathing Stops)

Most diving fatalities result from drowning. The causes are many and varied. Exhaustion of air supply, panic, inability to snorkel, lack of fitness, poor dive planning, diving too deep and being overcome by nitrogen narcosis may all lead to inhalation of water and ultimately death if the unconscious diver is not quickly recovered. Poisonous bites, such as blue-ringed octopus bite, will cause paralysis of respiratory muscles and hence respiratory failure. Other causes of respiratory failure are choking, suffocation, strangulation, drug overdose, electric shock and pneumonia.

Signs and Symptoms: If a person ceases to breathe, oxygen will no longer reach the tissues and unconsciousness quickly follows. As the supply of oxygen diminishes, cyanosis or blueness of the face, lips and finger nail beds becomes evident. When breathing ceases there will be no visible chest movement, no breathing sounds, and no flow of air from the mouth will be felt, i.e. breathing cannot be felt, seen or heard.

First Aid: Expired air resuscitation must be commenced immediately using mouth to mouth or mouth to nose method (see section 3H).

3G: 3 Cardiac Arrest (Heart Stops)

Cause: Shortly after cessation of breathing cardiac arrest will occur due to lack of oxygen reaching the heart. This may result from drowning, asphyxia, heart attack or electric shock.

Signs and Symptoms: Lack of pulse, unconsciousness, and cyanosis indicate cardiac arrest. It is important to feel the pulse by locating the carotid artery. The carotid arteries are located in the neck and lie below the surface between the windpipe (trachea) and the muscle beside the throat.

When searching for a pulse it is important to use the tips of the fingers, not the thumb. The thumb has its own pulse, which may be mistaken for the patient's pulse. It is important to search for the carotid pulse rather than the radial (wrist) pulse because the radial pulse may be weak or difficult to find due to hypothermia or restriction caused by the wet suit. Another sign of cardiac arrest is dilated pupils, that is pupils which do not respond to light. Normally when the eye is opened the pupil, the black centre portion of the eye, will contract in response. When checking for dilated pupils it is important to check both eyes. This is not a very reliable sign because persons suffering from shock, drug overdose or concussion will exhibit the same lack of response to light.

First Aid: When cardiac arrest is evident the circulation must be artificially restored immediately by commencing external cardiac compression (ECC) (see section 3H).

3G: 4 Shock

Cause: Physiological shock (a general state of collapse of the body's functions) is caused by a loss of circulating blood volume or fluid loss resulting in a lowering of the body's blood pressure.

Blood volume can be reduced in many ways. Severe bleeding will lead to a direct loss of blood volume. Burns, vomiting, diarrhoea and exposure will cause excess fluid loss and hence affect blood volume and pressure. Painful injuries, poison, heart attack, infection and severe fright may cause the body to reduce blood volume and hence the blood pressure.

Shock can result from any injury, no matter how insignificant or severe that injury may be, and in fact can itself be the cause of death.

Observation, treatment and reassurance should be given no matter what the patient says. Your own examination of the physiological evidence should be given more importance than the patient's words such as "It's all right" or "I'm OK".

Signs and Symptoms: A victim of shock will appear pale, often complain of faintness or nausea, and may vomit. Breathing will appear rapid and shallow. Skin will feel cold and clammy, and pulse will be weak and rapid. Unconsciousness, respiratory and cardiac arrest may also follow.

First Aid: Persons suffering from shock should be placed on their side,

reassured and observed for unconsciousness, respiratory and cardiac arrest. Resuscitation should be performed as necessary. Tight clothing around the neck and chest should be loosened and the patient protected from exposure. On a hot day the patient should be shaded and on a cold day protected with blankets. Alcohol will only worsen the condition because of its effect on the circulatory system. If the patient complains of thirst only let him rinse his mouth with water. If surgery appears necessary it is important to give nothing by mouth, as this will delay the administration of anaesthetic. Medical aid is imperative. However, the patient should not be moved unnecessarily. A record of the patient's condition, pulse and respiration should be kept and given to a qualified medical person.

After shock has been treated other specific first aid should be administered.

Section 3: MEDICAL CONSIDERATIONS

3H: Resuscitation

1. Expired Air Resuscitation
2. External Cardiac Compression
3. Cardio-Pulmonary Resuscitation

Section 3 MEDICAL CONSIDERATIONS

3H: 1 Expired Air Resuscitation

1. **Lie** the casualty on a flat surface.
2. **Release** any tight clothing restricting chest movement.
3. **Tilt** the head back and to one side and clear any obstruction from the mouth and throat. Kneel beside the casualty's head.
4. **Ensure a clear airway** be extending the casualty's head back, and lifting the jaw, so that air can enter the lungs. Maximum jaw lift can be achieved by using the pistol grip on the casualty's chin and pulling upwards. The other hand should be pressing gently on the forehead down and back.
5. **Pinch** the casualty's nostrils between your thumb and forefinger.
6. **Take** a deep breath and **seal** your lips over the casualty's mouth.
7. **Breathe** out firmly and watch the chest rise out of the corner of your eye. The chest rise should be similar to that of normal inspiration.
8. **Remove** your mouth and tilt your head to watch the casualty's chest fall while listening to and feeling the expired air.
9. **Turn** your head back and **repeat** the sequence.
10. **Give** first 3-5 breaths rapidly. Thereafter the **rate** is governed by the rise and fall of the casualty's chest (approximately 12 breaths per minute).
11. **Check** carotid pulse regularly. If absent, commence ECC.
12. **Continue** EAR until casualty begins breathing unaided or until medical help arrives.
13. On **revival**, place the casualty in the **recovery position**, treat for shock, and observe.

Notes:— For babies and young children seal around the mouth and nose and **puff** only.
— For elderly people adjust force of inflation as necessary.

— If an obstruction is lodged in the casualty's throat which cannot be removed with the fingers, roll the casualty onto one side and slap firmly between the shoulder blades.
— If casualty vomits, clear mouth and nose again.
— If the casualty's stomach becomes inflated, check jaw lift and **reduce** the **volume** and **force** of **inflation.**

3H: 2 External Cardiac Compression

1. **Lie** the casualty on a **firm, flat** surface and kneel beside the chest.
2. **Locate** the position of the heart (situated behind the lower half of the breastbone in the centre of the chest).
3. Place the **heel** of one hand on the lower ⅓ of the breastbone, keeping the palm and fingers raised from the chest.
4. Cover this hand with the heel of the other so that the hands are crossed.
5. **Keeping the arms straight** with the shoulders vertically above the hands **press** briskly down on the breastbone (breastbone depression should be approximately 5 cm for adults; 2 cm for children, using one arm; 1 cm for babies, using only two fingers).
6. Rock backwards releasing the pressure but maintaining constant contact with the breastbone.
7. Release and reapply the pressure **once per second** for adults; more frequently for children and babies.
8. Check effectiveness by watching for improvement in colour and presence of carotid pulse.

Note: ECC should not be practised on a live subject since this may upset the normal working of the heart and may cause death.

3H: 3 Cardio-Pulmonary Resuscitation (CPR): Combined EAR and ECC

Rates: One operator should alternate two breaths with fifteen compressions at four to six cycles per minute.

Two operators should give one breath every five compressions at ten to fifteen cycles per minute.

Continue CPR until the pulse is restored, after each EAR alone is performed until breathing is restored. Then treat casualty for shock.

Maintain CPR until medical help arrives.

If you wish to practise resuscitation techniques on a mannikin contact your local dive store.

Section 4: DIVE PLANNING

4A: Dangerous Marine Animals

1. Bites
2. Puncture Wounds
3. Stings
4. Electric Shock
5. Internal Poisoning

4B: Understanding Water Movement

1. Tides
2. Currents
3. Waves

4C: The Dive

1. Dive Planning
2. The Buddy System
3. Calculation of Air Consumption

4D: Specialist Diving

1. Boat Diving
2. Night Diving
3. Wreck Diving
4. Fresh Water Diving
   (Cave and Sink Hole Diving)
5. Deep Diving
6. Decompression Diving

Section 4: DIVE PLANNING

4A: Dangerous Marine Animals

1. Bites
2. Puncture Wounds
3. Stings
4. Electric Shock
5. Internal Poisoning

Section 4 DIVE PLANNING

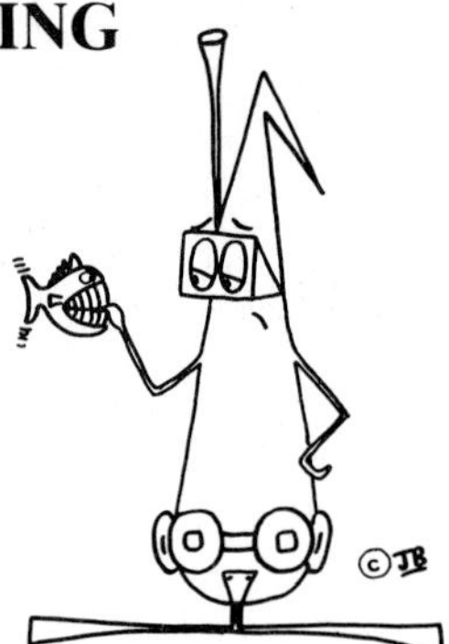

4A Dangerous Marine Animals

Most animals have evolved a means of protection from potential predators, or the means to be efficient predators. Spines, teeth, speed, cryptic colourations, and a huge range of irritants and toxins which can act either externally or internally, are examples of adaptations of these ways of life.

Naturally one or more of these attributes can be equally effective against man. Consequently, there are certain animals of which we need to be aware, respect, and avoid. If, due to mis-management or ignorance they are not avoided, it is important to know what to expect as a result, and what to do after the encounter.

The type of injury resulting from an unfavourable encounter can be divided into five categories.

1) Bites
2) Puncture wounds
3) Stings
4) Electric Shocks
5) Internal Poisoning

4A: 1 Bites: These may result from a number of animals.

a. There are bites **without** venom injection. Some marine animals such as moray eels, barracuda, groper, and more particularly sharks are known to attack divers.

The wounds from bites — particularly shark — are generally extensive with ragged edges. Tissue injury and haemorrhage is usually severe. Blood loss, shock and secondary infection are the main features causing concern. The death rate appears to be proportional to the number of large arteries severed. In severe cases, quick and efficient first aid is of vital importance.

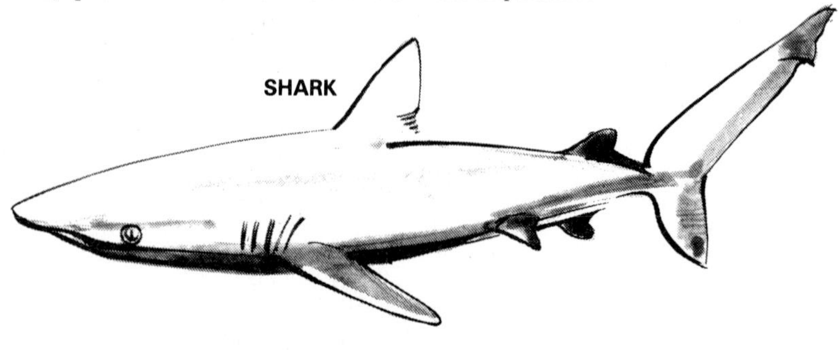

BARRACUDA

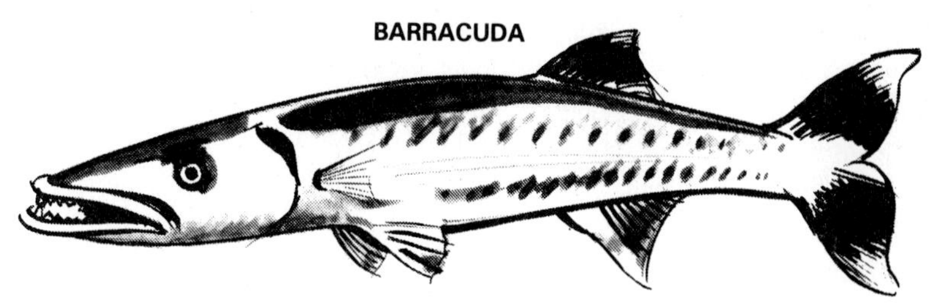

MORAY EEL

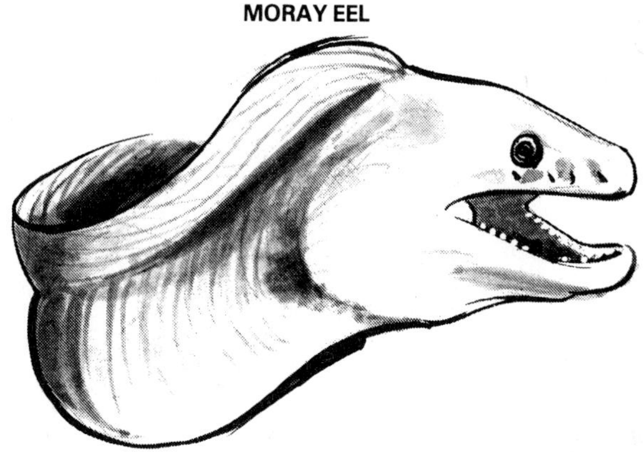

Boat Propellor

First Aid: Immediately control bleeding. The patient should be removed from the water, and only as far up the beach as is necessary to prevent drowning. **DO NOT rush the patient to hospital. SEND for medical help — including an ambulance.** Local pressure, to stop bleeding, should be applied while still in the water. Direct pressure should be applied to the injured limb to prevent further blood loss. The patient should be reassured and positioned with the head lowermost. Do not give the patient anything by mouth since an anaesthetic may need to be administered at the hospital. The patient should remain unmoved for at least 30 minutes or until visible signs of shock have disappeared. Many patients who die do so because of over-zealous transport to hospital.

b. There are also bites **with** venom injection. In Australia two animals are known to bite causing injection of venom into the wound. They are the Blue-ringed octopus and the Sea Snake.

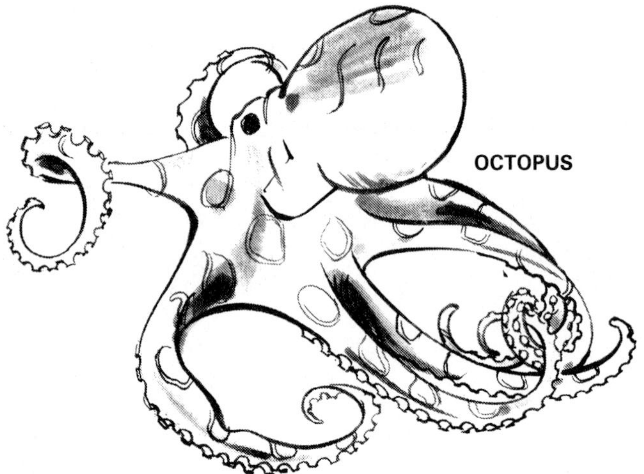

(i) Blue-ringed Octopus: When undisturbed, this animal is a yellowish-brown colour with dull ringed markings on the tentacles and stripes on the body. When disturbed, these dull markings become irridescent blue. The initial bite is almost painless. After about 15 minutes the bite becomes swollen, resembling a mosquito bite. A few minutes after the bite a rapid, painless paralysis results. The symptoms progress as follows:

- Numbness around the mouth and neck, which may cause difficulties in swallowing, nausea and vomiting.
- Breathing difficulties arise fairly quickly.
- The eye muscles gradually become paralysed.
- General weakness and difficulty with co-ordination lead to complete paralysis which persists for 4 to 12 hours.

(ii) Sea Snakes: There are a number of different species of this marine reptile, some being more dangerous than others. The toxins interfere with nerve and muscle function. The initial puncture is noticed but is not painful. Symptoms may take 10 minutes to several hours to manifest themselves. Restlessness, nausea and vomiting may occur, followed by a generalised stiffening and aching. Weakness develops into paralysis and spreads. This may be preceded by muscular twitchings and spasms. Respiratory and cardiac distress and failure may also occur.

First Aid: A broad pressure bandage (75mm crepe bandage) should be applied to the limb (over the bite if possible). Don't remove wet suit as removal will assist the entry of venom into the blood stream. The bandage should be as tight as would be applied to a sprain and extend up the limb as high as possible. The limb must be immobilized by a firmly bound splint using a second bandage.

The limb should feel comfortable if the bandage and splint are applied correctly. The bandage and splint can remain in place for several hours. They should only be removed by a doctor when the injected venom that will move into the blood stream has been treated. It is important that the limb be kept still. With the onset of paralysis, EAR must be initiated and maintained, often for several hours. ECC may also be necessary. Medical aid should be enlisted as soon as possible. The patient should be reassured since he may be aware of what is happening but be totally unable to respond because of the paralysis. In the case of sea snake bite the animal should be kept for identification if possible.

4A: 2 Puncture Wounds

These generally result from spines or darts. They may be complicated by toxins or irritants.

a. There are puncture wounds **without** venom injection. This type of wound is probably the most common injury resulting from contact with a marine animal. These wounds often occur while cleaning fish, exploring reefs, and while handling specimens.

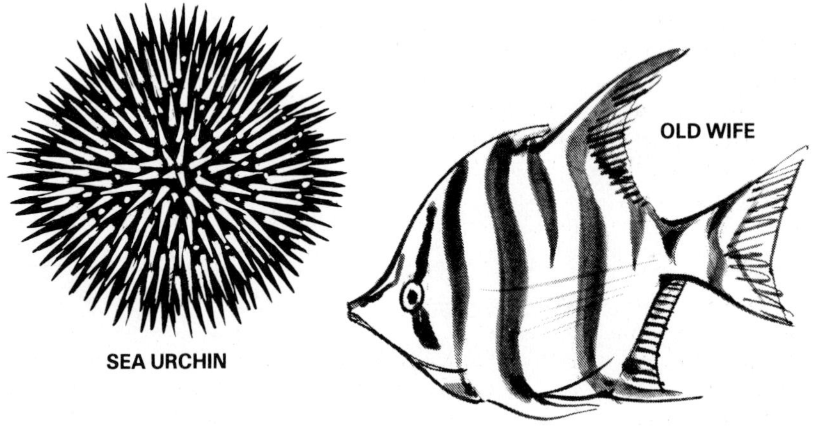

(i) Fish with spines: A common example is the Old Wife. These fish have long, strong spines as part of their fins. The presence of venom is doubtful. The puncture takes the form of a sharp prick. This may develop into an ache, or severe pain extending from the site of injury to include the whole limb. Bleeding is variable depending on the wound. The ache may last for several hours.

(ii) Sea urchins: Sea urchins are the most common marine animal encountered by divers that cause a puncture wound.

The spines of these animals are long, sharp and brittle. The spines tend to break off within the tissues. Severe pain occurs immediately after penetration. Swelling or inflammation usually occurs. The area of inflammation may increase and begin to ache. This ache can extend to involve the whole limb. The lymph glands become tender and swollen. General weakness and shock may result.

First Aid: The affected area should be placed in an elevated position and the wound washed and any debris removed.

Local application of weak solutions of potassium permanganate (Condy's Crystals), sodium bicarbonate, ammonia or acidic substances may relieve pain. Application of local anaesthetic sprays and cream will help relieve pain. Treatment with antibiotic cream or capsules may be indicated, particularly in remote areas. Cover the wound with a clean dressing and seek medical aid.

With sea urchin spines, removal **should not be attempted** unless removal can be accomplished without breaking the spine. If a spine is irretrievable embedded, it may be crushed by pummelling the area, and this may relieve pain and aid absorption. Drawing pastes (e.g. Magnoplasm) may be of use.

b. Puncture wounds **with** venom injection may also be suffered.

(i) Fish with spines: Many fish are particularly well endowed with spines. The Butterfly Cod, Stonefish, and Catfish are common examples found within tropical waters.

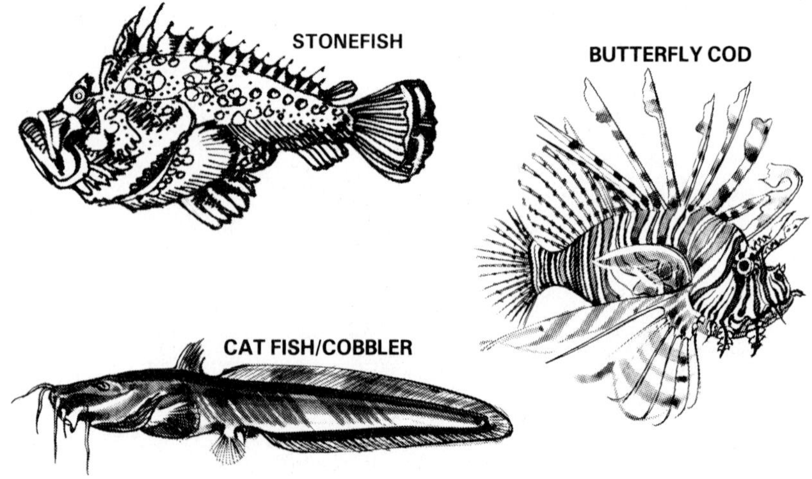

In these fish, the spines are covered by a sheath which is pierced and displaced when contact is made with the victim. Venom then passes along the spine into the wound. Severe pain is experienced at the affected site. This gradually increases in intensity. The intense pain lasts for several hours and may persist as a dull ache for a few days. The wound is susceptible to secondary infection.

Pain may extend to the lymph glands of the groin and armpit. Distress as a result of the pain may lead to mild delirium. Nausea, vomiting, sweating, fever and shock may result. Respiratory failure may occur. Weakness and exhaustion may last for several days. It is unlikely to be fatal except in the case of the Stonefish.

These fish have short stout spines covering the head and gill covers which may inflict a simple puncture wound.

(ii) Cone Shells: Although more prevalent in tropical waters, cone shells are found in temperate waters. These animals have a minute, rasp-like feeding appendage (radula) which can be thrust out of the narrow end of the shell. The radula has a series of 1-20 teeth which penetrate the skin and inject the venom. These specialised teeth are generally used for immobilising prey items, but may also be used for protection. The shell must never be picked up at the narrow end, and only carefully at the broad end.

The toxins injected affect the nerve muscle function. The initial puncture may be painless or associated with excruciating pain. Numbness and tingling may ascend from the bite to involve the whole body, particularly the mouth and lips. This process takes around 10 minutes. Mild to severe muscular paralysis may result within 10-30 minutes, including respiratory paralysis. Cardiac arrest may also occur. The patient's general condition deteriorates for 1-6 hours, after which improvement is likely.

(iii) Stingrays: Stingrays have a large serrated spine situated towards the posterior end of the tail. The 'stinging' response of the animal follows pressure on the posterior one third of the animal's back. The tail is thrust upward and forward, driving the spine into the victim. A sheath over the spine is ruptured during the process. Some stingrays have associated venom which passes down the spine and into the wound.

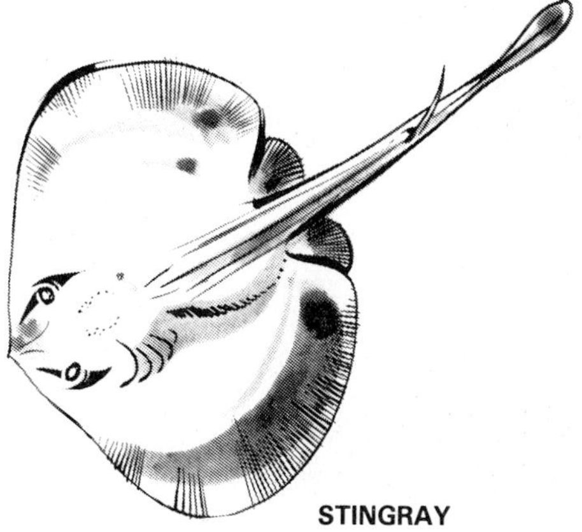

STINGRAY

The wound may vary from a puncture to a laceration up to 15 cm in length. Pain is immediate and increases over the first hour or two. There is some easing after 6-12 hours but pain may persist for some days. Bleeding is variable depending on the type of wound.

Nausea, vomiting, diarrhoea, fever, fainting and excessive salivation may occur. Pain may extend to the lymph glands of the groin and armpit. Respiratory depression, coughing and pain on inspiration may complicate matters, particularly in those cases where a venom has been injected.

First Aid: Treatment is identical to that described in the preceding section for treatment of bites with injection of venom, except for **stonefish**. When applying first aid to a victim of stonefish spine **do not** attempt to restrict the flow of the toxin. Pain relief may be achieved by bathing in warm water, or by local or general anaesthesia. Antivenene is available. Try to remove spine before applying pressure bandage.

However, depending on the nature of the toxin, cardiac arrest and respiratory failure may result. Consequently, the person administering first aid should be prepared to apply ECC and EAR. This may need to be kept up for many hours. Indeed, it should be maintained until advised by a medical practitioner. In those cases where a general paralysis occurs, it is necessary to reassure the patient who may be able to hear but may be unable to communicate.

4A: 3 Stings

Animals with tentacles coated with stinging cells (nematocysts)belong to a group of creatures called the Coelenterates (hollow gutted animals) and include corals, anemones, hydroids and jellyfish.

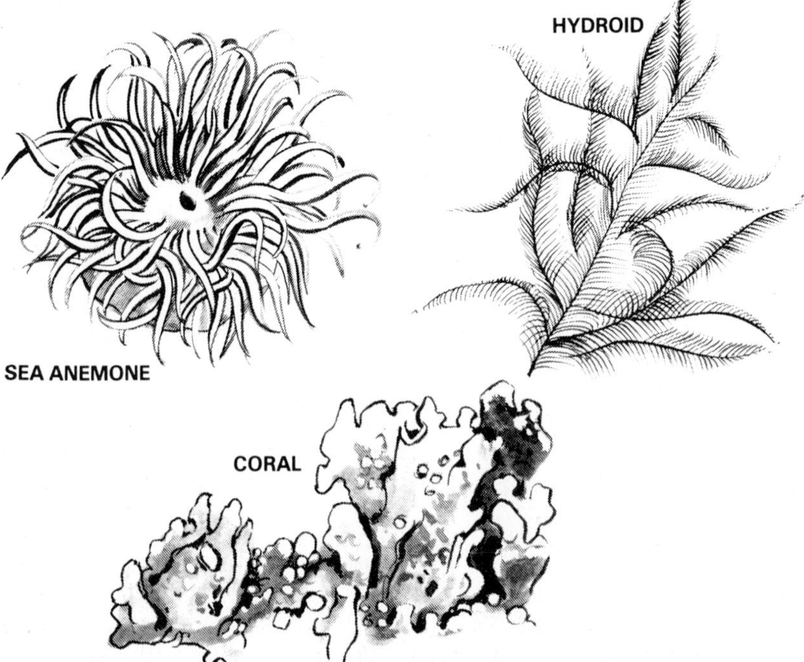

(i) Jellyfish: Examples of the better known species are Blue-bottle, Portuguese Man-of-War, Mauve Stinger, Jimble, and the most dangerous of all, the Sea Wasp.

Generally, a few seconds after contact, a stinging sensation is felt and this increases in intensity for a few minutes. A red coloured reaction surrounds the area of contact, and may raise up in the form of a pimple. Lesions, weals and blisters often result, the shape of which may be characteristic of the animal responsible. The pain may extend to the lymph glands of the groin and armpit.

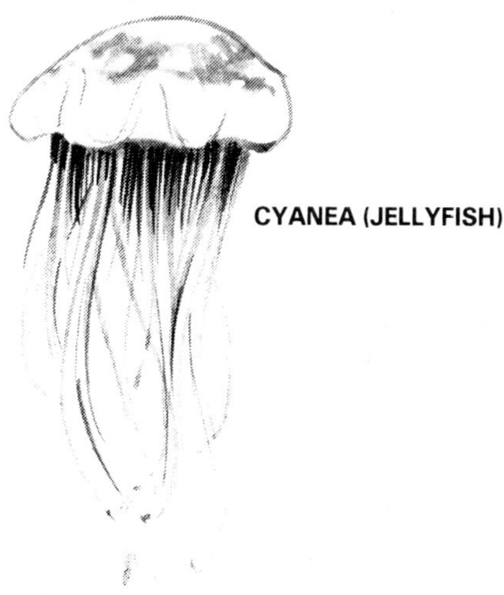

CYANEA (JELLYFISH)

General symptoms include abdominal pains, cramp, muscular aches, respiratory distress, sweating, anxiety and restlessness. Nausea and vomiting may also occur. Symptoms generally diminish within 4-12 hours. Convalescence may take up to a week. In the case of the Sea Wasp, if death occurs it usually occurs within the first 10 minutes.

(ii) Anemones (including corals and hydroids in general): The initial symptoms vary from a prickly sensation over the affected area to a severe burning pain. This occurs immediately on contact and may increase over the next few minutes. It may extend up the limb and involve the regional lymph glands in the groin and armpit. Pain generally lessens in a few hours but a residual ache or itch may persist for weeks.

Small blisters may develop. In severe cases, ulcerations may result. Secondary infection may be a problem. Nausea, fever, chills, thirst, abdominal pain and cramps may also result. In severe cases, shock and respiratory distress may be manifest.

First Aid: The patient should be removed from the water, reassured and laid down. **Vinegar** should be applied externally to inactivate the remaining nematocysts, although it does little to alleviate the initial pain. The tentacles may then be removed by gently shaving the area with a diver's knife. **Do not rub the affected area**. A few minutes after application of the vinegar a local anaesthetic should be used. Lignocaine 5% ointment is suitable. The patient's cardiovascular and respiratory functions should be monitored regularly. Resuscitate as necessary and seek medical aid.

4A: 4 Electric Shocks

Electric rays or numbfish are slow and ineffective swimmers. The electric discharge varies from 8 to 220 volts. The ray can deliver a successive series of shocks. The electric shock may be disabling, a major threat coming from drowning. Recovery is uneventful and treatment is not usually required.

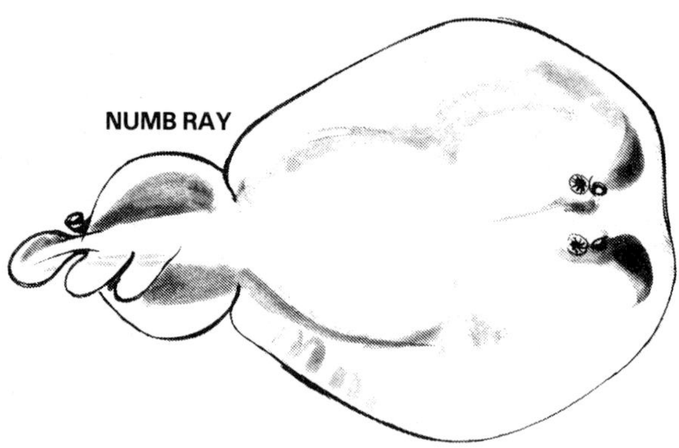

4A: 5 Internal Poisoning

Many fish are known to be poisonous when eaten. The most common belong to the family of fish called Tetradons. These include Toadfish, Puffers, Porcupine Fish and Sunfish.

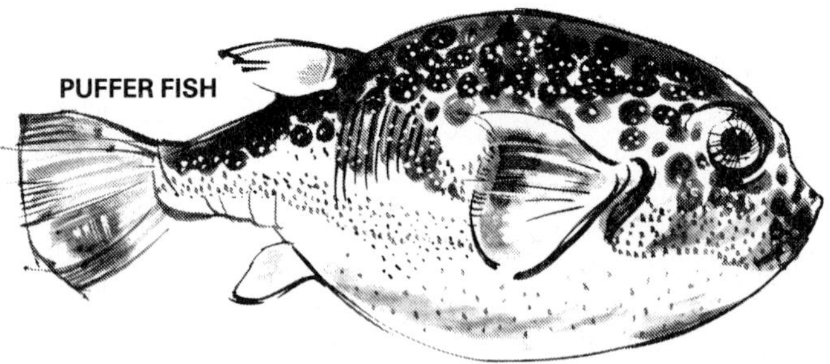

The onset of symptoms vary according to the toxin ingested. They include general weakness, dizziness, inco-ordination, numbness and cramps. Sweating, chest pain, headache, nausea, vomiting and diarrhoea may also be noted. Respiratory distress may also occur.

First Aid: In any sort of food poisoning episode, particularly in the early stages, vomiting should be induced by placing a finger against the back of the throat or ingesting a solution of mustard or salt in warm water. The patient should be rested and reassured. Respiratory and cardiovascular function should be monitored and appropriate action taken if these fail. Medical aid and hospitalisation should be obtained as quickly as possible.

In those cases where diarrhoea and vomiting are present, maintenance of fluid and salt balance in the body is important. Adequate liquid should be ingested. Balanced salt drinks such as 'Staminade' would be preferable. If nothing else, ingestion of salt tablets will help. This should only be attempted if medical aid is absent.

If food poisoning results from any source — particularly something that is not really known — note should be taken of what was eaten, when, how much, and if possible, save some of the food. This should be given to the doctor on hospitalisation.

Dangerous Marine Animals and First Aid in Remote Areas

In the situation where medical aid is unavailable for some hours, extra care must be taken to avoid the potential threats from marine organisms. Dive organisers have the responsibility to know the location and relevant telephone numbers of the nearest medical facilities and emergency services. They should also ensure the presence of a comprehensive First Aid Kit which should be put together in consultation with a doctor who is aware of the added problems associated with diving and entering the marine world. Included in the kit should be a copy of *Dangerous Marine Animals of the Indo Pacific Region* by Edmonds, 1975, and a Red Cross First Aid Manual. The presence of oxygen equipment is also highly recommended. (See Appendix G).

Finally, the responsibility rests with the individual to avoid any situation which may lead to injury. This is particularly important in remote areas. Animals which are unknown should be left alone and not touched or eaten. Similarly, the diver should stay well within his or her capabilities.

Section 4: DIVE PLANNING

4B: Understanding Water Movement

1. Tides
2. Currents
3. Waves

Section 4 DIVE PLANNING

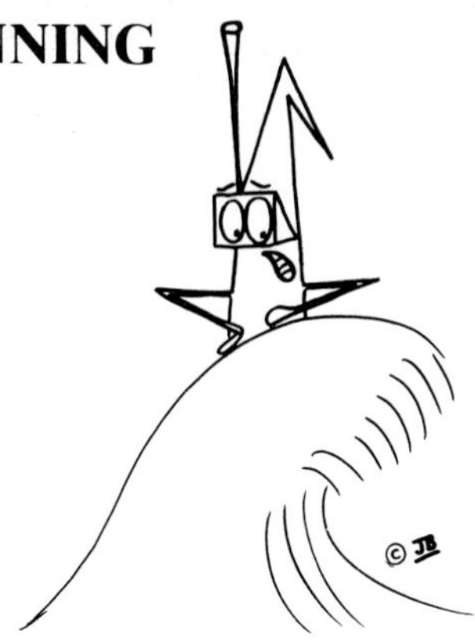

4B Understanding Water Movement

Tides, currents, land formations, and ocean reefs all have their own particular effect on the diver. As we enter the marine environment, we must forget our old relationship with our surroundings and replace terms like wind with current, rain and fog with turbidity and silting, mountains and valleys with wave surfaces. This section is not an attempt to explain all factors of water movement, but simply a cause and effect explanation for persons who will be involving themselves with water movement as a diver.

4B: 1 Tides

The tides are the regular rise and fall of the ocean water levels. Tides are as predictable as day and night, and should be checked so that the dive can be planned to coincide with appropriate tidal rhythms.

The moon, due to its close proximity to the earth, has the greatest influence on our tides, although both the sun and the earth's rotation also have an effect. If we imagine the earth to be a sphere completely enveloped in water, the effects of the moon and the sun can readily be seen. The outcome of the sun and the moon is a gravitational force bulging the earth's oceans.

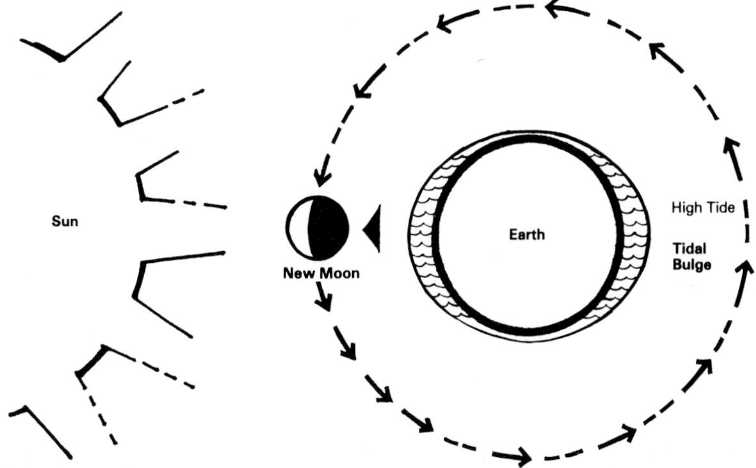

The sun and moon cause a gravitational pull on the earth's oceans so causing high and low tides.

In one rotation of the earth we experience two high tides and two low tides, the range of which are determined by the relative positions of the sun and the moon.

Spring tides result from the sun and the moon pulling either together or in opposite directions at full or new moon.

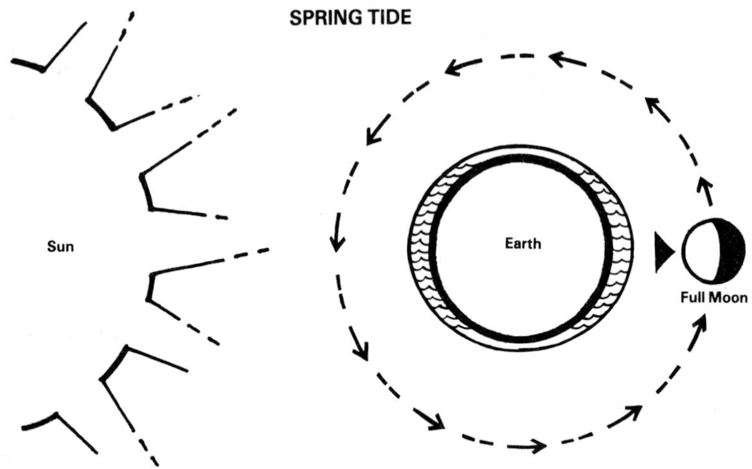

During spring tides, high water is higher than normal and low water is lower than normal.

Neap tides result from the sun and the moon pulling at right angles during the moon's first and last quarter.

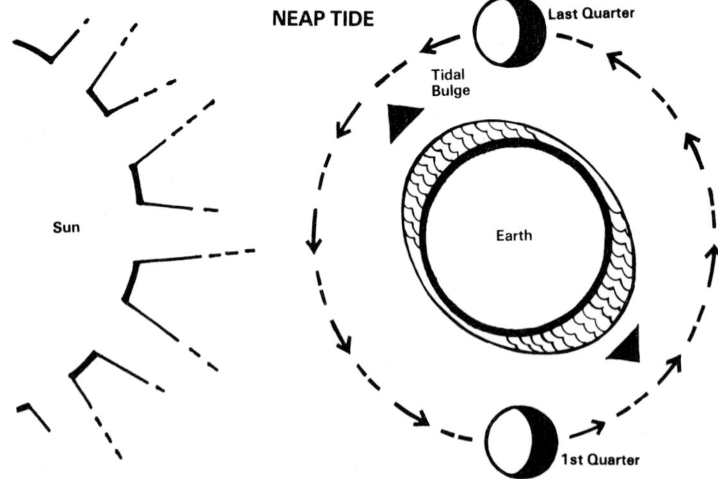

The moon builds up a high tide but the sun drags water across horizontally. During neap tides, high water is not as high as normal and low water is not as low as normal.

Although the diver will find that visibility is generally enhanced by high tide conditions, many other factors must be considered. Wave action can be increased by an outgoing tide. Entries and exits are generally influenced by the rise and fall of the tide. A tidal change can make a safe entry a hazardous exit. During low tide a small roll or swell can become a breaking wave as the reef becomes exposed. Outgoing tidal flow, particularly during spring tides, may be impossible to swim against and may literally wash a diver out to sea.

Avoiding problems associated with tides involves learning to read tide tables, relating prior knowledge of the sea in relation to theoretical aspects, and by seeking advice from local fishermen and divers. The local dive shop is a great source of information.

4B: 2 Currents

A current is a large-scale, sustained movement in a fluid mass.

Moving water masses (currents) are driven by three major forces — wind, gravity, and the tidal forces of the sun and the moon. The earth's ocean circulation is controlled by such currents as the Gulf Stream (Mexico and North America), the North Pacific (North America), the Kuroshio (Japan), and the Southern Equatorial (N.S.W. and Victoria).

These currents provide the major factor in determining the type of marine life a particular coast will support. Marine life is probably the foremost reason we dive, whether it be for photography, a source of food, or merely to revel in the enjoyment of observation.

Water movements, if properly understood, can make a marvellous experience of a properly planned dive, or a disaster out of a bravado attempt to fight against it. For this reason, divers must be familiar with the most commonly confronted currents, namely long-shore currents and rip currents.

a. Long-shore Currents: The long-shore current runs parallel to the coast.

LONG SHORE CURRENT

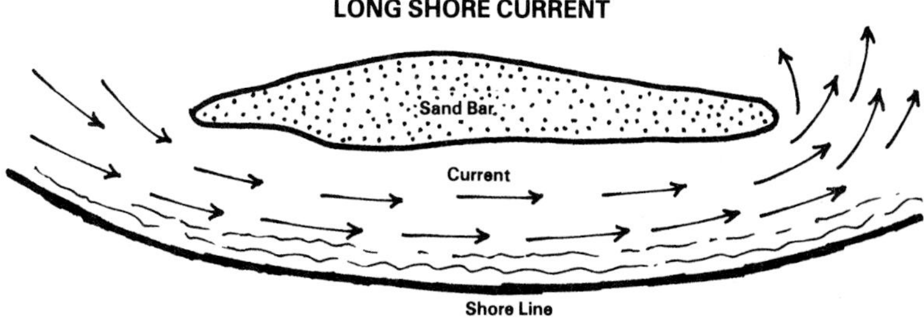

Divers can use this current to do coastal sweeps or decide entry or exit areas. Remember, if diving in a limited area, always swim directly into an up-current so as to return with the current to the exit area to avoid fatigue.

To determine the direction and strength of current movement, observe the movement of floating objects and foam in the water. Take your time and remember the wind can be a deceiving factor on light objects.

b. Rip Currents: Rip currents are water masses moving out to sea. They are the second greatest cause of drownings, the first greatest cause being over-estimation of ability.

RIP CURRENT

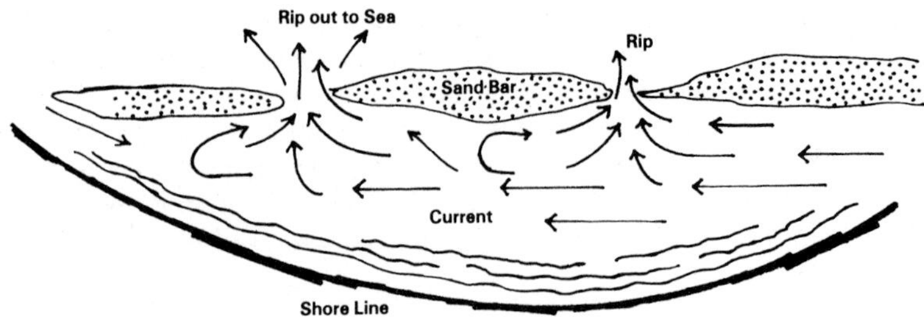

Water, as with most things, runs in the direction of least resistance. When waves, wind and long-shore current action "pile-up" waters on a headland or beach, this excess water mass begins to seek an "exit point". This exit point in turn generates the rip current. The energy a rip has is totally dependent upon the amount of water feeding it.

How to recognise a rip:

Look for a possible cause or reason for water to start moving out to sea, such as headlands, reefs, river mouths, and sand channels (mainly on sandy beaches).

Decreased swell movement and confused surface chop indicates rip activity.

"Brown" or dirty water in a surface zone or out to sea indicates shoreline water full of sediment being carried out to sea.

Surface movement of foam and objects — as with our earlier recognition of current — indicate rip activity.

If caught in a rip current:

1. Don't panic.
2. Inflate buoyancy compensator.
3. Assess the situation.
4. If current is weak, you may be able to fin "across current" to "good" water.
5. If current is strong, relax on your buoyancy compensator until current eases, then swim downcoast and plot an exit course.
6. Do not hesitate to ditch your gear.

Even though rip currents are shortlived, **do not** attempt to swim against them.

4B: 3 Waves:

Different types of waves are generated by different forces, but the motion beneath the water in all waves is similar. Wind driven waves are formed by storms or winds that blow in a given direction for a distance long enough to send out vibration (energy waves) in that given direction. A simple analogy is when we blow on a hot liquid to cool it. The ripples formed are small waves.

Seismic sea waves (wrongly called "tidal waves") are much less frequent than wind waves as they are caused by seismic activity in the earth's crust. Geological activity such as submarine landslides, fault slippage and volcanic eruption produce vibration which in turn starts the seismic sea wave off on its travels to some distant sea, beach or island. Predicting the arrival of such waves is under investigation due to their often destructive power.

Waves formed either by wind or submarine disturbance, have a common life cycle formed by an energy centre. They set out first confused and are then joined and coordinated. After flattening out they travel until they reach coastal shelves or reefs where they begin to "feel" bottom. As the wave enters shallow waters, its height is increased until finally the wave breaks. This area now becomes a surf zone as the travelled waves spend their energy entrapping air and rushing up the beach or over the reef.

WAVES BREAKING

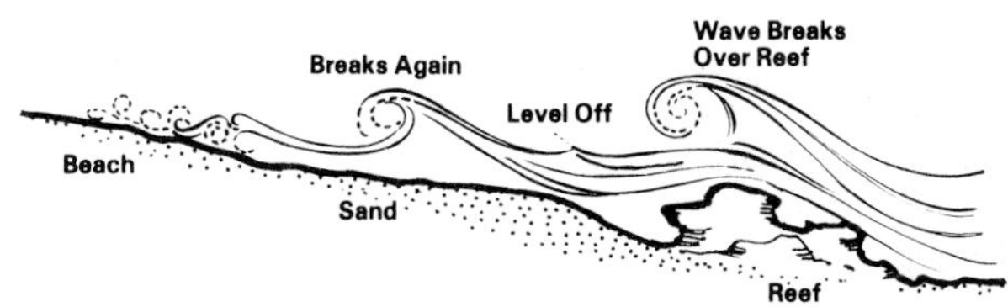

Wave energy is transmitted in orbital motion from molecule to molecule. Below is a diagram demonstrating this orbital transfer in waves.

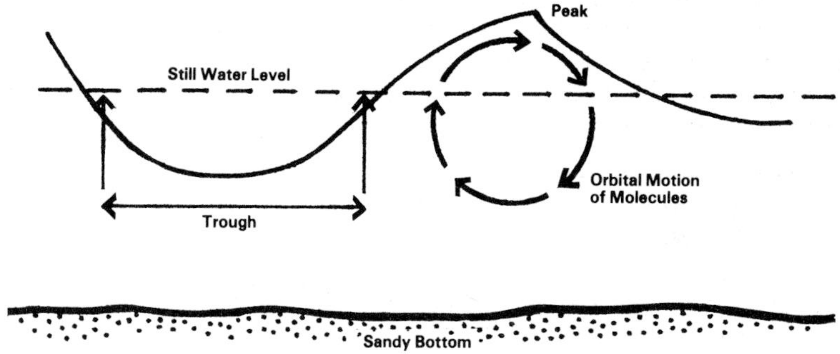

Wave sets, or surf beat, is the phenomenon of waves arriving in groups of two to five waves of which several will be large and wash well up the beach. By observing possible entry areas, you can time the duration and number of waves to a set and plan your entry on the backwash of the final wave in a set. Exits can be planned by following the water a final-set wave takes with it, then holding on till the water subsides and crawling to a safe position up the beach or reef.

Waves, as beautiful as they may be, can be equally destructive if surf, diver, and rocks, reef or beach happen to meet unexpectedly. Here are a few rules to remember when encountering waves.

1. Large surf stirs up silt and sand making visibility poor, and this, compounded by surge, makes diving unpleasant.
2. Waves potentially have a great deal of power and can rise very suddenly. Watch your dive area for a few wave sets before being satisfied with your dive plan.

3. Entries and exits done through surf can be especially dangerous and special care should be taken. These are the only entries you should do without your vest inflated, due to the buoyancy properties and high degree of wave energy towards the top of the wave. Beach entries through the surf should be carried out according to the following procedure.

(i) **Prior to dive:** Total gear and buddy checkout as to procedure.

(ii) **Ready to dive:** Regulator in mouth, enter water, walking backwards into surf zone to avoid tripping over your fins. **Watch** for oncoming waves.

(iii) **In the water:** Once in water too deep to walk in, dive under next wave and kick close to bottom. Then regroup just outside surf line, rest on your vests, and commence your dive.

(iv) **Entries are not** to be done by body-surfing waves. Broken necks, straying cylinders, and skull fractures result!

Section 4: DIVE PLANNING

4C: The Dive

1. Dive Planning
2. The Buddy System
3. Calculation of Air Consumption

Section 4 DIVE PLANNING

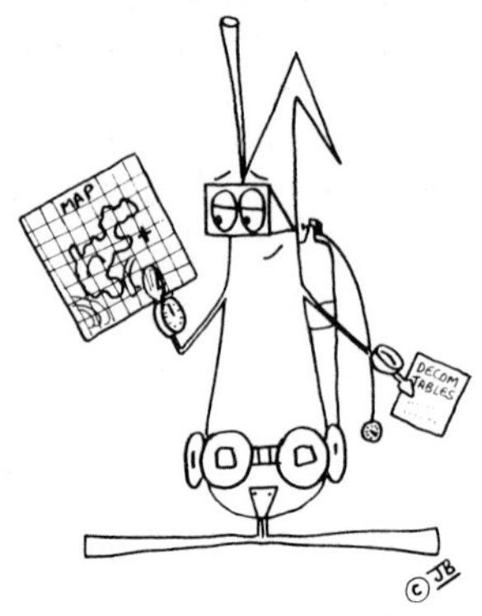

4C: The Dive

The climax of learning to dive is the actual pleasure dive itself. However, all the best training in the world will not overcome the hazards of a poorly planned dive. Good dive planning results mainly from experience, but certain guidelines should always be followed, no matter what sort of dive is to be done.

Experience is best gained by making observations, asking questions, and diving. The best learning ground is, no doubt, at the club level. A good dive club will provide a host of experiences not normally available to the individual diver.

4C: 1 Dive Planning

Good dive planning is conducted at three levels: in advance; on site; and post dive assessment.

a. Planning in Advance: Dive planning will usually begin in conversation among friends or club members. During this very first step in dive planning, a date, time and location will be chosen.

It is important when planning a dive to ensure that everyones' qualifications and experience are compatible with the chosen location. The best guide is usually the least experienced member. Can they handle the dive?

Charts, tide tables and information on the emergency services available in the area should be obtained to ensure adequate knowledge of the dive location. It is also useful to speak to divers who have dived the site before.

An alternative dive location is always a sensible precaution should foul weather interrupt plans. In the days preceding the dive, weather patterns should be observed by reading or listening to forecasts and from personal observations. If the prime location is going to be weather-affected, then an alternative site can be chosen in advance. This will avoid the disappointment of a long drive only to find conditions are too bad for **safe** diving.

Organise and check your gear well before the day of the dive. This will save the last minute rush to the local dive shop to buy a new mask strap, snorkel holder, or such items that can ruin a good day's diving.

Before leaving for the dive site, notify a friend or relative of your intentions and the estimated time of your return.

b. On-site Planning and Preparation: After considering the prevailing conditions such as weather, swell, and current, make a final decision as to the suitability of the site. Never be afraid to terminate the dive.

Once the decision to dive has been made, a sensible entry point and at least two alternative exits should be determined.

Before gearing up, check medical and physical fitness, and in particular, make sure that Eustachian tube function is normal. Decompression tables should be consulted to determine maximum depth and bottom time. Calculate the estimated air consumption (see Section 4C: 3) to ensure adequate air is available to complete the dive safely.

The diver's flag — International Code Flag 'A' — must be erected in a prominent position to indicate the presence of a diver to other boat drivers.

Organise the buddy system so that divers of equal ability are together. On new or unusual dives it is wise to have a more experienced diver leading the less experienced novice. A mutual understanding of hand signals (see appendix), lost buddy procedures, and recall is essential.

When gearing up it is imperative to check the following items:

Buoyancy Compensator — emergency gas supply and function
— oral inflation function
— dump valve function
Cylinder — contents
— test date
Regulator — function (purge and breathing)
Back Pack — quick releases
— twisted harness
Weight belt — does it clear all other harnesses?

The same checks should be done on the buddy and a final revision of the dive plan discussed before entry. Remember, "Be the buddy you wish to dive with".

During the dive the buddy system (see Section 4C: 2) must be maintained at all times. Never alter the dive plan during the dive unless for emergency reasons. Always "plan your dive and dive to your plan".

c. Post Dive Procedure: Upon exiting the water, three very important items should be recorded: the exit time, indicating the beginning of surface interval; bottom time; and maximum depth. All this information is important for the calculation of repetitive dive times.

Remove and correctly stow your gear. Do not leave it lying around where it can be damaged or covered in sand.

A group analysis of the dive will aid future dive plans as well as providing entertaining conversation.

Exit time, bottom time, and maximum depth is the minimum information your log book should contain. Although the comments made in a log are personal, recorded information regarding the dive will be useful should the dive-site be revisited in the future.

The medical condition of all divers should be checked on completion of the dive and minor signs and symptoms should be diagnosed as they may indicate more serious problems which may manifest themselves at a later time.

DATE: 15/5/81		PLACE: Blue Bay		
DEPTH 10 MTRS.	WIND S.E.	CURRENT NIL	VISIBILITY 8 MTRS.	DIVE TIME 55 MINS.
Comments: Boat dive. Back roll entry with Bill. checked anchor. Found nice reef. Plenty of marine life. Took great photo of pair 'old wives'. Bill had trouble with mask. Returned to boat.				
Bill Smith. BUDDY'S SIGNATURE			ACCUMULATED DIVE TIME 28 HRS.	

DATE: 29/5/81		PLACE: Stragglers.		
DEPTH 15 MTRS	WIND E.	CURRENT Slight	VISIBILITY 7 MTRS.	DIVE TIME 50 MIN.
Comments: Boat dive. Back roll entry. Interesting terrain lots of nice pot holes + caves. Saw many crayfish, mostly small. Found a nice Cowrie Shell in cave.				
G. R. Parker BUDDY'S SIGNATURE			ACCUMULATED DIVE TIME 28.50	

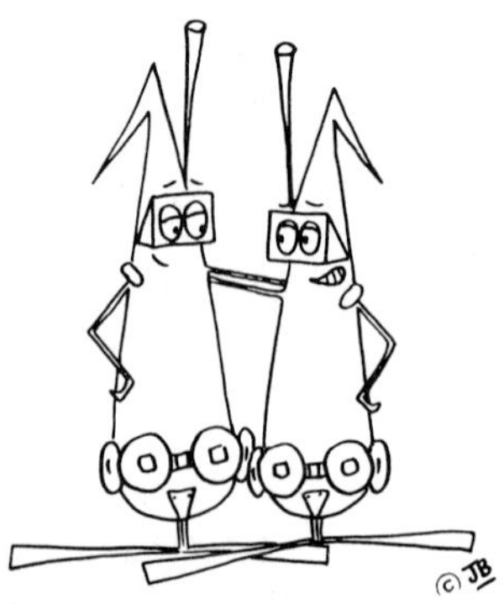

4C: 2 The Buddy System

The practice of diving alone should always be avoided. Problems may often occur where the presence or absence of a buddy can often mean the difference between life and death.

A good buddy must be adequately trained, physically fit, and have similar interests. It is imperative that they be aware of each other at all times. Although one will often act as a leader, the pair must function as a unit.

A good buddy is sufficiently well trained to be able to perform an adequate rescue should trouble occur, so confidence in each other's knowledge, abilities and judgement is paramount.

To be in the same ocean as each other is not adequate. It is imperative that visual or tactile contact be maintained throughout the dive. In most cases, eye contact is sufficient. However, with new buddies or in more trying conditions, more direct contact, such as holding of hands or contents gauges, is preferable.

In conditions of limited visibility the use of buddy-lines is sometimes advocated. A buddy-line is a 1-2 m length of 5-8 mm line connected via a quick release armband. However, if buddy-lines are used, familiarity with the use of them must be obtained by proper instruction and training in a pool or other safe environment. The ocean emergency situation is not the time or place to learn the use of buddy-lines.

BUDDY LINE

A good buddy system is a skill to be practised as much as any other skill in diving, and should become more automatic as experience with each other is gained.

Often the need will arise for a buddy to communicate with the other buddy. A set of standard hand signals (see appendix) should be known for safety reasons, although a series of personally used signals may be developed by the buddy pair. These signals should be simple to avoid confusion. All signals should be promptly answered or returned to ensure mutual understanding of intentions.

In the event of an emergency occurring, it is vital that the buddy pair have some prepared procedure to cope with the problem. Usually this will mean surfacing and exit from the water. The skills of buddy-breathing, and of using an octopus demand valve, will overcome the problem of failure of air supply. However, occasionally a diver may be forced to surface without an air supply, in which case a "free ascent" will be required.

Free ascents should **not** be practised, as failure to perform the correct procedure may negate the necessity for a second try. The free ascent is the practice whereby a diver surfaces, expelling the expanding air from the lungs via the mouth at a steady rate. The dangers include pulmonary barotrauma of ascent due to rapidly expanding gases.

Of the many hazards in the marine environment, the greatest threat comes from the diver himself. It is the diver's responsibility to be familiar with the signs, symptoms, first aid, and prevention of diving injuries, as well as to be efficient in rescue procedures.

Be The Buddy You Wish To Dive With

4C: 3 Calculation of Air Consumption

As part of dive planning, a diver must be able to calculate the amount of air he will consume during a dive. This will determine whether or not the dive can be performed safely.

a. Calculation of Cylinder Capacity: Since 1 litre of water weighs 1 kilogram, the cylinder water capacity (W.C.) can be converted directly to internal volume in litres at atmospheric pressure. Knowing the cylinder's volume at one atmosphere will allow us to compute the volume of air in the cylinder at any gauge pressure (G.P.) by simple multiplication. The cylinder gauge pressure must be read in atmospheres. The same calculation can be done using kilopascals by dividing the answer by 100: (1 atm = 100 kilopascals), i.e.:-

Cylinder capacity (litres) = water capacity (kilograms) × gauge pressure (atmospheres)

$$(C.C.) = (W.C.) \times (G.P.)$$

Example:

Consider an AS1777 cylinder with a water capacity of 11.15 kilograms, filled to a pressure of 200 atmospheres:
Now, C.C. = W.C. (kg) × G.P. (atm)
Therefore, C.C. = 11.15 × 200 = 2230 litres
N.B. The same calculation can be done on older cylinders by converting water capacity from pounds and ounces into kilograms. See appendix for conversion factors.

b. Calculation of Air Consumption: During a scuba dive, as depth (ambient pressure) increases, the density of air being delivered to the lungs will also increase. Therefore, each lungfull of air will contain more molecules. At 10 metres the lungs will contain twice as many molecules of air as they would at the surface. The net result is that cylinder contents will be consumed at a greater rate. Of course, this rate increases with increasing ambient pressure or depth.

At the surface, the average rate of air consumption is approximately 30 litres per minute at moderate work. This is referred to as Respiratory Minute Volume (R.M.V.). To calculate the amount of air needed for a dive, two further pieces of information are needed: the total dive time (T), and the absolute pressure (P) planned for the dive.

(i) Total Dive Time (T):

Total Dive Time (T) (minutes) = Bottom Time (B.T.) + Ascent Time (A.T.) + Decompression Time (D.T.)

$$T = B.T. + A.T. + D.T.$$

Remember, Bottom Time (B.T.) is descent time plus time spent at depth.

(ii) Absolute Pressure (P):

$$\text{Absolute Pressure (P) (atmospheres absolute)} = \frac{\text{Depth (metres)}}{10} + 1$$

To calculate air consumption, multiply Total Dive Time, Absolute Pressure, and Respiratory Minute Volume, i.e.

$$\text{Air consumed (litres)} = T \times P \times RMV$$

N.B. Respiratory minute volume (RMV) can be assumed to be 30 litres per minute unless otherwise known.

Note that R.M.V. can be increased dramatically by a number of factors including hypothermia, exertion and anxiety. If your dive includes any factors which will increase your R.M.V. your calculation must allow for it. For safety, at least 10-15% of calculated air consumed should be left in reserve after each dive.

Problem: A diver plans to dive to 20 metres for a bottom time of 39 minutes using a cylinder containing 2000 litres of air. Can this dive be performed safely?

Solution: Assume RMV of 30 litres per minute.
Assume a normal rate of ascent, 20 metres per minute.
Total Dive Time = Bottom Time + Ascent Time + Decompression Time

Bottom Time (B.T.) = 39 minutes
Ascent Time (A.T.) = 1 minute
Decompression Time (D.T.) = 0 minutes
Total Dive Time (T.) = 40 minutes

$$\text{Absolute Pressure (P)} = \frac{20}{10} + 1 = 3 \text{ atmospheres absolute}$$

Using the formula: Air Consumed = T × P × RMV
A.C. = 40 × 3 × 30 = **3600 litres**

It is quite obvious that this dive will not be completed safely. Either depth or bottom time or both must be reduced.

Problem: A diver plans to dive to 40 metres for an 18 minute bottom time. During ascent he requires 15 minutes of decompression (R.N. Tables). His respiratory minute volume is 20 litres per minute. Can this dive be carried out safely using twin 2000 litre cylinders?

Solution: RMV = 20 litres per minute
Assume a normal rate of ascent, 20 metres per minute.

$$\text{Total dive time (T)} = \text{B.T.} + \text{A.T.} + \text{D.T.}$$

$$\text{B.T.} = 18 \text{ minutes}$$

$$\text{A.T.} = 2 \text{ minutes}$$

D.T. = **15** minutes (Royal Navy)

$$\text{(T)} = 35 \text{ minutes}$$

$$\text{Absolute Pressure (P)} = \frac{40}{10} + 1 = 5 \text{ atmospheres absolute}$$

Using the formula: Air consumed = T × P × RMV

A.C. = 35 × 5 × 20 = **3500 litres**

The diver can do this dive safely. Bearing in mind that the air consumption is over estimated, there is more than a 10% safety margin.

The method of calculation of air consumption described above is a simplified one. If further accuracy is required, the calculation should be broken into three basic components:

1. Air consumed during descent and ascent
2. Air consumed at depth
3. Air consumed during decompressions stops.

c. Calculation of Respiratory Minute Volume (RMV): Under controlled conditions, we can determine our air consumption by monitoring our pressure gauge and time spent at a particular depth. For instance, if a cylinder holds 2000 litres of air at a gauge pressure of 200 atmospheres, it must hold 1000 litres at a pressure of 100 atmospheres. To work out respiratory minute volume, time how long it takes to consume 1000 litres at a particular depth and substitute the relevant information in the restated Air Consumption formula. To restate the formula, divide both sides by T × P.

A.C. = T × P × RMV . . . divide both sides by T × P

$$\text{Therefore: } \frac{\text{A.C.}}{\text{T} \times \text{P}} = \frac{\text{T} \times \text{P}}{\text{T} \times \text{P}} \times \text{RMV} \; . . . \; \frac{\text{T} \times \text{P}}{\text{T} \times \text{P}} = 1$$

$$\text{Hence: RMV} = \frac{\text{A.C.}}{\text{T} \times \text{P}}$$

Problem: During a dive to 10 metres a diver notices his pressure gauge reads 180 atmospheres. Thirty minutes later, his gauge reads 60 atmospheres. After the dive, he notices the water capacity of his cylinder is 10 kg. What is the diver's RMV?

Solution: Using the formula, Cylinder contents = Water capacity × gauge pressure

we find: a. Cylinder contents at beginning of dive = 180 × 10 = 1800 litres

b. Cylinder contents at end of 30 mins. = 60 × 10 = 600 litres

Therefore: air consumed = 1800 − 600 = **1200 litres**

Total time (T) = 30 minutes

$$\text{Absolute Pressure (P)} = \frac{10}{10} + 1 = 2 \text{ ata}$$

$$\text{Calculation of RMV: Using RMV} = \frac{\text{A.C.}}{\text{T} \times \text{P}}$$

$$\text{the RMV} = \frac{1200}{30 \times 2}$$

$$= 20 \text{ litres per minute.}$$

If a diver knows his RMV then he can calculate his air consumption for a given dive with greater accuracy.

Section 4: DIVE PLANNING

4D: Specialist Diving

1. Boat Diving
2. Night Diving
3. Wreck Diving
4. Fresh Water Diving
   (Cave and Sink Hole Diving)
5. Deep Diving
6. Decompression Diving

Section 4 DIVE PLANNING

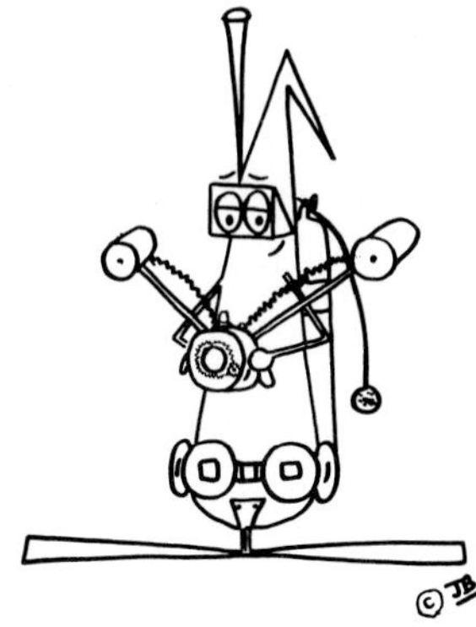

4D: Specialist Diving

Once training and the initial ocean dives have been completed, many divers begin to look towards other activities for greater excitement and interest. However, most of these types of diving have inherent dangers not encountered under normal circumstances. It is essential that the diver be made aware of these dangers.

Specialist diving includes:

- Boat diving
- Night diving
- Wreck diving
- Fresh water diving
- Deep diving
- Decompression diving

4D: 1 Boat Diving

Boat diving provides a greater range of diving locations offshore, and for this reason most divers prefer to dive from a boat. Diving from a boat offers many advantages. The diver need not carry equipment over difficult terrain or long distances. One may merely exit the boat over the selected site.

However, the use of the boat requires more precise dive planning. It is impossible to dive safely from a boat in adverse weather conditions. A detailed weather forecast should be obtained for the area. If any doubts exist as to the suitability of conditions, the dive should not be attempted.

Upon arrival at the site the boat must be anchored in such a position that if a wind or current change occurs, the boat is not likely to swing into rocks. Approximately three times the depth of water, as measured on the anchor rope, should be paid out to allow the anchor to grip and the boat to ride up over a swell. When anchoring the boat, do not switch the motor off until the anchor is secured. The boat will usually align itself with the wind, which may disguise the presence of a strong current. It is important to determine the strength of the current. This can be achieved by trailing a small buoy attached to approximately 30 metres of line (sometimes reffered to as a "mermaid catcher") off the stern of the boat. This will indicate the direction and speed of the current at the surface and will help to avoid the risk of a diver being swept away by the current.

Before entry, erect the International Code 'A' flag which signifies that a diver is below. After entry, usually by a backward roll, check the strength of the current, and descend the anchor line to check and secure the anchor. To avoid having to snorkel against the current upon completion of the dive, it is important to swim directly up-current at the start of the dive. Returning to the boat with the current will avoid unnecessary exhaustion.

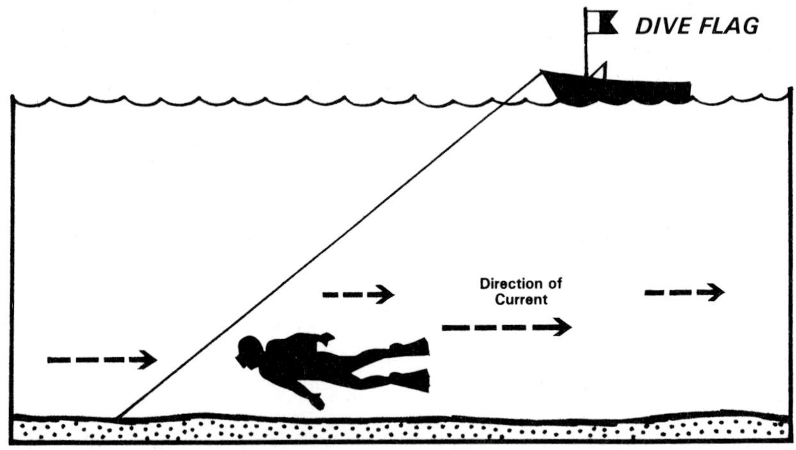

ANCHOR BOAT AND SWIM UP CURRENT

Further considerations to note when diving from a boat include ensuring that essential safety equipment required by law is on board and in working order.

4D: 2 Night Diving

Diving at night has rapidly become one of the most popular diving activities. The greater range of animals to be seen at night combined with the kaleidescope of colours revealed by the diver's torch often turn the drab daytime scene into an enjoyable experience. Underwater photography is aided by the ease with which sleeping fish can be photographed. Many invertebrate animals are also far more obvious and active during the hours of darkness. The diving site, however, must be viewed in daylight for any potential hazard such as fishing line, which may not be readily noticeable at night. Strong currents automatically eliminate some areas as safe night-diving sites.

Once the site has been chosen it is important to ensure that equipment to be used is in good condition and adequate for the task. At least one proper underwater torch per diver is a must, while inclusion of a chemical light stick such as "Cyalume" is handy in the event of torch failure, recognition, and pick-up of a lost diver.

The correct use of a compass will ensure the diver stays close to the diving base which should be marked with an easily seen marked light to allow a ready return.

Diver communication at night using hand signals is aided by ensuring that the torch illuminates the hand signal. Do not shine the torch directly into your buddy's eyes, as his vision will be impaired for several minutes.

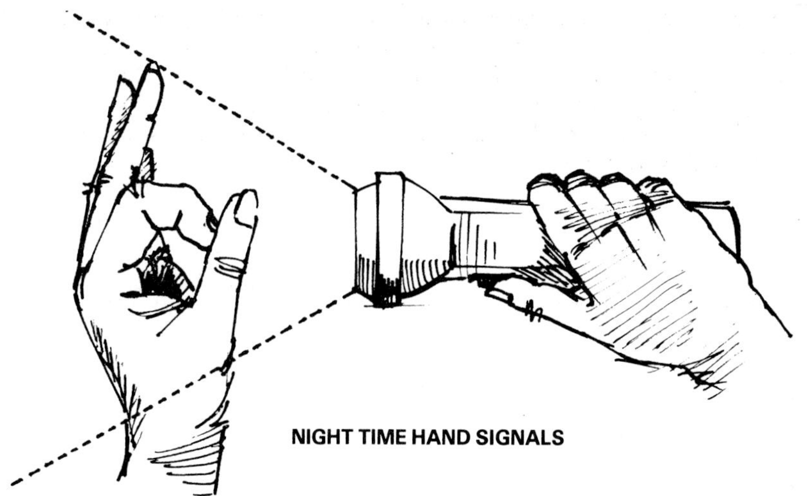
NIGHT TIME HAND SIGNALS

Night diving from a boat should not be attempted until several shore-based night dives have been successfully completed.

4D: 3 Wreck Diving

Most ships are wrecked in shallow, turbulent water and they very quickly become reduced to a pile of twisted metal and rubble. Wrecks often present problems in respect to entanglements, surf and surge, reduced and sometimes nil visibility. Wrecks also often present ideal locations for fishermen and so become entangled with fishing lines and nets. It is important to carry a sharp knife and make every endeavour to avoid entrapment. Should entanglement occur, the diver should remain calm while his buddy gently removes the entangling materials.

ENTANGLEMENT AND HAZARDS

Often rough conditions are associated with shallow water wreck sites so the diver must try to select the calmest possible conditions. If surge is encountered, it is often better to move with the surge than to fight it. This may mean bumping against objects underwater, but trying to fight surge often leads to exhaustion.

A torch is often required to allow illumination of the inner parts of the wreck.

Wrecks in deeper water do not usually break up as readily and can provide the diver with access into the hull. Due to the size of most ships and the presence of silt, a line, reel and tether will be required for safe underwater entry and exit of the wreck.

In Australia, it is illegal to remove artifacts from any pre-1900 wreck. Most local museums are very happy to inform divers regarding regulations pertaining to historic wrecks.

4D: 4 Freshwater Diving: (Cave and Sinkhole Diving)

The world has many freshwater lakes, sinkholes, and caves that create ideal diving sites when ocean conditions are adverse. Many factors, such as silting, buoyance, cold, depth, altitude and the necessity for relevant qualifications must be considered when diving in such locations.

Inland waters usually have large concentrations of silt which is easily stirred up causing reduced visibility. To overcome the problem, divers should be neutrally buoyant, and keep well off the bottom, at the same time ensuring that finning is kept to a minimum. If silting occurs the diver should ascend until clear water is encountered.

Due to the lower density of fresh water, less lead is required and greater attention paid to buoyancy control using the buoyancy compensator.

Inland waters are often characterised by layers of water of different temperature. The interface between the layers is referred to as "thermocline". The water below the thermocline is generally significantly colder, which presents a problem of adjustment. Thermoclines will also often reduce vertical visibility thus causing problems with buddy location. Due to its cooler temperature, the likelihood of hypothermia is greatly increased when diving in fresh water. When diving at altitude, adjustment for decompression problems is essential, due to the lower atmospheric pressure.

Cave and sinkhole diving in many regions are controlled by Cave Diver's Associations. Diving in these areas requires special training, certification and equipment which is beyond that required for SCUBA diver awards. Further information related to this type of diving should be sought from your local dive store.

4D: 5 Deep Diving

When diving at depths greater than 10 metres, both a watch and a depth gauge are essential. Particular care must be taken to adjust buoyancy. When ascending, a diver must not exceed the speed of his slowest visible bubbles and particular emphasis must be placed on finning to the surface.

Avoid Decompression Dives At All Times

Often divers will experience loss of orientation when in mid-water when neither the surface nor the bottom are visible. This is referred to as "blue orb syndrome" and occurs because our eyes cannot focus on an object. To avoid this syndrome, ensure that your eyes are focused on the anchor rope of the dive boat or on your buddy.

4D: 6 Decompression Diving

Decompression diving should be avoided because the surface is not readily attainable without the subsequent risk of decompression sickness, should problems occur. However, if decompression is required, the following equipment is absolutely necessary.

a. **Air Decompression Tables:** Adequate decompression requires the use of an air decompression table which can be obtained printed on plastic. Even though a set of tables should be carried by the diver, all calculations should be completed before the dive begins. Decompression meters are not a substitute for correct use of the tables.

b. **Octopus Demand Valve:** In the advent of air supply failure, buddy-breathing is not a satisfactory alternative and so the use of an octopus demand valve should be mastered.

c. **Shot Line:** A depth gauge is not an accurate method of determining the depth of a decompression stop. A weighted shot line, marked at 3, 6, and 9 metre intervals should be suspended from the stern of the boat where movement is minimal. The anchor line is only second best due to the pitching motion of the boat caused by a swell.

d. **Spare SCUBA Unit:** In the event of lack of primary air supply, a spare SCUBA unit should be attached at the first scheduled decompression stop.

e. **Oxygen:** Some means by which oxygen can be administered to a diver in the advent of decompression sickness should be included. (See Appendix G.)

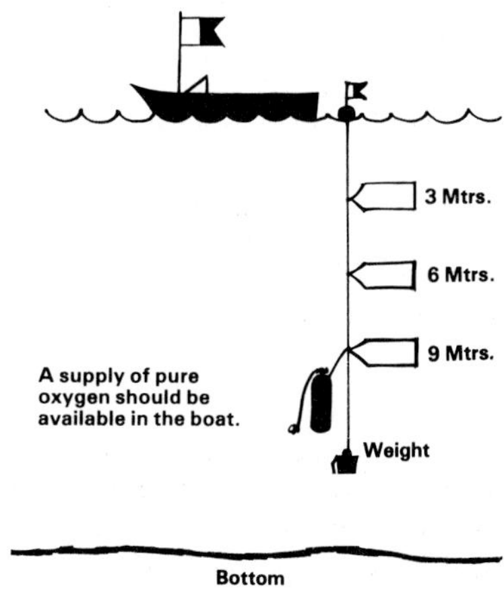

In addition to the above requirements, a knowledge of the nearest recompression chamber, transport, emergency services, and medical personnel is essential.

Appendix A **USEFUL ADDRESSES**

Confederation Mondiale Des Activities Subaquatiques (CMAS)
(World Underwater Federation)

Headquarters:— 34, Rue du Colisee, F — 75008 Paris, FRANCE

Australia

Australian National Qualification System (N.Q.S.)
P.O. Box 246, Tuart Hill, Western Australia 6060

Federation of Australian Underwater Instructors (F.A.U.I.)
P.O. Box 246, Tuart Hill, Western Australia 6060

South Pacific Underwater Medicine Society (S.P.U.M.S.)
81 Wellington Pde., Melbourne, Victoria 3002

Great Britain

British Sub Aqua Club (B.S.A.C.)
Headquarters:— 70 Brompton Road, London SW3 1HA

New Zealand

New Zealand Underwater Association (N.Z.U.A.)
P.O. Box 875, Auckland, New Zealand

United States of America

International Diving Educators Association (I.D.E.A.)
P.O. Box 17374, Jacksonville, Florida 32216

National Association of Scuba Diving Schools (N.A.S.D.S.)
641 W. Willow St., Long Beach, California 91763

National Association of Underwater Instructors (N.A.U.I.)
P.O. Box 14650, Montclair, California 91763

National Y.M.C.A. Centre for U/W Activities (Y.M.C.A.)
P.O. Box 1547, Key West, Florida 33040

Professional Association of Diving Instructors (P.A.D.I.)
1243E Warner Avenue, Santa Ana, California 92705

Scuba Schools International (S.S.I.)
2619 Canton Court, Ft. Collins, Colorado 80525

Appendix B DIVING METRICS

Pressure Conversion Factors:

1 atmosphere = 101 (100) kilopascals kPa (0·1 megapascals MPa)
= 10.07 (10) metres sea water
= 33·05 (33) feet sea water
= 33·95 (34) feet fresh water
= 1·033 (1) kg/cm^2
= 14·7 (15) lbs/in^2
= 1·013 (1) bar (1000 millibars)
= 760 millimetre mercury, mmHg
= 760 Torr

Mass:

SI base unit = kilogram (kg)
1000 micrograms= 1 milligram (mg)
1000 milligrams = 1 gram (g)
1000 grams = 1 kilogram (kg)
1000 kilograms = 1 tonne (t)

Volume:

SI base unit = cubic metre (m^3)
1000 cubic millimetres = 1 cubic centimetre (cm^3)
1000 cubic centimetres = 1 cubic decimetre (dm^3)
1000 cubic decimetres = 1 cubic metre (m^3)

Volume (for fluids only):

1000 millilitres (ml) = 1 litre (l)
1000 litres = 1 kilolitre (kl)

Length:

SI base unit = metre (m)
10 millimetres (mm) = 1 centimetre (m)
10 centimetres = 1 decimetre (dm)
10 decimetres = 1 metre (m)
10 metres = 1 decametre (dm)
10 decametres = 1 hecotmetre (Hm)
10 hectometres = 1 kilometre (km)

Area:

SI base unit = square metre (m^2)
100 square millimetres = 1 square centimetre (cm^2)
10000 square centimetres = square metre (m^2)

Conversion:

1 metre	=	39·37 inches
1 gram	=	weight of a cubic centimetre of water
1 litre	=	1 cubic decimetre
	=	1000 cubic centimetres
	=	1000 grams
1 litre of fresh water	=	1 kilogram
1 litre of sea water	=	1·025 kilogram.

Appendix C HAND SIGNALS

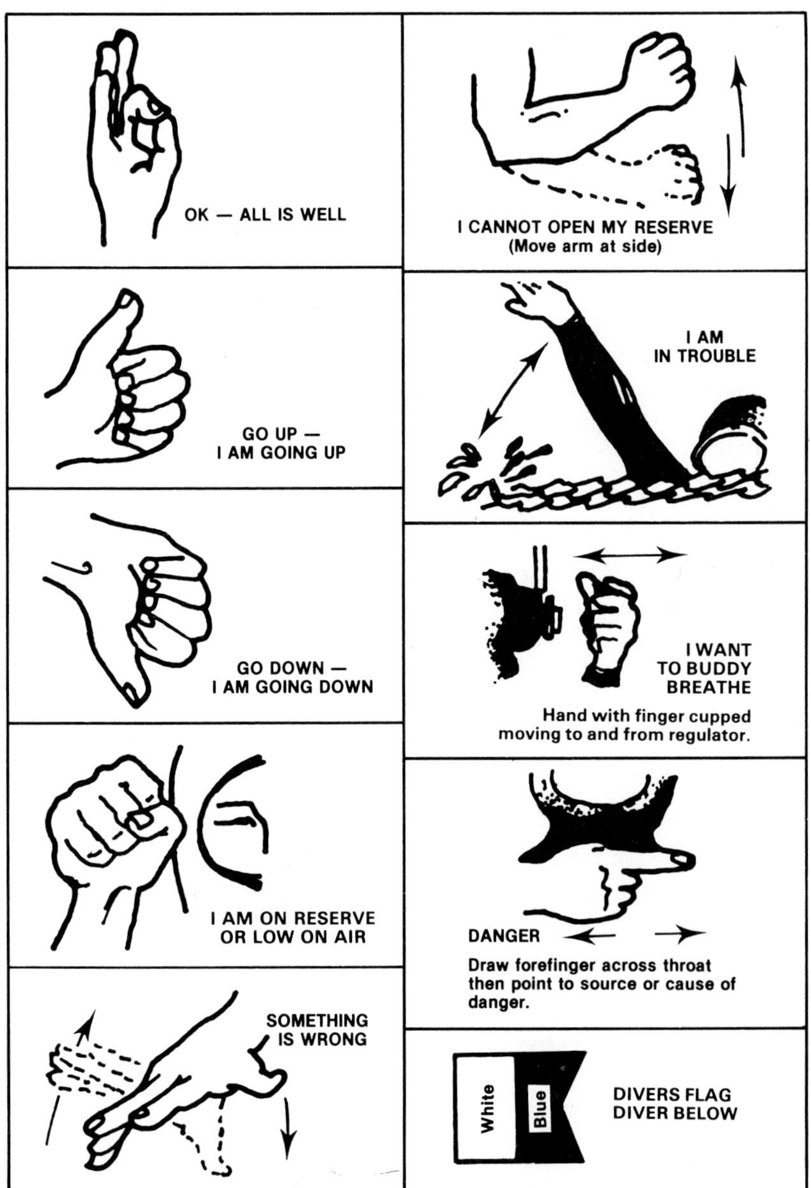
OK — ALL IS WELL
I CANNOT OPEN MY RESERVE
(Move arm at side)
I AM
IN TROUBLE
GO UP —
I AM GOING UP
GO DOWN —
I AM GOING DOWN
I WANT
TO BUDDY
BREATHE
Hand with finger cupped
moving to and from regulator.
I AM ON RESERVE
OR LOW ON AIR
DANGER
Draw forefinger across throat
then point to source or cause of
danger.
SOMETHING
IS WRONG
White
Blue
DIVERS FLAG
DIVER BELOW

Appendix D **DECOMPRESSION CHAMBERS**

In the case of an emergency occuring that requires recompression, prompt action is essential.

Listed below are the major contacts for information on the nearest recompression facilities.

Australia

24 hours a day — R.A.N. School of Underwater Medicine,
H.M.A.S. Penguin,
Balmoral, Sydney, New South Wales
(02) 9600321
Request: "The Diving Medical Officer"

Great Britain

(a) Business Hours — Portsmouth (0705) 22351, Extension 872375
Request: "The Superintendent of Diving".

(b) Other times — Portsmouth (0705) 22351, Extension 872413/4/5
Request: "The Duty Lieutenant Commander".

United States of America

Contact nearest United States Coast Guard by telephone or by radio either

V.H.F. Channel 16
or
H.F. 2182 KHz.

State: "This is a diving accident requiring recompression".

Remember the first aid for decompression sickness and pulmonary barotrauma is:

1. **OXYGEN (100%, high flow)**
2. **FLUIDS (salted and sweetened 1 litre/hour only if conscious)**
3. **ASPIRIN (two tablets only if conscious)**
4. **OBTAIN EXPERT ADVICE i.e. contact your nearest recompression facility.**

KNOW WHERE YOUR NEAREST CHAMBER IS!

Appendix E BIBLIOGRAPHY

Australian Standards AS2299 (1979). Underwater air breathing, appendix A. Medical standards for divers. Standards Association of Australia, Sydney.

Barada, Bill (1970) Let's go diving. U.S. Divers Co., Santa Ana, California.

British Sub Aqua Club (1972) The British sub aqua club diving manual. B.S.A.C.

Council for National Cooperation in Aquatics (1974) The new science of skin and scuba diving. Follett, Chicago.

Cropp, Benjamin (1974) Handbook for skindivers. Pollard, North Sydney, N.S.W.

Dueker, Christopher Wayne (1970) Medical aspects of diving. A.S. Barnes, New York.

Edmonds, C. (1974) Dangerous marine animals of the Indo-Pacific region. Diving Medical Centre, Sydney.

Edmonds, C., Freeman, P., Thomas, R., Tonkin, J. and Blackwood, F. (1973) Otological aspects of diving. Australasian Medical Publ., Sydney.

Edmonds, C., Lowry, C., and Pennefather, J. (1981) Diving and subaquatic medicine. Diving Medical Center.

Foley, J. (1979) How to find your way; a divers navigational manual. Dacor Corp., Northfield, Ill.

Gonsett, Bob (1975) Scuba regulators; air pressure reduction valves for diving. NAUI, Colton, Calif.

Gonsett, Bob (1973) Scuba tanks; high pressure cylinders for diving. NAUI, Colton, Calif.

Halstead, B.L. (1959) Dangerous marine animals. Cornell Maritime Press, Cambridge, Maryland.

Miles, S., MacKay, D.E. (1976) Underwater medicine. Granada, London.

National Association of Underwater Instructors (n.d.) Instructors Handbook.

P.A.D.I. (1977) 1977 standards and procedures manual. P.A.D.I., Santa Ana, Calif.

Reseck, John (1975) SCUBA safe and simple. Prentice-Hall, New Jersey.

Royal Life-Saving Society — Australia (1976) Manual of water safety and lifesaving. R.L.S.S.A., Chatswood, N.S.W.

Royal Navy Diving Manual (1972) BR 2806. H.M.S.O., London.

Roydhouse, Noel (1975) Scuba diving and the ear, nose and throat. T.B. Roydhouse, Auckland.

Silvester, B. (1979) The down-under S.C.U.B.A. diver. Ian McNiel.

Sport Diver Manual (1975) Jeppesen Sanderson, Denver, Colo.

Strykowski, Joe (1971) Diving For Fun. A complete textbook for students, instructors, and advanced divers. Dacor Corp., Northfield, Ill.

Thomas, R. and MacKenzie, B. (1981) The diver's medical companion. Diving Medical Centre, Sydney.

United States. Department of Commerce (1977) United States underwater fatality statistics — 1975. Report No. URI — SSR — 77-11, March.

United States. Navy Department. (1979) U.S. Navy diving manual. Vol.1.: air diving. Best Publ., Carson, Calif.

Walker, D. (1974) Provisional report: diving deaths in Australian water in 1974. *Federation of Australian Underwater Instructors Technical Bulletin.*

Zanelli, Leo and Skuse, George (1976) Sub-aqua illustrated dictionary. Kaye and Ward, London.

Appendix F

DECOMPRESSION TABLES

(i) DECOMPRESSION PROCEDURES AND TABLES FROM ROYAL NAVY DIVING MANUAL (BR 2806)

5102. Methods Available.

1. Decompression may be carried out in one of three ways:
   a. In the water while the diver is ascending on a shot rope or lazy shot.
   b. In a compression chamber on the surface.
   c. In a submersible compression chamber.
2. In each case the method used may be varied by the type of gas the diver is breathing.
3. The simplest of these methods and the the one most commonly used with dives of relatively short duration is decompression in the water.
4. Compression chambers are used with the surface-decompression technique and during advanced operations involving the use of submersible compression chambers.
5. Whichever method is used a common factor is the decompression schedule. Different schedules are available depending on the circumstances, most of them relying on 'stage' decompression, i.e. ascending to a calculated depth or stage for a given time and then ascending to a further stage. These stages are set out in the decompression tables.

5103. Hard Work — Increased Decompression.

1. When a diver exerts himself under pressure, his body absorbs more gas than usual and he will require a longer period of decompression to eliminate this gas.
2. On all occasions, therefore, when hard physical work is carried out by a diver, the decompression routine for the dive is to be taken as that for the next longer time increment for the dive, as given in the decompression tables.

5104. Procedure After Diving in Excess of 35 Metres.

1. A diver who has carried out a dive deeper than 35m for a period above the limiting line in Table 11 is to remain within four hours' travelling time of a compression chamber for 12 hours after completing the dive.
2. A diver who has carried out a dive of 35m or more for a period below the limiting line in Table 11 must remain in the immediate vicinity of a compression chamber (i.e. on board) for a period of four hours after completing the dive, and within four hours' travelling time of a chamber for a further 12 hours.
3. If no compression chamber is available, the diver should be kept under observation on board for the first four hours quoted in para. 2 above.

5111. Repetitive Dives.

1. Dives to depths of less than 10 metres, or equivalent air depths of 10 metres, have no time restriction or requirement for further decompression when preceded

by deeper dives and do not count as 'dives' in the terms of this article.
2. Dives carried out breathing pure oxygen may be followed by deeper dives without modification of the appropriate decompression schedule.
3. A diver who carried out a dive to depths greater than 42 metres or dived below the limiting line is not to carry out a further dive within 12 hours of surfacing.
4. If the time interval between dives about the limiting line exceeds six hours, then no modification of decompression is required *provided the second dive does not exceed 42 metres.*
5. If the time interval between dives above the limiting line is less than six hours, the procedure for combined dives above the limiting line is less than six hours, the procedure for combined dives must be followed as in Article 5112.

5112. Stops for a Combined Dive

1. The stops for a combined dive are obtained by adding together the duration of the first and each subsequent dive to obtain a total time for the combined dives. This total time and the depth of the deepest dive made are used to obtain the stops in the relevant table as for a single dive.
2. The total time of the combined dives (i.e. the sum of successive durations is not to be allowed to exceed a total time for decompression (Column 4 or 6 in the appropriate table) of 75 minutes or the next lower figure in this column if 75 is not quoted.
3. Dives carried out using pure oxygen are not to be included in this calculation.

5113. Diving Below the Limiting Line

1. That part of each depth section above the limiting line is the ordinary working table where the risk of decompression sickness is negligible. Diving for periods below the line carries a greater risk of decompression sickness, and this risk increases with an increase of duration below the line. Intentional diving below the limiting line should be undertaken only when a compression chamber is available on the site and even then only when circumstances justify the risk. This risk is in no way diminished by the use of oxygen during decompression.
2. A diver who has carried out a dive below the limiting line is not to carry out a further dive within 12 hours.
3. He is also to remain within the vicinity of a compression chamber and under surveillance for four hours (Article 5104, para. 2).

5121. Diving at Altitude

1. Most diving takes place at sea level where the pressure on the surface is one bar absolute (one ATA).
2. If a dive is carried out at altitude (e.g. in a mountain lake), the surface pressure is less than one bar absolute. Because of this, decompression schedules must be adjusted to prevent the onset of decompression sickness in the rarefied atmosphere.
3. Water will invariably be fresh, but stoppages should be used as though it were salt, so increasing the safety margin of the schedule.

4. Adjustments should be made to the schedules as follows:
   a. Dives between altitudes of 100m and 300m: Add 0.25 of the depth the depth of the dive.
   b. Dives between altitudes of 300m and 2000m: Add 0.3 of the depth to give the depth of the dive.
   c. Dives between altitudes of 2000m and 3000m: Add 0.5 of the depth to give the depth of the dive.

5. For example, a dive to a depth of 24m from an altitude of 1000m should be treated in the decompression tables as a dive to a depth of 32m.
6. No adjustments are required for altitudes of less than 100m.

5122. Decompression Sickness — Flying Restrictions

1. To avoid the risk of contracting decompression sickness by flying after having dived, the following rules, applicable to commercial cabin altitude, normally between the equivalents of 5000 and 9000 feet, are to be applied:

Type of dive	*Period before flying*
No-stop dive	2 hours
Dive involving stoppages	24 hours

DECOMPRESSION IN THE WATER

5201. General

1. When carrying out decompression in the water, the diver must always be on a shot rope of lazy shot. To carry out decompression safely, the diver's maximum depth of dive and his depth at any moment during stops must be known accurately.
2. Stops are never to be carried out swimming free, even when a depth gauge is carried.
3. If a diver breaks surface before carrying out his full stops, he must be sent down immediately to complete them. An increased risk of subsequent decompression sickness must then be borne in mind.
4. The maximum depth of dive may be obtained by soundings, bearing in mind that if the diver is covering a wide area one sounding will not necessarily indicate his maximum depth of dive. Maximum depth may also be obtained from the markings on the lifeline — which includes the air hose of the SDDE — the depth indicated by the markings erring on the safe side as the diver moves away from the attendant. If the diver has a depth gauge and is in telephone communication with the attendant, he can inform the surface of his maximum depth.
5. The attended diver's depth while he is ascending on a shot rope, as indicated by the markings on the lifeline or shot rope, will be accurate only when the shot rope is vertical in the water. If the shot is laid out from a boat swinging with wind or tide, the shot rope may be out at an angle from the boat; in this case the shot may be lifted off the bottom to hang as a lazy shot or a separate lazy shot may be used, as described in Article 3342.

DECOMPRESSION TABLE

5602. Application of Diving Tables

1. Different diving tables are provided for different sets of circumstances, but their format and application are nonetheless similar.
2. Their limitations are also similar. Therefore, in cases where either the depth of duration of the dive is in doubt, stoppages for the next greater figure in the appropriate column are to be employed.

5611. Table 11: Air Table

1. Table 11 is employed for dives down to depths of 55m.
2. The table is applied as described in Article 5602.

ROYAL NAVY AIR DECOMPRESSION TABLES
Table 11
Air Table

(1) Depth not exceeding (metres)	(2) Duration time leaving surface to beginning of ascent not exceeding (min.)		(3) Stoppages at different depths (min.)					(4) Total time for decompression (min.)
			15 m	12 m	9 m	6 m	3 m	
9	No limit		—	—	—	—	—	—
		135	—	—	—	—	—	—
		165	—	—	—	—	5	5
		195	—	—	—	—	10	10
		225	—	—	—	—	15	15
12		255	—	—	—	—	20	20
		330	—	—	—	—	25	25
		390	—	—	—	—	30	30
		660	—	—	—	—	35	35
	Limiting Line							
		over 660	—	—	—	—	40	40
		85	—	—	—	—	—	—
		105	—	—	—	—	5	5
		120	—	—	—	—	10	10
		135	—	—	—	—	15	15
		145	—	—	—	—	20	20
		160	—	—	—	—	25	25
		170	—	—	—	5	25	30
15		190	—	—	—	5	30	35
	Limiting Line							
		240	—	—	—	10	40	50
		360	—	—	—	30	40	70
		450	—	—	—	35	40	75
		over 450	—	—	—	35	45	80
		60	—	—	—	—	—	—
		70	—	—	—	—	5	5
		80	—	—	—	5	5	10
		90	—	—	—	5	10	15
		100	—	—	—	5	15	20
		110	—	—	—	5	20	25
		120	—	—	—	5	25	30
		130	—	—	—	5	30	35
	Limiting Line							
18		140	—	—	—	10	30	40
		150	—	—	—	10	40	50
		160	—	—	—	15	40	55
		180	—	—	—	20	40	60
		200	—	—	5	30	40	75
		255	—	—	10	35	45	90
		325	—	—	20	40	45	105
		495	—	—	35	40	45	120
		over 495	—	—	35	40	50	125
		40	—	—	—	—	—	—
		55	—	—	—	—	5	5
		60	—	—	—	5	5	10
		70	—	—	—	5	10	15
		75	—	—	—	5	15	20
21		85	—	—	—	5	20	25
		90	—	—	—	5	25	30
		95	—	—	5	5	25	35
	Limiting Line							
		105	—	—	5	5	35	45
		120	—	—	5	10	40	55
		135	—	—	5	20	45	70
		150	—	—	5	30	45	80
		165	—	—	10	30	50	90
		180	—	—	15	35	50	100
		210	—	—	25	40	50	115
		240	—	5	30	40	50	125

(1) Depth not exceeding (metres)	(2) Duration time leaving surface to beginning of ascent not exceeding (min.)		(3) Stoppages at different depths (min.)					(4) Total time for decompression (min.)
			15 m	12 m	9 m	6 m	3 m	
		30	—	—	—	—	—	—
		40	—	—	—	—	5	5
		50	—	—	—	5	5	10
		55	—	—	—	5	10	15
		60	—	—	—	5	15	20
		70	—	—	—	5	20	25
		75	—	—	—	5	25	30
24	Limiting Line							
		80	—	—	5	5	30	40
		90	—	—	5	10	35	50
		105	—	—	5	20	40	65
		120	—	5	5	30	45	85
		140	—	5	10	35	50	100
		160	—	10	30	40	50	130
		25	—	—	—	—	—	—
		30	—	—	—	—	5	5
		40	—	—	—	5	5	10
		45	—	—	—	5	10	15
		50	—	—	—	5	15	20
		55	—	—	—	5	20	25
		60	—	—	5	5	20	30
		65	—	—	5	5	25	35
27	Limiting Line							
		70	—	—	5	10	30	45
		75	—	—	5	15	30	50
		80	—	—	5	20	35	60
		90	—	—	5	25	40	70
		100	—	—	5	30	45	80
		110	—	5	15	35	45	100
		120	—	5	20	35	50	110
		135	5	5	25	40	50	125
		150	5	10	35	40	50	140
		20	—	—	—	—	—	—
		25	—	—	—	—	5	5
		30	—	—	—	5	5	10
		35	—	—	—	5	10	15
		40	—	—	—	5	15	20
		45	—	—	—	5	20	25
		50	—	—	5	5	20	30
		55	—	—	5	5	25	35
30	Limiting Line							
		60	—	—	5	10	30	45
		70	—	—	5	20	35	60
		75	—	5	5	20	40	70
		80	—	5	5	30	40	80
		90	—	5	15	30	45	95
		105	—	5	25	35	50	115
		120	5	10	30	40	50	135

(1) Depth not exceeding (metres)	(2) Duration time leaving surface to beginning of ascent not exceeding (min.)	(3) Stoppages at different depths (min.) 18 m	15 m	12 m	9 m	6 m	3 m	(4) Total time for decompression (min.)
33	17	—	—	—	—	—	—	—
	20	—	—	—	—	—	5	5
	25	—	—	—	—	5	5	10
	30	—	—	—	—	5	10	15
	35	—	—	—	—	5	15	20
	40	—	—	—	—	5	20	25
	45	—	—	—	5	5	20	30
	Limiting Line							
	50	—	—	—	5	10	25	40
	55	—	—	—	5	15	30	50
	60	—	—	—	5	20	35	60
	65	—	—	5	5	20	40	70
	70	—	—	5	10	20	45	80
	75	—	—	5	15	25	45	90
	80	—	—	5	20	30	45	100
	90	—	5	5	20	40	45	115
	100	—	5	10	25	40	50	130
	110	—	5	20	30	45	50	150
	120	5	5	25	40	45	50	170
36	14	—	—	—	—	—	—	—
	20	—	—	—	—	—	5	5
	25	—	—	—	—	5	5	10
	30	—	—	—	—	5	15	20
	35	—	—	—	—	5	20	25
	40	—	—	—	5	5	25	35
	Limiting Line							
	45	—	—	—	5	10	25	40
	50	—	—	—	5	15	30	50
	55	—	—	5	5	20	35	65
	60	—	—	5	10	25	40	80
	70	—	—	5	20	30	45	100
	75	—	5	5	20	35	45	110
	80	—	5	10	25	35	45	120
	90	—	5	15	30	40	50	140
	100	5	5	20	35	45	50	160
	110	5	15	25	40	45	50	180
	120	5	20	30	40	45	50	195

(1) Depth not exceeding (metres)	(2) Duration time leaving surface to beginning of ascent not exceeding (min.)	(3) Stoppages at different depths (min.) 21 m	18 m	15 m	12 m	9 m	6 m	3 m	(4) Total time for decompression (min.)
39	11	—	—	—	—	—	—	—	—
	15	—	—	—	—	—	—	5	5
	20	—	—	—	—	—	5	5	10
	25	—	—	—	—	—	5	10	15
	30	—	—	—	—	—	5	20	25
	35	—	—	—	—	5	5	20	30
	Limiting Line								
	40	—	—	—	—	5	10	25	40
	45	—	—	—	5	5	15	30	55
	50	—	—	—	5	5	20	35	65
	55	—	—	—	5	10	25	40	80
	60	—	—	—	5	15	30	45	95
	70	—	—	5	10	20	30	50	115
	75	—	—	5	15	25	40	50	135
	80	—	—	5	20	30	45	50	150
	90	—	5	5	25	40	45	50	170
	100	5	5	15	30	40	45	50	190
	110	5	10	25	30	45	45	50	210
	120	5	15	30	40	45	45	50	230

(1) Depth not exceeding (metres)	(2) Duration time leaving surface to beginning ascent not exceeding (min.)		(3) Stoppages at different depths (min.)							(4) Total time for decompression (min.)
			21 m	18 m	15 m	12 m	9 m	6 m	3 m	
		9	—	—	—	—	—	—	—	—
		10	—	—	—	—	—	—	5	5
		15	—	—	—	—	—	5	5	10
		20	—	—	—	—	—	5	10	15
		25	—	—	—	—	—	5	15	20
		30	—	—	—	—	5	5	20	30
	Limiting Line									
		35	—	—	—	—	5	10	25	40
		40	—	—	—	5	5	15	30	55
42		45	—	—	—	5	10	15	35	65
		50	—	—	—	5	15	20	40	80
		55	—	—	5	5	15	25	45	95
		60	—	—	5	5	20	35	45	110
		65	—	—	5	10	25	40	45	125
		70	—	—	5	15	30	40	50	140
		75	—	5	5	20	30	45	50	155
		80	—	5	10	20	35	45	50	165
		85	—	5	15	25	40	45	50	180
		95	5	5	20	35	40	45	50	200
		105	5	15	25	35	45	45	50	220
		115	5	20	35	40	45	45	50	240
		8	—	—	—	—	—	—	—	—
		10	—	—	—	—	—	—	5	5
		15	—	—	—	—	—	5	5	10
		20	—	—	—	—	—	5	15	20
		25	—	—	—	—	5	5	20	30
	Limiting Line									
		30	—	—	—	—	5	10	25	40
		35	—	—	—	5	5	10	30	50
		40	—	—	—	5	10	15	35	65
45		45	—	—	—	5	15	20	40	80
		50	—	—	5	5	15	25	45	95
		55	—	—	5	10	20	30	50	115
		60	—	—	5	15	25	35	50	130
		65	—	5	5	15	30	40	50	145
		70	—	5	10	20	30	45	50	160
		75	—	5	15	25	35	45	50	175
		80	5	5	20	30	40	45	50	195
		85	5	10	25	35	40	45	50	210
		90	5	15	30	40	45	45	50	230
		10	—	—	—	—	—	5	5	10
		15	—	—	—	—	—	5	10	15
		20	—	—	—	—	5	5	15	25
		25	—	—	—	—	5	10	20	35
	Limiting Line									
		30	—	—	—	5	5	10	25	45
		35	—	—	—	5	10	15	30	60
		40	—	—	—	5	10	20	40	75
48		45	—	—	5	5	15	25	45	95
		50	—	—	5	10	20	30	45	110
		55	—	—	5	15	25	40	45	130
		60	—	5	5	20	25	40	50	145
		65	—	5	10	20	35	45	50	165
		70	—	5	15	25	40	45	50	180
		75	5	5	20	30	40	45	50	195
		80	5	10	25	35	40	45	50	210
		85	5	15	30	40	45	45	50	230

(ii) DECOMPRESSION PROCEDURES AND TABLES FROM U.S. NAVY DIVING MANUAL

Depth (metres)	*Depth (feet)*	*Bottom time (min)*	*Time to first stop (min:sec)*	*Decompression stops (feet)*					*Total ascent (min:sec)*	*Repetitive group*
				50	40	30	20	10		
12	40	200	—	—	—	—	—	0	0:40	(*)
		210	0:30	—	—	—	—	2	2:40	N
		230	0:30	—	—	—	—	7	7:40	N
		250	0:30	—	—	—	—	11	11:40	O
		270	0:30	—	—	—	—	15	15:40	O
		300	0:30	—	—	—	—	19	19:40	Z
15	50	100	—	—	—	—	—	0	0:50	(*)
		110	0:40	—	—	—	—	3	3:50	L
		120	0:40	—	—	—	—	5	5:50	M
		140	0:40	—	—	—	—	10	10:50	M
		160	0:40	—	—	—	—	21	21:50	N
		180	0:40	—	—	—	—	29	29:50	O
		200	0:40	—	—	—	—	35	35:50	O
		220	0:40	—	—	—	—	40	40:50	Z
		240	0:40	—	—	—	—	47	47:50	Z
18	60	60	—	—	—	—	—	0	1:00	(*)
		70	0:50	—	—	—	—	2	3:00	K
		80	0:50	—	—	—	—	7	8:00	L
		100	0:50	—	—	—	—	14	15:00	M
		120	0:50	—	—	—	—	26	27:00	N
		140	0:50	—	—	—	—	39	40:00	O
		160	0:50	—	—	—	—	48	49:00	Z
		180	0:50	—	—	—	—	56	57:00	Z
		200	0:40	—	—	—	1	69	71:00	Z
21	70	50	—	—	—	—	—	0	1:10	(*)
		60	1:00	—	—	—	—	8	9:10	K
		70	1:00	—	—	—	—	14	15:10	L
		80	1:00	—	—	—	—	18	19:10	M
		90	1:00	—	—	—	—	23	24:10	N
		100	1:00	—	—	—	—	33	34:10	N
		110	0:50	—	—	—	2	41	44:10	O
		120	0:50	—	—	—	4	47	52:10	O
		130	0:50	—	—	—	6	52	59:10	O
		140	0:50	—	—	—	8	56	65:10	Z
		150	0:50	—	—	—	9	61	71:10	Z
		160	0:50	—	—	—	13	72	86:10	Z
		170	0:50	—	—	—	19	79	99:10	Z
24	80	40	—	—	—	—	—	0	1:20	(*)
		50	1:10	—	—	—	—	10	11:20	K
		60	1:10	—	—	—	—	17	18:20	L
		70	1:10	—	—	—	—	23	24:20	M
		80	1:00	—	—	—	2	31	34:20	N
		90	1:00	—	—	—	7	39	47:20	N
		100	1:00	—	—	—	11	46	58:20	O
		110	1:00	—	—	—	13	53	67:20	O
		120	1:00	—	—	—	17	56	74:20	Z
		130	1:00	—	—	—	19	63	83:20	Z
		140	1:00	—	—	—	26	69	96:20	Z
		150	1:00	—	—	—	32	77	110:20	Z
27	90	30	—	—	—	—	—	0	1:30	(*)
		40	1:20	—	—	—	—	7	8:30	J
		50	1:20	—	—	—	—	18	19:30	L
		60	1:20	—	—	—	—	25	26:30	M
		70	1:10	—	—	—	7	30	38:30	N
		80	1:10	—	—	—	13	40	54:30	N
		90	1:10	—	—	—	18	48	67:30	O
		100	1:10	—	—	—	21	54	76:30	Z
		110	1:10	—	—	—	24	61	86:30	Z
		120	1:10	—	—	—	32	68	101:30	Z
		130	1:00	—	—	5	36	74	116:30	Z
30	100	25	—	—	—	—	—	0	1:40	(*)
		30	1:30	—	—	—	—	3	4:40	I
		40	1:30	—	—	—	—	15	16:40	K
		50	1:20	—	—	—	2	24	27:40	L
		60	1:20	—	—	—	9	28	38:40	N
		70	1:20	—	—	—	17	39	57:40	O
		80	1:20	—	—	—	23	48	72:40	O
		90	1:10	—	—	3	23	57	84:40	Z
		100	1:10	—	—	7	23	66	97:40	Z
		110	1:10	—	—	10	34	72	117:40	Z
		120	1:10	—	—	12	41	78	132:40	Z

Depth (metres)	Depth (feet)	Bottom time (min)	Time to first stop (min:sec)	Decompression stops (feet)					Total ascent (min:sec)	Repeti-tive group
				50	40	30	20	10		
33	110	20	—	—	—	—	—	0	1:50	(*)
		25	1:40	—	—	—	—	3	4:50	H
		30	1:40	—	—	—	—	7	8:50	J
		40	1:30	—	—	—	2	21	24:50	L
		50	1:30	—	—	—	8	26	35:50	M
		60	1:30	—	—	—	18	36	55:50	N
		70	1:20	—	—	1	23	48	73:50	O
		80	1:20	—	—	7	23	57	88:50	Z
		90	1:20	—	—	12	30	64	107:50	Z
		100	1:20	—	—	15	37	72	125:50	Z
36	120	15	—	—	—	—	—	0	2:00	(*)
		20	1:50	—	—	—	—	2	4:00	H
		25	1:50	—	—	—	—	6	8:00	I
		30	1:50	—	—	—	—	14	16:00	J
		40	1:40	—	—	—	5	25	32:00	L
		50	1:40	—	—	—	15	31	48:00	N
		60	1:30	—	—	2	22	45	71:00	O
		70	1:30	—	—	9	23	55	89:00	O
		80	1:30	—	—	15	27	63	107:00	Z
		90	1:30	—	—	19	37	74	132:00	Z
		100	1:30	—	—	23	45	80	150:00	Z
39	130	10	—	—	—	—	—	0	2:10	(*)
		15	2:00	—	—	—	—	1	3:10	F
		20	2:00	—	—	—	—	4	6:10	H
		25	2:00	—	—	—	—	10	12:10	J
		30	1:50	—	—	—	3	18	23:10	M
		40	1:50	—	—	—	10	25	37:10	N
		50	1:40	—	—	3	21	37	63:10	O
		60	1:40	—	—	9	23	52	86:10	Z
		70	1:40	—	—	16	24	61	103:10	Z
		80	1:30	—	3	19	35	72	131:10	Z
		90	1:30	—	8	19	45	80	154:10	Z
42	140	10	—	—	—	—	—	0	2:20	(*)
		15	2:10	—	—	—	—	2	4:20	G
		20	2:10	—	—	—	—	6	8:20	I
		25	2:00	—	—	—	2	14	18:20	J
		30	2:00	—	—	—	5	21	28:20	K
		40	1:50	—	—	2	16	26	46:20	N
		50	1:50	—	—	6	24	44	76:20	O
		60	1:50	—	—	16	23	56	97:20	Z
		70	1:40	—	4	19	32	68	125:20	Z
		80	1:40	—	10	23	41	79	155:20	Z
45	150	5	—	—	—	—	—	0	2:30	C
		10	2:20	—	—	—	—	1	3:30	E
		15	2:20	—	—	—	—	3	5:30	G
		20	2:10	—	—	—	2	7	11:30	H
		25	2:10	—	—	—	4	17	23:30	K
		30	2:10	—	—	—	8	24	34:30	L
		40	2:00	—	—	5	19	33	59:30	N
		50	2:00	—	—	12	23	51	88:30	O
		60	1:50	—	3	19	26	62	112:30	Z
		70	1:50	—	11	19	39	75	146:30	Z
		80	1:40	1	17	19	50	84	173:30	Z
48	160	5	—	—	—	—	—	0	2:40	D
		10	2:30	—	—	—	—	1	3:40	F
		15	2:20	—	—	—	1	4	7:40	H
		20	2:20	—	—	—	3	11	16:40	J
		25	2:20	—	—	—	7	20	29:40	K
		30	2:10	—	—	2	11	25	40:40	M
		40	2:10	—	—	7	23	39	71:40	N
		50	2:00	—	2	16	23	55	98:40	Z
		60	2:00	—	9	19	33	69	132:40	Z
		70	1:50	1	17	22	44	80	166:40	Z
51	170	5	—	—	—	—	—	0	2:50	D
		10	2:40	—	—	—	—	2	4:50	F
		15	2:30	—	—	—	2	5	9:50	H
		20	2:30	—	—	—	4	15	21:50	J
		25	2:20	—	—	2	7	23	34:50	L
		30	2:20	—	—	4	13	26	45:50	M
		40	2:10	—	1	10	23	45	81:50	O
		50	2:10	—	5	18	23	61	109:50	Z
		60	2:00	2	15	22	37	74	152:50	Z
		70	2:00	8	17	19	51	86	183:50	Z

Depth (metres)	*Depth (feet)*	*Bottom time (min)*	*Time to first stop (min:sec)*	*Decompression stops (feet)*					*Total ascent (min:sec)*	*Repetitive group*
				50	40	30	20	10		
54	180	5	—	—	—	—	—	0	3:00	D
		10	2:50	—	—	—	—	3	6:00	F
		15	2:40	—	—	—	3	6	12:00	I
		20	2:30	—	—	1	5	17	26:00	K
		25	2:30	—	—	3	10	24	40:00	L
		30	2:30	—	—	6	17	27	53:00	N
		40	2:20	—	3	14	23	50	93:00	O
		50	2:10	2	9	19	30	65	128:00	Z
		60	2:10	5	16	19	44	81	168:00	Z
57	190	5	—	—	—	—	—	0	3:10	D
		10	2:50	—	—	—	1	3	7:10	G
		15	2:50	—	—	—	4	7	14:10	I
		20	2:40	—	—	2	6	20	31:10	K
		25	2:40	—	—	5	11	25	44:10	M
		30	2:30	—	1	8	19	32	63:10	N
		40	2:30	—	8	14	23	55	103:10	O
		50	2:20	4	13	22	33	72	147:10	Z
		60	2:20	10	17	19	50	84	183:10	Z

* See table 1–11 for repetitive groups in no-decompression dives.

Instructions for Use

1. No-decompression limits:

   This column shows at various depths greater than 30 feet the allowable diving times (in minutes) which permit surfacing directly at 60 feet a minute with no decompression stops. Longer exposure times require the use of the Standard Air Decompression Table (table 1-10).

2. Repetitive group designation table:

   The tabulated exposure times (or bottom times) are in minutes. The times at the various depths in each vertical column are the maximum exposure during which a diver will remain within the group listed at the head of the column.

   To find the repetitive group designation at surfacing for dives involving exposures up to and including the no-decompression limits: Enter the table on the *exact or next greater depth* than that to which exposed and select the listed exposure time *exact or next greater* than the actual exposure time. The repetitive group designation is indicated by the letter at the head of the vertical column where the selected exposure time is listed.

   For example: A dive was to 32 feet for 45 minutes. Enter the table along the 35-foot-depth line since it is next greater than 32 feet. The table shows that since group D is left after 40 minutes' exposure and group E after 50 minutes, group E (at the head of the column where the 50-minute exposure is listed) is the proper selection.

   Exposure times for depths less than 40 feet are listed only up to approximately 5 hours since this is considered to be beyond field requirements for this table.

TABLE 1-11.—*NO-DECOMPRESSION LIMITS AND REPETITIVE GROUP DESIGNATION TABLE FOR NO-DECOMPRESSION AIR DIVES*

Depth (feet)	*No-decompression limits (min)*	*Repetitive groups (air dives)*														
		A	B	C	D	E	F	G	H	I	J	K	L	M	N	O
10	—	60	120	210	300	—	—	—	—	—	—	—	—	—	—	—
15	—	35	70	110	160	225	350	—	—	—	—	—	—	—	—	—
20	—	25	50	75	100	135	180	240	325	—	—	—	—	—	—	—
25	—	20	35	55	75	100	125	160	195	245	315	—	—	—	—	—
30	—	15	30	45	60	75	95	120	145	170	205	250	310	—	—	—
35	310	5	15	25	40	50	60	80	100	120	140	160	190	220	270	310
40	200	5	15	25	30	40	50	70	80	100	110	130	150	170	200	—
50	100	—	10	15	25	30	40	50	60	70	80	90	100	—	—	—
60	60	—	10	15	20	25	30	40	50	55	60	—	—	—	—	—
70	50	—	5	10	15	20	30	35	40	45	50	—	—	—	—	—
80	40	—	5	10	15	20	25	30	35	40	—	—	—	—	—	—
90	30	—	5	10	12	15	20	25	30	—	—	—	—	—	—	—
100	25	—	5	7	10	15	20	22	25	—	—	—	—	—	—	—
110	20	—	—	5	10	13	15	20	—	—	—	—	—	—	—	—
120	15	—	—	5	10	12	15	—	—	—	—	—	—	—	—	—
130	10	—	—	5	8	10	—	—	—	—	—	—	—	—	—	—
140	10	—	—	5	7	10	—	—	—	—	—	—	—	—	—	—
150	5	—	—	5	—	—	—	—	—	—	—	—	—	—	—	—
160	5	—	—	—	5	—	—	—	—	—	—	—	—	—	—	—
170	5	—	—	—	5	—	—	—	—	—	—	—	—	—	—	—
180	5	—	—	—	5	—	—	—	—	—	—	—	—	—	—	—
190	5	—	—	—	5	—	—	—	—	—	—	—	—	—	—	—

TABLE 1-12. — *Surface Interval Credit Table for air decompression dives*
[Repetitive group at the end of the surface interval (air dive)]

Repetitive group at the beginning of the surface interval from previous dive

	Z	O	N	M	L	K	J	I	H	G	F	E	D	C	B	A
Z	0:10 0:22	0:23 0:34	0:35 0:48	0:49 1:02	1:03 1:18	1:19 1:36	1:37 1:55	1:56 2:17	2:18 2:42	2:43 3:10	3:11 3:45	3:46 4:29	4:30 5:27	5:28 6:56	6:57 10:05	10:06 12:00
O		0:10 0:23	0:24 0:36	0:37 0:51	0:52 1:07	1:08 1:24	1:25 1:43	1:44 2:04	2:05 2:29	2:30 2:59	3:00 3:33	3:34 4:17	4:18 5:16	5:17 6:44	6:45 9:54	9:55 12:00
N			0:10 0:24	0:25 0:39	0:40 0:54	0:55 1:11	1:12 1:30	1:31 1:53	1:54 2:18	2:19 2:47	2:48 3:22	3:23 4:04	4:05 5:03	5:04 6:32	6:33 9:43	9:44 12:00
M				0:10 0:25	0:26 0:42	0:43 0:59	1:00 1:18	1:19 1:39	1:40 2:05	2:06 2:34	2:35 3:08	3:09 3:52	3:53 4:49	4:50 6:18	6:19 9:28	9:29 12:00
L					0:10 0:26	0:27 0:45	0:46 1:04	1:05 1:25	1:26 1:49	1:50 2:19	2:20 2:53	2:54 3:36	3:37 4:35	4:36 6:02	6:03 9:12	9:13 12:00
K						0:10 0:28	0:29 0:49	0:50 1:11	1:12 1:35	1:36 2:03	2:04 2:38	2:39 3:21	3:22 4:19	4:20 5:48	5:49 8:58	8:59 12:00
J							0:10 0:31	0:32 0:54	0:55 1:19	1:20 1:47	1:48 2:20	2:21 3:04	3:05 4:02	4:03 5:40	5:41 8:40	8:41 12:00
I								0:10 0:33	0:34 0:59	1:00 1:29	1:30 2:02	2:03 2:44	2:45 3:43	3:44 5:12	5:13 8:21	8:22 12:00
H									0:10 0:36	0:37 1:06	1:07 1:41	1:42 2:23	2:24 3:20	3:21 4:49	4:50 7:59	8:00 12:00
G										0:10 0:40	0:41 1:15	1:16 1:59	2:00 2:58	2:59 4:25	4:26 7:35	7:36 12:00
F											0:10 0:45	0:46 1:29	1:30 2:28	2:29 3:57	3:58 7:05	7:06 12:00
E												0:10 0:54	0:55 1:57	1:58 3:22	3:23 6:32	6:33 12:00
D													0:10 1:09	1:10 2:38	2:39 5:48	5:49 12:00
C														0:10 1:39	1:40 2:49	2:50 12:00
B															0:10 2:10	2:11 12:00
A																0:10 12:00

Instructions for Use

Surface interval time in the table is in *hours* and *minutes* (7.59 means 7 hours and 59 minutes). The surface interval must be at least 10 minutes.

Find the *repetitive group designation letter* (from the previous dive schedule) on the diagonal slope. Enter the table horizontally to select the surface interval time that is exactly between the actual surface interval times shown. The repetitive group designation for the *end* of the surface interval is at the head of the vertical column where the selected surface interval time is listed. For example, a previous dive was to 110 feet for 30 minutes. The diver remains on the surface 1 hour and 30 minutes and wishes to find the new repetitive group designation. The repetitive group from the last column of the 110/30 schedule in the Standard Air Decompression Tables is "J". Enter the surface interval credit table along the horizontal line labelled "J". The 1-hour-and-30-minute surface interval lies between the times 1:20 and 1:47. Therefore, the diver has lost sufficient inert gas to place him in group "G" (at the head of the vertical column selected).

*NOTE — Dives following surface intervals of *more* than 12 hours are not considered repetitive dives. *Actual* bottom times in the Standard Air Decompression Tables may be used in computing decompression for such dives.

TABLE 1-13.—*Repetitive dive timetable for air dives*

Repetitive groups	*Repetitive dive depth (ft) (air dives)*															
	40	50	60	70	80	90	100	110	120	130	140	150	160	170	180	190
A	7	6	5	4	4	3	3	3	3	3	2	2	2	2	2	2
B	17	13	11	9	8	7	7	6	6	6	5	5	4	4	4	4
C	25	21	17	15	13	11	10	10	9	8	7	7	6	6	6	6
D	37	29	24	20	18	16	14	13	12	11	10	9	9	8	8	8
E	49	38	30	26	23	20	18	16	15	13	12	12	11	10	10	10
F	61	47	36	31	28	24	22	20	18	16	15	14	13	13	12	11
G	73	56	44	37	32	29	26	24	21	19	18	17	16	15	14	13
H	87	66	52	43	38	33	30	27	25	22	20	19	18	17	16	15
I	101	76	61	50	43	38	34	31	28	25	23	22	20	19	18	17
J	116	87	70	57	48	43	38	34	32	28	26	24	23	22	20	19
K	138	99	79	64	54	47	43	38	35	31	29	27	26	24	22	21
L	161	111	88	72	61	53	48	42	39	35	32	30	28	26	25	24
M	187	124	97	80	68	58	52	47	43	38	35	32	31	29	27	26
N	213	142	107	87	73	64	57	51	46	40	38	35	33	31	29	28
O	241	160	117	96	80	70	62	55	50	44	40	38	36	34	31	30
Z	257	169	122	100	84	73	64	57	52	46	42	40	37	35	32	31

Instructions for Use

The bottom times listed in this table are called "residual nitrogen times" and are the times a diver is to consider he has *already* spent on bottom when he *starts* a repetitive dive to a specific depth. They are in minutes.

Enter the table horizontally with the repetitive group designation from the Surface Interval Credit Table. The time in each vertical column is the number of minutes that would be required (at the depth listed at the head of the column) to saturate to the particular group.

Appendix G

PROCEDURES FOR ADMINISTRATION OF PURE OXYGEN

(i) ADMINISTRATION OF OXYGEN USING STANDARD EQUIPMENT

Oxygen administration for diving accidents requires the following:

1. **Oxygen Cylinder**

   This must be at least a D size (1.5 m^3). This can be expected to last about 1½ hours at 15 litres a minute. C size (0.44 m^3) can only be expected to last a little over 20 minutes at the same rate.

2. **Regulator with Contents Gauge**

   CIG Minireg (part number 518515) fits D and larger sizes. A spanner is required to tighten it securely in place.

3. **Flowmeter**

   CIG bobbin type (TM 105) is recommended. With this a small black ball floats in a vertical tube, which is marked in litres per minute flow. The flow reading is the number opposite the ball. It has an outlet to which a plastic tube can be attached to take the oxygen to the patient.

4. **Plastic Tubing**

   Approximately two metres of plastic tubing to fit the outlet of the flowmeter and the male fitting on the end of the nasal catheters.

5. **Nasal Catheters**

   It has recently been shown by Dr. David Komesaroff that the easiest way to give extra oxygen to a person who is not breathing is to put plastic nasal oxygen cannulae into the victim's nose and run in oxygen (5 litres a minute) while giving mouth to mouth resuscitation (EAR). This gives the patient an oxygen concentration of about 60%.

POSITION FOR
NASAL CATHETERS AND E.A.R.

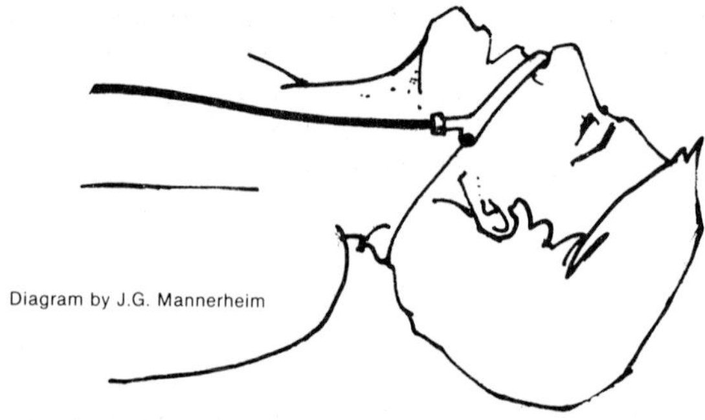

Head tilted back with Nasal catheter in place ready for Expired Air Resuscitation.

6. **Adaptor to take Diving Regulator**

Experience has shown that most people have problems getting an airtight seal on the face with a resuscitation mask (see 7 below). Dr. Mike Davis, of Christchurch, New Zealand, has designed an adaptor which screws into a D or larger oxygen cylinder and allows a diving regulator first stage to be attached. The diver then puts his regulator into his mouth and breathes through it. It may be necessary for him to hold his nose or wear a nose clip to make sure that he does not dilute the oxygen with air.

The adaptor is made from the standard bull-nose fitting that screws into all large cylinders of oxygen and other industrial gases by brazing on the top of a diving pillar valve. This is illustrated below.

ADAPTOR TO FIT A DIVING REGULATOR TO A LARGE OXYGEN CYLINDER

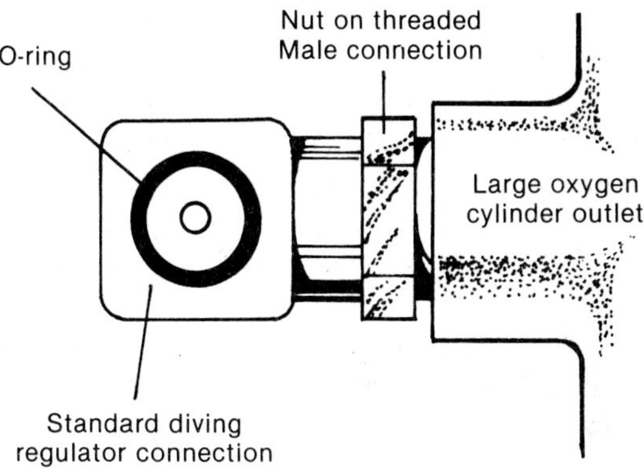

After a diving accident the diver is either breathing or not breathing. If he is not breathing, oxygen should be given by nasal catheters while E.A.R. is performed. As soon as he starts to breathe, and if he is breathing when rescued, he should be given oxygen to breathe through a diving regulator. If the party contains someone who is good at getting a seal between resuscitation mask and face, such as an anaesthetist or a mobile intensive care ambulance officer, the following items may be of use.

7. **Face Mask**

CIG Medishield Resuscitation Mask (M 1110) is made of hard clear plastic with a rubber cushion to enable it to adjust to the face. This allows the attendants to observe the patient's face better than an all rubber mask.

8. **Exhale Valve**

CIG Medishield Exhale Valve (with side inlet) (DF 6555) has an inlet for the oxygen and an attachment for the mask and one for the reservoir bag. (See figure below).

The patient breathes in from the reservoir bag and his expired gas passes out through the exhale valve. The grey knob should be fully open. In this position there is very little resistance to expiration. If the flowmeter is set at 14 litres a minute there will be no rebreathing.

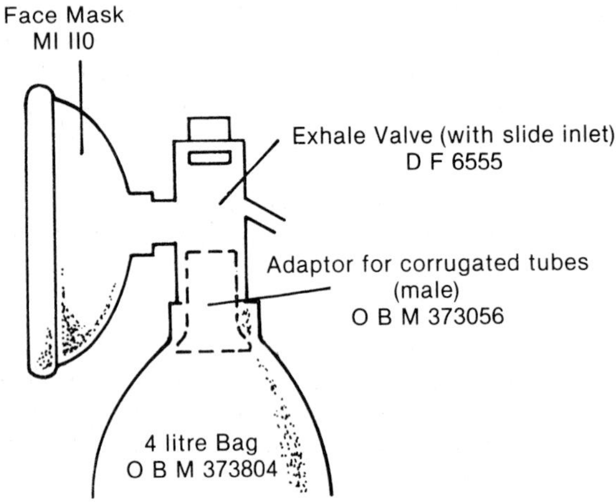

9. **Reservoir Bag**

A black rubber reservoir bag (OBM 373804) is needed to hold a reservoir of oxygen for the patient to breathe in from. It attaches to the exhale valve by item 8.

10. **Adaptor**

CIG Medishield adaptor for corrugated rubber tubes (male) (OBM 373056) is recommended as it is made from plastic and does not corrode. The bag is put over the ridged end and the male fitting plugs into the female fitting on the exhale valve.

11. **Head Harness**

This is used to hold the mask tightly to the patient's face. Clausen's Head Harness (OBM 301061) is what is normally used by anaesthetists. It has three tails that hook onto the mask. One comes over the top of the head and the other two round the sides of the jaw.

The two diagrams are reproduced from the South Pacific Underwater Medicine Society Journal, April to June 1981 issue.

(ii) ADMINISTRATION OF OXYGEN USING NON STANDARD EQUIPMENT

General

Oxygen therapy is an essential part of the treatment of most diving ailments. The procurement of oxygen must be one of the first tasks assigned to an assistant once a diving problem has arisen. Often this may entail the assistant visiting the most unlikely premises and needing to assemble what can only be termed make shift equipment. However, such is the importance of oxygen therapy, particularly in the treatment of decompression sickness and pulmonary barotrauma, that any effort made, will often aid the long term outcome of a diving problem.

In the absence of medical oxygen, the use of industrial oxygen is recommended. The major difference in terms of purity between medical and industrial oxygen is not in the oxygen itself which in both cases is 99.5% pure with the impurities mainly consisting of argon and nitrogen, but in the standard of cleanliness of the filling apparatus.

With medical oxygen the cylinders are evacuated and checked for cleanliness while with industrial oxygen the cylinders are merely topped up.

Availability of Oxygen

In the advent of adaquate oxygen resuscitation equipment not being available at the site of the diving accident then oxygen can be procured from a variety of sources. Industrial oxygen is often available in the form of an oxy-acetylene system and this oxygen is perfectly adequate for the purposes of resuscitation. The diver must avoid bare cylinders with no attachments, while cylinders with manifolds and attached hoses can usually be modified easily to allow for the administration of oxygen (see Adaptions Required for the Use of Industrial Oxygen below).

Sources of Oxygen may include:-

- Veterinary clinics
- Public swimming pools
- Air Ports
- Surf life saving Clubs
- Garages, welding shops and industrial sites for oxy-acetylene
- Aquarium shops
- Dentist
- High school manual arts centre.

Adaptions Required for the Use of Industrial Oxygen

Once a cylinder of oxygen has been located, the diver has one of three choices available to him.

(a) The oxygen system will already be set up for resuscitation and need only be used as per (appendix G section i. 7-11)

(b) An adaptor as shown in appendix G section i. 6, needs to be fitted to the cylinder to enable the divers normal demand valve to be used.

(c) Provided the cylinder is supplied with a reduction valve as used with oxy-acetylene equipment, the valve can be reset to deliver a minimum supply of oxygen and all attachments such as oxy-acetylene hand sets are removed. The diver now has a cylinder with a reduction valve and pipe for delivery. **Note:** Oxygen can be delivered via the oxy-acetylene hand piece if tools are not available.

Preparation of Divers for Oxygen Therapy

Once all preliminary resuscitation efforts prior to the arrival of oxygen have been made, the diver in charge of the emergency should record all relevent details of the accident. Eye witness accounts and all predisposing factors need to be documented. Symptoms exhibited by the patient should be recorded, as well as the time that oxygen resuscitation is commenced. Throughout the administration of the oxygen resuscitation, any changes in symptoms should be recorded also.

Administration of Oxygen

Once the oxygen cylinder has been modified to deliver a steady flow at minimal pressure, the diver in charge of the accident should then ascertain whether the patient is breathing or not.

If breathing the oxygen can be delivered to the patient by placing the diver's mask completely over the patient's face, covering both mouth and nose. The oxygen supply hose is placed under the skirt of the mask and allowed to free flow across the diver's face. It is essential that adequate oxygen pressure be available to ensure that a continued recycling of expired carbon dioxide does not occur. Adequate pressure can be readily ascertained by allowing sufficient oxygen pressure to feather the edges of the mask outward. When the patient breathes inwards there should be no suction of the mask onto the face. Using this method the patient should now be breathing in excess of 40-50% oxygen. The oxygen hose can be taped to the patient's cheek so freeing the attendant's hands to allow monitoring and recording of changes in the patient's condition.

If unconcious the delivery of oxygen will need to be via mouth to mouth resuscitation. Under these circumstances the outlet pipe for the oxygen equipment can be placed into the patients mouth or nose (see Appendix G Section i. 5) while the attendant diver administers Expired Air Resuscitation (see Section 3 page 126-127).

Problems of sealing around the mouth may arise, in which case the use of tape to hold the oxygen hose in place may help. Using this method oxygen levels to the patient may rise by as much as 15% to effectively be delivering 25-35% to the lungs.

When Pulmonary Barotrauma is suspected, the use of positive pressure oxygen therapy must normally be avoided. If the patient is not breathing however, Expired Air Resuscitation is essential. The use of oxygen via the side of the mouth as described above will not increase the risk of further tissue damage. It is not advisable however, to use the oxygen via an oxy-viva as this may cause further damage. If the diver is breathing and has a suspected Pulmonary Barotrauma then oxygen via the face mask or using the divers own regulator is perfectly acceptable.

Conclusion

These brief notes are by no means intended to be a definitive statement regarding oxygen resuscitation. They should be taken more as a suggested guide and hopefully they will stimulate further thought and discussion.

Oxygen therapy is often mentioned but very little is ever written regarding **how** the diver undertakes the task at an isolated location without the aid of an expensive and often complex oxygen resuscitation unit. Under most circumstances the administration of oxygen via any of the above mentioned methods is preferable to no oxygen at all.

INDEX

Absolute Pressure 3, 153
Absorption 11
  Light 11, 14
  Nitrogen 102
Age 104
Air
  Contents 23
  Embolism 87
  Consumption Calculation 152-154
Alternobaric Vertigo 85-86
Alveoli 76, 77, 78, 87, 98, 117
Ambient Pressure 4
Ammonia 134
Analgesics 117
Anoxia 96
  Latent 97
Aorta 77, 78
Artery 77, 121
  Carotid 78
Artifacts — Wrecks 160
Ascent Rate 107
Aseptic Bone Necrosis 105
Aspiration — Salt Water 117
Atrium 78

Back Pack 52-53
Balanced Regulator 55-56
Barotrauma 21, 80-93
  Ear 82-86
  Gastro Intestinal 92-93
  Inner Ear 84
  Mask 92
  Middle Ear 82-84
  Pulmonary 86-91, 152
  Sinus 91
  Tooth 92
Bends — See Decompression
  Sickness 102, 103
Belts, Weight 39
Bites 130-131
Blackout — Shallow Water 97-98
Bleeding 121
Blue Bottle 137
Blue Ringed Octopus 122, 132-133
Boat Diving 157-158
Body Temperature 10
Bone Necrosis 105
Bottom Time 106
Bourdon Tube 63
Boyle's Law 18, 19, 20, 21, 25, 80, 87
Bronchioles 76

Buddy Line 151
Buddy System 150
Buoyancy 6
Buoyancy Compensators 9, 42, 46, 84, 160
Butterfly Cod 134

C.P.R. 127
Caisson Disease
  (Decompression Sickness) 102
Calculation of Air Consumption 152-154
Capillaries 76, 77
Capillary Tube 63
Carbon Dioxide 76, 78, 95, 96-98
Carbon Dioxide Cartridge 42, 43, 70
Carbon Monoxide 66, 95, 99, 115
Cardiac Arrest 123
Carotid Artery 78
Cat Fish 134
Cave Diving 160
Chambers Recompression 104
Charles' Law 22, 23
Chemoreceptors 78, 97
Chokes (Decompression Sickness) 102, 103
Circulation 75
Coelenterates 136-137
Compass 64-65
Compensators, Buoyancy 9, 42-46, 84, 160
Compressor 99-100
Conductivity, Thermal 10, 113
Cone Shells 135
Contamination, Air 99
Contents Gauge 4, 48
Coral 136-137
Core Temperature 10, 113
Cousteau Jacques-Yves 48
Currents 143
  Long Shore 143
  Rip 143-144
  Diving 158
Cyalume 158
Cyanosis 87, 91, 122
Cylinder 48
  Capacity 51, 152
  Value 51
  Testing 50
  Codes 49

Dalton's Law 23, 24, 25
Dangerous Marine Animals 130-139
  First Aid 139

Dead Space 75
Decompression Sickness 27, 29, 64, 102-105, 160
- Bends 102
- Caisson Disease 102
- Chokes 102
- Diving 161
- Desaturation 29
- Itches 102
- Meters 64, 105
- Necrosis of Bone 105
- Niggles 102
- Repetitive Dive 107
- Schedules 107
- Staggers 102
- Stops 107
- Tables 106-111
- Temperatures 115

Deep Diving 160-161
Demand Valve 48, 54
Density 7
Depth 106
Depth-Pressure Relationship 3
Depth Gauges 4, 62-63
Diaphragm (Regulator) 55
Diarrhoea 139
Diffusion 26, 27
- Into Blood 76

Dive 148
- Boat 157-158
- Cave 160
- Decompression 161
- Deep 160-161
- Night 158-159
- Planning 148-149
- Specialist 157
- Wreck 159-160

Downstream Valve 58
Dysbaric Osteonecrosis 105

E.A.R. 88, 98, 121, 126-127, 133
E.C.C. 88, 121, 123, 127
Ear 21,82
- Barotrauma 82-86
- Otitis Externa 117-118
- Outer Ear Infection 117-118

Electric Shock 138
Embolism 87-88, 89
Emphysema 89
- Mediastinal 89
- Subcutaneous 90

Equalisation 82
Equilibrium 28, 29
Eustachian Tube 20, 21, 82
Exhaustion 113
- Cold Water 113
- Heat 118

Expiration 77
Expired Air Resuscitation 88, 98
Eye 12-13

Filtration, Compressor 99
Fins 35-36
- Grips 35

First Aid 121
- Dangerous Marine Animals 139

Flag, Dive 66, 149, 158
Flashing 99
Fresh Water Diving 160

Gagnon, Emile 48
Gases 17
- Poisonings 29, 66, 95

Gastro Intestinal Barotrauma 92-93
Gauges 145
- Bourdon Tube 63
- Capillary 63
- Depth 62-63
- Oil Filled Gauges 63
- Submersible Contents Gauges 59-60

Grips, Fin 35
Gut Squeeze 92-93

Headache 97
Heat Exhaustion 118
Henry's Law 27, 28, 29, 89, 102
Hookah 58, 66-67
Hydroid 136-137
Hyperbaric 3, 88, 100
Hyperventilation 78, 97-98
Hypothermia 11, 89, 99, 113-115, 123
- Mild 114
- Severe 114

Hypoxia 95-96
- Carbon Monoxide Induced 99

Inert Gas Narcosis 98-99
Inflation, Oral 42
Inspiration 77
Insulation, Thermal 11
Itches (Decompression Sickness) 102

J Valve 51-52
Jelly Fish 136-137
Jimble 137

K Valve 51-52
Kilopascals 3
Knife 40, 159

Latent Anoxia 97
Light 11
  Absorption 11
  Reflection 11
  Refraction 11
Line Pressure 54
Long Shore Current 143
Lung Physiology 75-77
  Pressure Injury 86-91
  Squeeze 86

Maintenance (Regulators) 69-70
Man-O-War 137
Marine Animals 130-139
  Bites 130-131
  Stings 136-138
Mask 13, 32-33, 34
  Barotrauma 92
  Corrective Lenses 33
Mauve Stingers 137
Mediastinal Emphysema 89
Mermaid Catcher 157
Meters, Decompression 64, 105
Monoxide, Carbon 66, 95, 99

Narcosis, Nitrogen 29, 98-99
Nausea 83, 97, 99, 103
Neap Tides 142
Necrosis, Bone 105
Nematocysts 136
Neoprene 8, 37
Niggles, Decompression Sickness 102, 103
Night Diving 158-159
Nitrogen 29, 98-99
  Absorption 102
  Narcosis 29, 95, 98-99
  Residual 108
No Decompression Dives 107, 108-109
  Calculation 109
  Limit 107
Non Return Valve 58
Numb Ray 138
Nylon 37

Octopus, Sea Blue Ringed Octopus 132
Octopus Regulators 63, 161
Old Wife 134
Osteonecrosis 105
Otitis Externa 117-118
Oxygen 95, 161
  Acute 95-96
  Chronic 95
  Decompression Diving 161
  Poisoning 95

Pack, Back 52
Partial Pressure 24, 25, 98
Parts, Spare 67
Pascal's Principle 17, 18
Physics of Diving 3
Pin Cushion Effect 13
Piston Regulator 55
Plasma 78, 100
Pleura 76, 90-91
Pneumothorax 90-91
Poisonings 29
  Gas 29
  Internal 138
Porcupine Fish 138
Portuguese Man-O-War 137
Potassium Permanganate 134
Pressure 3
  Absolute 3, 153
  Ambient 3
  Depth — Relationship 3
  Partial 24, 25, 98
  Points 121-122
Puffer Fish 138
Pulmonary Artery 77, 78
Pulmonary Barotrauma 86-91
Pulse 123
Puncture Wounds 133-136

R.M.V. 152
Rate of Ascent 107
Recompression Chamber 89, 103-104
Reflection, Light 11
Refraction, Light 11, 12-13
Regulators 53-59
  Balanced Diaphragm 56
  Balanced Piston 56-57
  Demand Valve 54
  Diaphragm 55
  Fault Finding 54
  First Stage 55
  Function 54
  Lever Valve (Downstream) 58
  Octopus 63-64
  Piston 55
  Second Stage 58-59
  Tilt Valve (Upstream) 57
  Twin Hose 53, 54
Repetitive Dive 107
  Group Designation 107
  Procedure 109
  R.N. Tables 109, 168
  U.S. Tables 109, 176
Residual Nitrogen 108
Residual Volume 77, 86
Respiration 75
  Arrest 122
  Respiratory Minute Volume 77, 152, 154

Response, Cold 113
Resuscitation 88, 98, 121, 124, 126-127
Rates 126-127
Reverse Ear Squeeze 84
Reverse Squeeze 81
Rip Currents 143

Salt Water Aspiration 98, 117
Saturation 27, 102
Scuba 48
Cylinder 48
Unit 48
Sea Anemone 136
Sea Sickness 89, 118-119
Sea Snake 133
Sea Urchin 134
Sea Wasp 137
Sharks 130
Shock 123-124
Shock, Electric 138
Shot Line 161
Sickness, Sea 89, 118-119
Silicone 70
Sink Hole Diving 160
Sinus 80-81, 91
Barotrauma 91
Skindiving Equipment 32
Skip Breathing 97
Snake, Sea 133
Snorkel 34-35
Sound, Speed 15
Spare Parts Kit 67
Specialist Diving 157
Spring Tides 142
Squeeze 81
Gut 92-93
Lung 86
Middle Ear 82
Reverse 81
Reverse Ear 84
Sinus 91
Stabilizer Jacket 43, 45
Staggers (Decompression Sickness) 102, 103
Standards, Australian 48, 49
Stingray 135
Stings 136, 138
Stonefish 134, 136
Stops, Decompression 107
Subcutaneous Emphysema 90
Submersible Contents Gauge 59-60
Sunburn 118
Sunfish 138

Tables 106-111
Decompression 161
Tanks 48-52
Teeth, Barotrauma 92
Temperature 10
Body 10, 113
Charles' Law 10
Conductivity 10
Core 10, 113
Test Stations 50
Tetradons 138
Therapeutic Recompression 88
Thermoclines 160
Tides 141
Neap 142
Spring 142
Tilt Valve 57
Toadfish 138
Torches 65-66, 158-159
Trachea 75

Upstream Valve 57
Urchin, Sea 134

Valsalva Manoeuvre 82
Valve 51
J 51, 52
K 51, 52
Vasoconstriction 113
Vasodilation 113, 114
Veins 77
Ventricle 77, 78
Vertigo 83, 85-86
Vinegar 137
Vital Capacity 77
Volume, Residual 77, 86

Wasp, Sea 137
Watches 64
Waves 144-146
Entry 145-146
Weight Belts 39
Wetsuit 9, 37, 38
Compression 9
Insulation 11
Wreck 159-160
Act 160
Artifacts 160

X Ray 105